D1053585

# The Revolution Generation

ALSO BY JOSH TICKELL

**Kiss the Ground:**
How the Food You Eat Can Reverse Climate Change,
Heal Your Body & Ultimately Save Our World

**Biodiesel America:**
How to Achieve Energy Security, Free America from
Middle-East Oil Dependence and Make Money Growing Fuel

**From the Fryer to the Fuel Tank:**
The Complete Guide to Using Vegetable Oil
as an Alternative Fuel

# The Revolution Generation

HOW
MILLENNIALS
CAN SAVE
AMERICA
AND THE WORLD
(BEFORE IT'S TOO LATE)

## JOSH TICKELL

**ENLIVEN BOOKS**
—
**ATRIA**
NEW YORK   LONDON   TORONTO   SYDNEY   NEW DELHI

ENLIVEN
ATRIA

An Imprint of Simon & Schuster, Inc.
1230 Avenue of the Americas
New York, NY 10020

First Enliven Books hardcover edition September 2018

For information about special discounts for bulk purchases, please contact Simon & Schuster Special Sales at 1-866-506-1949 or business@simonandschuster.com.

The Simon & Schuster Speakers Bureau can bring authors to your live event. For more information or to book an event, contact the Simon & Schuster Speakers Bureau at 1-866-248-3049 or visit our website at www.simonspeakers.com.

Interior design by Laura Levatino

Manufactured in the United States of America

10  9  8  7  6  5  4  3  2  1

Library of Congress Cataloging-in-Publication Data

Names: Tickell, Joshua, author.
Title: The revolution generation : how millennials can save America and the world (before it's too late) / Josh Tickell.
Description: New York, NY : Enliven Books, [2018] | Includes bibliographical references.
Identifiers: LCCN 2018016448 (print) | LCCN 2018017343 (ebook) | ISBN 9781501146114 (ebook) | ISBN 9781501146091 (hardcover) | ISBN 9781501146107 (pbk.)
Subjects: LCSH: Generation Y—United States—Social conditions. | Young adults—Political activity—United States. | Social action. | Political participation.
Classification: LCC HQ799.7 (ebook) | LCC HQ799.7 .T53 2018 (print) | DDC 305.20973—dc23
LC record available at https://lccn.loc.gov/2018016448

ISBN 978-1-5011-4609-1
ISBN 978-1-5011-4611-4 (ebook)

*Revolutio*

Latin root word for "revolution."

Original meaning:

"rotation, revolving, or turning."

**DISCLAIMER:** If you picked up this book hoping for the latest how-to-sell-more-garbage-to-young-people guide, then I'm going to save you some time. Stop reading here. There is an ever-growing stack of books about how to market to Millennials. This isn't one of them.

# CONTENTS

# The Revolution Generation

# INTRODUCTION

Millennials, I have bad news and good news.

The bad news is, according to the media, you are the most lazy, narcissistic, entitled, self-absorbed generation ever to walk the earth.

The good news?

This entire book is about you.

But here's why it's different from everything else you've probably read.

The vast majority of what is published about your generation is an overt or covert attempt to teach people older than you how to hack your brain to make you do something, sell you something, or convert you to some form of belief system. I know this because I've surveyed literally thousands of articles, books, websites, and blogs on Millennials. And it's safe to say, Millennials, that you have been strategically targeted by the largest corporate-controlled media manipulation machine in history.

And that is just the beginning.

Even the established frame of reference for you, Millennials, the one in which you are lazy, narcissistic, entitled, and self-absorbed, is a purpose-driven creation. Behind its rinse-lather-repeat retelling by the media machine is an insidious goal—to disenfranchise, disempower, and shut you down before you even walk through the door.

That's why this book is a deviation from the mountains of regurgitated clickbait about you. Instead, it's a formula for how you accelerate, amplify, and strengthen what you are consciously and unconsciously doing: disrupting the world we once knew.

## THE GREAT MILLENNIAL AWAKENING

By the time these words are printed, *all the members of your generation will have crossed the threshold into voting age.* By 2020, when the next US presidential election takes place, along with hundreds of state and local elections and the redrawing of countless voting districts, you, Millennials, will be the largest voting bloc in the United States.

> On the morning of November 9, 2016, one thing came into sharp focus: our democracy is an illusion.

For Millennials and people of all generations living in the United States, the 2016 US presidential election was a clarion call for action. On the morning of November 9, 2016, one thing came into sharp focus: our democracy is an illusion.

In our republic, and the money for which it stands, there are approximately four hundred registered lobbyists for every member of the House and Senate.[1] A seat in the House costs about $1 million. The Senate is around $40 million,[2] and the presidency? Well, that will set you back $1 billion.[3]

Thus, in 2016, the popular vote, also known as the will of the people, was ignored. Whether you love her, hate her, or are indifferent, the fact remains that Hillary Clinton received over 2.5 million more votes than her opponent. But the woman Americans elected by popular vote did not become their president. Instead, a real estate mogul named Donald Trump was placed in the White House by a rigged system.

But the powers that be didn't count on one thing: they didn't realize that in rigging an election, they would awaken a sleeping leviathan.

More than any other group of people, your generation holds the power to determine the future.

With so much responsibility and so much at stake in our world, there are signs that a Great Millennial Awakening is under way. Inside of this awakening, more and more of you are finding your passion and marrying it with educations and jobs in which you are actively altering the structures of power. For millions of others, who find yourselves either unemployed or in a gig or job that doesn't change the world, you are engaging in online platforms from Change.org to Facebook initiatives.

This is why your Millennial Awakening is totally different from that of your parents', the people known as the Baby Boomer generation. In contrast to the Boomers, whose movements tended to be confrontational, the pragmatic optimism that runs strong in the veins of your generation finds many of you blending into the systems of power you wish to alter. So much of your civic tsunami is a silent and powerful undercurrent. Like one of those puzzle pictures, you can see it only when you know what to look for.

Your generation is taking over the world. In so doing, you are already revolutionizing old systems. But your biggest revolution is yet to materialize. I'm talking about the one in which you use your power to change the political course of history.

On the whole, the Millennial political activists, a number of whom you will meet in the coming pages, are equal parts pragmatists, team players, builders of things, and idealists. If it is to take place, your Millennial revolution will be based in the practical, in compromise, in tangible solutions, and in bold new models. That's a good thing, because there has never been a greater need for compassionate, large-scale change than now.

For all you interlopers reading this—i.e., Baby Boomers and Gen Xers who are still trying to figure out Millennials—get ready to get woke. This is the story of an underdog generation that is dealing with collective trauma, catharsis, and empowerment and, most important, one that is about to pull its sword from the stone.

Steven Olikara, a first-generation Indian American Millennial, heads up the Millennial Action Project (millennialaction.org), a bipartisan group of about five hundred young elected officials at every level of office across the country. Says Olikara, "The definition of leadership involves bringing up people behind you. So, if you're a Baby Boomer or Gen Xer, one of the great legacies you can leave is to build the next generation of leadership: mentor, advise, cultivate, invest in the next generation of leaders."

After all, a positive future for you, Millennials, is a positive future for our country and quite possibly our civilization.

All futures being possible, the opposite pathway is also plausible. As our world hurtles toward what the United Nations tells us will be ten billion souls by 2050, you could turn out to be a generation that unveils, through a combination of action and inaction, unimaginable darkness for humanity.

But let's not do that, okay?

Due to your connectivity, Millennials, you can move quickly, en masse, and in a completely unexpected direction. This may prove to be your single most important tactical advantage.

To make the most of that advantage, especially in the thousands of pivotal city, state, and federal elections that will happen in the upcoming months and couple of years, which collectively may decide how we deal with the future of life as we know it, it is important to understand a few fundamentals of structural change.

## STRUCTURAL CHANGE

Think of this book as your training manual for how to make structural change.

Structural change is a term borrowed from economics that refers to bringing about a new order that forces businesses and the market itself to change. It often happens through politics when a new regime takes over or when major overhauls are made to laws that regulate business.[4]

The type of structural change of which I will speak in this book refers to deep, lasting change that alters the very structure of society itself. It's the kind of change that happened when the US Constitution was ratified and when the French Revolution took place.

On a foundational level, the structure of a society is its immutable commandments, core truths, inalienable rights, given norms, acceptable behaviors, allowable violations, and consequences for transgression of its rules. To be more specific, most societies, and especially modern societies, operate on three primary levels of structure.

1.  The underlying culture—the beliefs, ideologies, language(s), religion(s), iconography, fashions, memes, and traditions
2.  The political structures—the laws, governance, judicial system, punishment system, rules of business, and organization of commerce

3.  The infrastructure—the energy systems, transportation systems, agricultural systems, cities, bridges, freeways, schools, etc.

Each layer builds upon the previous one. A freeway, for instance, can be built only when sanctioned by a law that is, in turn, driven by the collective belief that we must have a way to move our cars. To build on that example, the energy system and pipelines that deliver fossil fuel to gas stations to fuel those cars can operate only through laws that give them power in a society that demands automobile transportation, regardless of the environmental or sociological impact. Infrastructure needs political power, which needs shared belief.

Now, here's the important part: to accomplish structural change, you must change all three layers.

Much of the Millennial Awakening has thus far failed to accomplish structural change because its change makers have targeted only the top layer—i.e., beliefs. This is the trap of many recent movements (think Occupy Wall Street, the Arab Spring, etc.). These and other widespread hearts-and-minds campaigns often begin with social media and engage tens and sometimes hundreds of millions of people. They bring to light dire injustices. They create petitions, there are protests, and they demand action. Yet, when all that collectivism alters neither the political landscape nor the social infrastructure, there is no structural change.

A telling example of this stagnation is America's gun control issue. It is unconscionable that, with all our technological wizardry in the second decade of the twenty-first century, we live in a society that willingly and knowingly puts semiautomatic weapons in the hands of unstable people who walk into our schools and shoot our children. The new conservative solution of putting guns into teachers' hands is symptomatic of a political leadership that has so wholly prostituted itself to special interests that our leaders are willing to sentence innocent children to die. It's also desperate, reckless, idiotic, barbaric, and . . . I could go on.

Meanwhile, recent polls show the majority of Democrats, Republicans, and Independents support stricter gun control.[5] So where are the laws, the codification, the infrastructure? How many years of congressional hearings, protests, and high school shootings do we need to live through before this issue is under control? How many more body bags filled with the dead bodies of our precious children will pile up, how many lives will be destroyed, and how many communities will be terrorized before the reasonable and sane and, let's just say it, *no-brainer* solution of genuine gun control is enacted?

My heart aches for the bereaved families and friends of the youth who have fallen at the hands of those who, in a functional democracy, would never have had access to guns in the first place. The politicians who ensure near-universal gun access are unpardonable and should be held to account. But inside the pain, the suffering, the fear, and the anger, there is a critical takeaway: we must no longer expect outcry alone to change policy.

*Beliefs* will not, by themselves, alter *policies*. Clicking is not voting—not yet, anyway. Tweeting is not engaging in the political process. Hashtagging is not running for office. Posting is not engaging voters in meaningful conversation. The Internet and smartphones are not the same as political reality. They are merely tools, and more often than not, they are tools of distraction.

And distracted is exactly how the powers that be want you, Millennials. That way they can keep vaporizing your votes, shutting you up, and shutting you down.

This is the truth: politics trumps every-

> Clicking is not voting—not yet, anyway. Tweeting is not engaging in the political process. Hashtagging is not running for office.

thing. (Yes, there's a pun in there somewhere.) No matter how loudly and how many you engage, or how intensely and how viscerally you demand change, our current version of paid-for democracy will only work against you until you take control of it, recode it, and reboot it.

The real question is not: When will our current flock of pay-to-play politicians work for the people? After all, puppets dance only for their masters. The real question is: How long are you, Millennials, going to wait before your revolution begins?

I say *you* because, as the largest voting bloc and the most Independent-registered generation at 50 percent, you are the change makers. Baby Boomers and Gen Xers who are also woke will champion you, coach you, mentor you, and support you. But there's no cavalry coming.

The revolution is wholly, completely, and 100 percent up to you.

Not only is the revolution up to you, but you are at an apex moment in history. With so much of our world in flux and with so much crisis, a critical window of opportunity is opening. All futures are possible right now. Everything is on the table. But mark my words, this open window won't last long.

I should know, because I've been doing my best to lay a little groundwork for your revolution my whole life.

## SO, WHO AM I, ANYWAY?

Glad you asked . . .

I grew up in Louisiana in the shadow of the 150 oil refineries that dot the landscape of that swampy state. Those refineries form a "cancer alley" where pollution is so intense that cancer rates there are up to seven hundred times the national average.[6] As a young boy, I watched members of my family get sick and die from pollution-related illness.

It was during my first high school science project that I initially saw the power of corrupt policy to hurt people. I tested the quality of local waterways only to find high levels of arsenic, lead, and other heavy poisons. But at the Louisiana State Science and Engineering Fair, a local EPA official, acting as one of the judges, disqualified my project because the results were "impossible."

The official who judged my project was part of a state organization that was, and still is, funded by the very industries it is supposed to police. It's no wonder that the data it had published on waterway pollution was a farce.

From there, I went to a very liberal liberal-arts school: New College of Florida. At the time, it was known for its lack of grades (pass/fail only) and its similar lack of clothes. I studied economics. But I became disillusioned when I learned that Adam Smith, the father of modern economics and the first theorist of capitalism, based his thesis on three deeply flawed assumptions: that slavery will always exist, that infinite consumption of resources is the basis for a healthy economy, and that greed is the central human motivation in a society.[7] Instead of becoming an economic hit man, I graduated with a degree in sustainable living.

The year was 1997, the Gulf War was still a topic of hot debate, and the issue of global warming was just heating up. I wanted to show that, instead of going to war for oil and baking the planet, perhaps there was another way to make fuel. If you were watching TV in the late '90s, you might have glimpsed a funny-looking, skinny kid driving a spray-painted Winnebago called the Veggie Van around the country, picking up used french fry oil from Kentucky Fried Chicken Dumpsters and turning it into biodiesel. Yep, that was me.

The Veggie Van turned into a lecture tour, which turned into making films about environmental topics. To date, my wife, Rebecca, and I have made seven major documentaries on issues that have to do with the environment.

By the way, the book you're reading is also a documentary by the same name: *The Revolution Generation*, which you can see at RevolutionGeneration.us. Whereas the book gives you detail beyond what is possible in a film, the film opens a window into the lives of many of the key characters in this book. I encourage you to watch it.

Over the course of my twenty years working as a journalist, researcher, and environmental advocate, I've spent more than ten thousand hours interviewing experts in the fields of poverty, water, climate, agriculture, sustainability, energy, environmental justice, political history, and policy. I've met with President Bill Clinton and have been in a meeting with President George W. Bush. I've spent time with military units and four-star generals. I've traveled deep into the jungles of Central America and Nigeria. I've walked the halls of Congress speaking to and interviewing countless senators and representatives, including one of the truly good ones, Representative Tulsi Gabbard (D-HI), who happens to be a Millennial and is interviewed in this book.

After all this, one thing is clear: the challenges we face are interconnected, and so are the solutions.

Christin "Cici" Battle, the director of People for the American Way Foundation's Young People For (YoungPeopleFor.org), a national youth leadership training program, says, "As a black woman in this country, my survival is tied to reproductive justice. My survival is tied to climate justice. My survival is tied to immigration reform, and access to education, and access to fair housing and so on." Cici maintains that she and many other Millennials share an urgency around these issues, not only because they are tied together, but because they are questions of life and death.

If there is one set of demands that unifies the Millennial leaders with whom I've spoken, it's to treat all humans—regardless of race, age, gender, creed, or origin—with dignity and respect, while at the same time ensuring that the planet that sustains us is protected and that greed and lust for profit are kept in check.

As the starting place for a true turning around or revolution, these demands give me great hope.

## READY? SET? GO!

Millennials, this book might depress you temporarily, shock you at least a little, infuriate you a lot, and, I hope, ultimately inspire you to great action.

While the term *youth culture* has existed for some time, never before has a generation had such universality in its connectedness. Unlike former generations, Millennials, you have your own faiths, iconography, linguistics, behaviors, communications systems, and social strata. Because a culture shares distinct forms of organization, language, and identity, and you, as Millennials, have these systems unto yourselves, I believe that you represent the first true global youth culture.

Your generation has so many powerful emerging leaders that one could write many books about them and still only scratch the surface. However, it is important to note that this is not an inspirational book *about* visionary Millennial leaders. Rather, this is a training manual *for* visionary young leaders. And as such, it contains a critical element that I believe was taken from your generation: your past. Let me explain.

The powerful leaders I've met—both in the

> This is not an inspirational book *about* visionary Millennial leaders. Rather, this is a training manual *for* visionary young leaders.

Millennial generation and among those who are older—have a nearly universal trait: they have a firm command of history. I believe that the instrument of true historical perspective, especially the actual events of the recent takeover of the American political system by corporate-backed interests, is the single biggest missing asset in the Great Millennial Awakening. Thus, this book unveils a largely covert sequence of political, social, and economic events that led to the current economic crisis in which you live. After all, in order to formulate an effective revolution, you must first understand how the current self-destructive economic and political models were created.

Your intense collectivism gives you a type of new youth power— power to heal, power to create, and power to destroy. It is possible, likely even, that your legacy will be to alter society so that it is unrecognizable to itself.

On a spiritual level, this book is an investigation into the soul of your generation. The French philosopher Voltaire wrote: "Each player must accept the cards life deals him or her: but once they are in hand, he or she alone must decide how to play the cards in order to win the game." In the game of history each generation begins its journey with unique advantages and disadvantages, faces perils far greater than those that came before, grapples with its demons, and, ultimately, forges the future into existence.

Millennials, before you can collectively play your hand on the world stage, you will have to come to terms with the depth of your generation's flaws and the enormity of the stakes of the game you are about to play.

If you were born in or after 1980, you stand at the precipice of a historical sea change in the course of our civilization. If you were born before 1980, this is your chance to support a generation that, by no fault of its own, has been shouldered with enormous social, economic, and environmental burdens. Millennials, in a very short time, the choices you make will determine the course of billions of human lives and, quite possibly, whether or not the next millennium of human history is one of abundance or apocalypse. It is my hope that, in some tiny way, this book contributes to your creating the good kind of future.

Regardless of the direction you choose, I am convinced, now more than ever, that you, the Millennials, are the generation that will forever change our world.

**CHAPTER ONE**

# Meet the Real Millennials

*Maybe there's a way out of the cage where you live*
*Maybe one of these days you can let the light in . . .*
—"Brave" by Sara Bareilles

I'm standing in the lobby of the Greco-Roman monolith known as Caesars Palace, watching a swarm of thousands of young people in black clothing. They have come to Las Vegas from towns and cities across America to attend the largest hair and makeup educational convention and party in the world. It's called Caper, and it's organized by Paul Mitchell Schools for the star students of their national trade schools.

At first glance this is the ultimate testament to self-indulgent Millennial narcissism. For several days this group of predominantly young, mostly women will learn how to replicate the cutting edge of beauty. Lecturers, runway shows, and experts will demonstrate every technique of applying products for that perfect look. The sea of faces bubbles with the effervescence of youth. It's almost impossible to find one of them without dazzling hair and airbrushed makeup.

By all measures, this crowd should be a shining beacon of vapid Millennial shallowness. But a closer look reveals that the narcissism stereotype only runs skin-deep.

My first introductions are to a couple of the event's motivational speakers. I meet Lizzie Velásquez. She is a Millennial author, speaker, and subject of a recent documentary. Lizzie is skinny. Really skinny. That's because she was born with a rare disease that prevents her from accumulating body fat. In 2006, she was dubbed the World's Ugliest Woman by a YouTube video. At the time, she was seventeen years old. She has since dedicated her life to speaking out against bullying and advocating for "going beyond looks to find your true source of happiness." Her TEDx Austin Women's talk has almost eleven million views. Velásquez brings her questions on the nature of beauty and judgment home with such poise, I wonder if the young beauticians to whom she is speaking feel a bit guilty. But from where I am sitting I can see only rapt faces, eyes wide, expressions hanging on her every word.

As if that wasn't humbling enough, I then spend a few minutes speaking with Kathy Buckley, a well-known deaf Gen X comedienne whose talk is about filling your heart with joy, removing labels, and respecting others. Onstage, Kathy speaks about the incredible obstacles she had to face on her road to becoming a deaf performer for those who hear. When she relates her experience of being derided, made fun of, and put down, sympathetic heads nod in the audience. It seems that these pierced, blue-haired, tattooed young people have also experienced the pain of being reduced to labels like *weird* and *different*. Buckley's end message about self-love and acceptance is stunningly beautiful. As she delivers her final words, I find myself wiping away tears. A quick glance at the youthful audience confirms I am not alone.

Many of these young people come from rough neighborhoods, tough families, and difficult backgrounds. Only a couple of the people I speak with have attended any college. They cite finances as the biggest detriment. A number of the young men I meet have come out of military service. When describing why they are here, the students don't talk much about hair or makeup or fashion. Instead, they use words like *opportunity, inspiration, community, connectedness, doing good,* and *contribution.*

On one hand, this event, like most things in Vegas, is about making money. In this case, it's about selling hair and beauty products and services. It's also very much about an industry that emphasizes appearance. But the emphasis from the stage and from the attendees isn't about outward beauty. Instead, their focus is on what it means to be a better human, what inner beauty is really about, and how to spread happiness.

> "We're a generation that wants to create change. We're more motivated by social impact than we are our paychecks. We're very interested in making our mark by making the world a better place."

This dichotomy and this particular cross section of young people is a good weathervane for the Millennial generation. More often than not, you are appearance-conscious, positive, hardworking, earnest, community-oriented, aspirational, and, yes, poor. The particular Millennials whom I am meeting all have something else in common, too: they desperately want a job. The opportunity to have a life in which they make a difference for others while having employment is by no means a given. It's their big dream.

This sentiment is echoed by many people in your generation. People like Lindsey Horvath, a bright, eloquent Millennial who recently held the position of mayor of West Hollywood (making her one of the youngest mayors in America). I meet her on a sweltering day in Los Angeles in her modest apartment (with no A/C), and we sit amid stacks of old campaign paraphernalia. Says Horvath, "People often say the Millennial Generation is the Me Generation and focused on themselves. But that's just simply not true. We're a generation that wants to create change. We're more motivated by social impact than we are our paychecks. We're very interested in making our mark by making the world a better place."

Horvath tells me she has a substantial amount of college debt, though she declines to tell me the exact amount, and that she basically put her life on hold for several years to serve in public office. Steven Olikara, head of the Millennial Action Project, says, "Some of my friends who even run for state office, they take out a second mortgage on their home just so they can run. Think about the sacrifices for their family that they're making."

The mixture of economic aspiration and desire to make a difference is precisely where your generation differs from the generations that preceded you.

## BIGGER, FASTER, STRONGER

If you were born between approximately 1980 and 2000, you are known as a Millennial or, to marketers, a member of Generation Y. Yours is a generation of eighty million strong and growing due to immigration in the United States, and 2.3 billion worldwide. The sheer magnitude of people in your age group dwarfs Generation X (fifty million US) and now eclipses the Baby Boomers (seventy-eight million US and declining due to death).

You've been born into an incredibly young period of human existence. *Half of the people alive on earth right now are under the age of thirty-five.* Yes, half. That's more people than made up the entire human race in 1950.

In general, you're the most educated, most female/male equal, most entrepreneurial, most mobile, most tech-savvy, most connected, most politically independent, most racially diverse as well as the most globally aware generation in history. As thirty-something-year-old Ana Kasparian, a lead reporter with the popular online news show *The Young Turks*, tells me, "Millennials are more socially liberal. They want gay rights. They want equality among races. And they're more likely to want these things as opposed to Baby Boomers." This is all very positive.

> **Half of the people alive on earth right now are under the age of thirty-five.**

However, you also suffer from being the most economically depressed,[1] most in debt ($37,000 average US college graduate debt),[2] least employed (35–40 percent actual unemployment in the United States),[3] most unmarried,[4] most single-parent generation[5] so far. Your economic prospects get grimmer with each passing day as the economic crisis caused by the Great Recession of 2008 drags on.

Marketers love to segment Generation Y into categories like *Lifepreneurs* and *Hip-ennials*. If you're a young person, this kind of stuff might make you throw up in your mouth a bit. Or at least it should. Because it completely misses the point of what your generation is experiencing.

When will older generations stop asking questions about how to sell to young people and start trying to understand them? If understanding is the goal, we might start by asking what is the actual demographic and social makeup of the Millennial generation.

## HERE ARE SOME BASIC GROUPINGS
## FOR THE PEOPLE IN YOUR GENERATION:

### Young Millennials Eighteen to Twenty-Two Years Old
- College age (twenty-nine million eighteen- to twenty-four-year-olds)[6]

### Unemployed, Working Poor, and in Poverty
- Unemployed (approximately 35 percent, or twenty-eight million)[7]
- Wage labor or gig economy poor (approximately thirty million)[8]
- Living in poverty (approximately 20 percent, or sixteen million)[9]

### College Degrees, Working, and Careers
- Total Millennial workforce: about 53.5 million[10]
    Of these, about thirty million are in some form of wage-labor job, and about twenty million are in some form of gainful employment.
- Those with college degrees (22 percent, or eighteen million)[11]

### Parents
- Approximately half, or forty million[12]

A number of stark economic realities separate you from other generations. You are by far the most impoverished generation. There are different ways to look at this, but basically the most optimistic data shows that no more than 36 percent[13] of your generation will graduate with a four-year college degree and some reports put your graduation rate as low as 22 percent.[14] That shiny and expensive degree is the single most important indicator as to your lifetime earning potential.

According to Tamara Draut, author of *Strapped: Why America's 20- and 30-Somethings Can't Get Ahead*, people without college degrees are likely to end up in wage-labor jobs or the gig economy. Draut says that about two-thirds of Millennials today are unlikely to progress beyond wage-labor jobs due to structural impediments in the economy that prohibit those without a four-year college degree from advancing.[15]

Another way to look at poverty is by household. Of the seventeen million households living in poverty, five million of them are headed by a Millennial. This is disproportionately high considering there are only about twenty million Millennial households.[16]

> Two-thirds of Millennials today are unlikely to progress beyond wage-labor jobs.

No matter how you cut it, somewhere between one-quarter and one-third of your generation is living below, near, or just above the poverty line. Millennials, while you probably knew this, to those of us not in your generation, this should be a sobering fact.

For those of you who are working, gainfully employed, or have a career, income is sliding backward compared with other generations.[17] Yes, *backward*. The defining hallmark of youth that *economic well-being increases* over time as you work your way up the Great American corporate ladder is, unfortunately for you Millennials, *reversed*. Ouch.

Millennial parents are particularly hard hit by your generation's economic catch-22, especially mothers. Of the twenty million or so Millennial moms, at least four million are single.[18] Even Millennial parents who are coupled find that economically speaking, they are struggling compared to those who do not have children. Although a higher percentage of families with small children have one parent working, they have lower incomes than families without children.[19] In other words, it's not that *expenses are higher*, it's that they actually *earn less*. Yet another defining hallmark of the once Great American economic system—the tax breaks, benefits, write-offs, etc. that used to help young parents with young children—is *reversed* for you, Millennials.[20]

The numbers don't lie. The Great Recession, the big short, derivative trading, and an economy built on greed and greed alone have left your generation high and dry. The only upside seems to be that because recreational marijuana is finally becoming legal in America, if you can't make money in the old economy, you might be able to pick up some extra hours at a pot shop. Like I said, high and dry.

Seriously, it's bleak. But your story is far from over. And, given some determination and hard work, great things *can* come from crisis.

In pinyin, which is a way of writing Chinese words with English letters, the Chinese word for "crisis" is written *wēijī*. While often mistranslated in America, it actually derives from two characters: *wēi*, which refers to "danger" or "precarious," while *jī* refers to "a point where things happen or change."[21]

If ever there was a generation experiencing mass *wēijī*, it is yours.

To understand why it's not just economics pushing you to make sweeping changes, we need to go deeper into what's really happening on the planet.

## THE REALLY, REALLY SCARY SHIT YOU ABSOLUTELY *HAVE* TO DEAL WITH

Millennials, you are coming of age at the culmination of the ten largest human and environmental crises in the history of our civilization. Many of these are existential threats, i.e., they threaten the very existence of humankind itself.

Historically speaking, your parents (the Baby Boomers) faced the first genuine human species–level existential threat. Thanks to the nuclear-tipped missiles that the United States and USSR amassed during the Cold War, by the late 1950s humanity had the power to completely extinguish itself. At the time, it was the scariest thing ever.

But one could contend that your world, Millennials, is ten times scarier. That's because you now face the following:

## TOP TEN SPECIES EXTINCTION THREATS

1. DESERTIFICATION. More than two-thirds of the world is turning to desert.[22] This is putting more pressure on overburdened and under-resourced cities, especially in Africa and Asia.[23]

2. OVERPOPULATION. Only a handful of developed countries are at low or negative population growth. The rest of the world continues on an exponential population growth curve.[24]

3. WATER SCARCITY. More than half the global aquifers are at or below critical levels.[25] Once aquifers are drained, they often cannot store the same quantity of water as before.

4. CLIMATE. Carbon dioxide levels in Earth's atmosphere are higher than they have been in three million years and climbing.[26] And that's when the oceans were thirty feet higher.

5. OCEAN ACIDIFICATION. Increased $CO_2$ in the atmosphere is turning ocean waters acidic.[27] The acidic waters kill the coral and phytoplankton that are responsible for making more than half the oxygen we breathe.[28]

6. CHEMICAL AGRICULTURE. Due to chemical agriculture, it is predicted that Earth will lose most of its remaining topsoil within a few decades.[29] As topsoil turns to dust, crop failure is increasing in many agricultural regions around the world. There are only an estimated sixty harvests left in the world.[30]

7. TERRORISM. For a relatively small price, terrorists now have access to bioweaponry,[31] suitcase-sized "dirty" nuclear bombs,[32] and debilitating cyber hacks and viruses.[33]

8. REFUGEES. The United Nations estimates that we will soon have one billion human refugees as a result of soil desertification and climate change.[34]

9. GLOBAL RECESSION. The economies of the world are likely to continue to experience inflation, recession, and constriction into the foreseeable future.[35]

10. MASS EXTINCTION. The number of species that are going extinct on Earth has now reached critical levels. Similar to the end of the ecosystem in which dinosaurs once lived, we are experiencing what scientists are calling the sixth major extinction.[36]

Given this future, it's a wonder that people ask why you, Millennials, are such a high-anxiety generation.

*How* you deal with the gigantic challenges before you will determine *what*, if any, civilization remains at the end of this century. In other words, what your generation does between now and 2050, when the United Nations estimates the world population will be almost ten billion people, may determine the very future of our species itself. It is not hard to imagine the aforementioned concurrent crises spiraling into an apocalypse.

Perhaps this is why there's a new genre of entertainment we could call "apocaphylia" that's being consumed by your generation as fast as it can be produced. From zombie outbreaks to *The Hunger Games* to video games based on killing the global population with plagues, the apocalypse is as titillating to Millennials as space travel was to the Baby Boomers (Boomers, think the original *Lost in Space*, *Star Trek*, and the televised version of *Buck Rogers in the 25th Century*).

While the heroes of the Boomer era were extensions of the technology-driven Cold War, with a thinly veiled aliens-as-Russians motif, the heroes of today use bows and arrows to survive in a future where the technocracy has collapsed, leaving in its wake poisoned oceans and an irradiated biosphere.

*The Hunger Games* heroine Katniss Everdeen has a lot to say about where your generation subconsciously thinks the world you are inheriting is headed.

If we Gen Xers and Baby Boomers were a bit more honest with you, we'd have given you the following pep talk as you became teenagers: "Now, here's your iPhone and here's your gas mask. Good luck, young Millennial, because in the disintegrating world we built for you, you're going to need them."

But that's not what we tell you. Instead, when it comes to Baby Boomers and Gen Xers, there're a lot of Millennial haters.

## WHY THEY HATE Y(OU)

If you're one of those Millennial people whom this book is about, then it's no secret: people who are older than you—especially people in the media—just love to hate on you.

"Why?" you might ask. After all, aren't those very same people the generation who birthed you? Aren't they the ones who put the "Baby on Board" signs on their minivans, who took you to soccer practice, and who made sure you did your best in school?

The answer I'm about to give will undoubtedly ruffle some Boomer and Gen Xer feathers. But it's true. And by the time you finish this book, you will agree that it is absolutely undeniable.

Here it is:

*This prevailing negative view of Millennials is no accident. Rather, it is a purpose-driven creation. The campaign against Millennials was, and still is, an effective tool to objectify you, to use you, to program you, to marginalize you, to disenfranchise you, and to push as many of you as possible into the wage-labor economy.*

**This prevailing negative view of Millennials is no accident. Rather, it is a purpose-driven creation.**

As we will discuss in the subsequent parts of this book, the social stigma that was strategically attached to Millennials at a young age has over time also become a powerful political weapon. It has cemented a disempowering context for a generation of young people. And it has paved the way for institutional ageism at many levels of our economy and civil society.

The disenfranchisement of the Millennial generation is bolstered through a rinse-lather-repeat messaging campaign that is insidious, ubiquitous, and surprisingly effective. My staff and I surveyed over two thousand articles written about Millennials and Generation Y from 2014 to 2016. The vast majority of them, over 95 percent, were about marketing to, or selling to, young people. Over 60 percent of the articles had negative words like "difficult," "different," "stay-at-home," or "low earner." These articles were not written by sociologists or demographers or even political groups; they were written by, and for, the marketing industry.

### HERE ARE A FEW HIGHLIGHTS FROM THE ARTICLES WE SURVEYED ON MILLENNIALS:

- "Sick of all the articles about the younger generation? Popular browser extension changes the word 'millennial' into 'snake person.'"[37]

- "Entitled, lazy, narcissistic, and addicted to social media. Those are just some of the common complaints about millennials . . ."[38]

- "Millennials in a hurry causing workplace conflict: Survey."[39]

*Snake person* definitely wins the prize. But it doesn't take too much reading on Millennials to conclude that, in addition to being the largest and most impoverished generation, yours is also the most loathed.

The campaign against Millennials actually began when you were just a twinkle in your Baby Boomer parents' eyes, but it really came to a head in 2013. That's when a *Time* magazine cover story deemed Millennials the "ME ME ME Generation." Joel Stein, a *Time* contributor, called Millennials "selfish, egotistical, and lazy." The cover story sparked a wave of criticism from young people and inspired counter blogs and videos.

Flipping the paradigm back on the Baby Boomers, who originated the campaign, Stephen Colbert used the magazine in his well-received graduation speech that year at UVA, saying:

> Your generation needs everything to be about you. And that's very upsetting to us Baby Boomers, because self-absorption is kind of our thing. We're the original "Me Generation"; we made the last fifty years all about us. We took all the money. We soaked up all the government services. And we've deep-fried nearly everything in the oceans. It may seem that all that's left for you is unpaid internships, Monday-to-Tuesday mail delivery, and, thanks to global warming, soon Semester at Sea will mean sailing the coast of Ohio.

Says Millennial researcher Jason Dorsey, "Any time change is coming about, especially driven by youth, older generations find it threatening, and that's why it's easier to point to the negativity."

On the Baby Boomer side there's a bit of guilt, a lot of justification, and a tremendous amount of judgment and prejudice toward members of the Millennial generation. The vitriol seems completely lopsided with Boomers really dishing out the majority of it.

Stan Brown's book *What's Wrong with Millennials? 50 Things You Need to Know About the Entitled Generation* really brings it home. Here are his top complaints:

1. YOU'RE ENTITLED.
2. IN YOUR WORLDVIEW, EVERYBODY WINS.
3. YOU THINK SHOWING UP IS ENOUGH.
4. YOU DON'T BELIEVE IN AN ABSOLUTE TRUTH—INSTEAD YOU THINK THAT TRUTH IS RELATIVE.
5. YOU THINK REALITY IS A CHOICE.
6. YOU DON'T GRASP THE IMPORTANCE OF HIERARCHY.
7. YOU SEE LIFE AS A SERIES OF UNLIMITED OPTIONS.
8. YOU'RE UNDER THE IMPRESSION THAT LIFE IS FAIR.
9. YOU THINK DRUGS ARE A NORMAL PART OF LIFE.
10. YOU ARE DISCONNECTED FROM THE CONSEQUENCES OF YOUR CHOICES.

And so on, and so on.

While some of these could be applied to young people of any era, here's the problem: no matter what kind of Millennial you may be, this is a fixed framework through which you are viewed.

Social frameworks can be dangerous things. They have a way of imposing a worldview that at best is limiting but at worst can be deadly (think ISIS). They also tend to be self-fulfilling and self-reinforcing. This is called confirmation bias, which, according to the *Oxford English Dictionary*, means "the tendency to interpret new evidence as confirmation of one's existing beliefs or theories."

Here is the part that really, really, really frustrates Boomers and Gen Xers about you: in spite of Matthew McConaughey trying, like, way too hard to sell you Lincolns, you just won't buy cars like you're supposed to. And even with all those new lines of credit, you keep not buying houses like you should.

> **"What Millennials emphasize more than material things are experiences."**

As the next generation of would-be consumers, you're a huge disappointment to an older generation who would feel much better if you just continued to buy, buy, buy, *buy.*

Millennial *Young Turks* reporter Ana Kasparian, a sharp, quick-witted young woman, tells me:

> There have been a number of negative articles written about Millennials because they refuse to be consumers. So, one of them that really stands out to me was this scathing article written about how Millennials don't buy diamonds anymore. Even if they could afford diamonds, what Millennials emphasize more than material things are experiences.

Because most of what is written about Millennials comes from frustrated marketers trying to "crack" the "Millennial code," they often conflate the meaning of a "social generation" with a "marketing segment." It's important to remember that they're completely different.

Marketers constantly claim they have discovered the next biggest generation. But what this actually means is the marketers themselves are getting older while the market segment they are targeting often gets younger.

A generation is not a marketing segment, it is something else entirely. And to understand your generation, you first have to understand where you fit into the mix of other generations.

## THE GENERATIONS

A social generation is a group of people born during a period of about two decades who age together and who, throughout their lives, experience a unique constellation of parenting trends, social situations, challenges, crises, triumphs, and cultural touchstones.

| GI | SILENT | BOOMER | GEN X | MILLENNIAL | GEN Z |
|---|---|---|---|---|---|
| born 1901-1924 | born 1925-1945 | born 1946-1964 | born 1965-1979 | born 1980-2000 | born 2001-2020 |
| 30 million | 40 million | 78 million | 50 million | 80 million | 73 million |
| WWI, WWII | WWII, Great Depression | Post WWII | Vietnam Era | 9/11, Iraq, etc. | Syrian Conflict |
| Taft/Wilson/Harding | Hoover/Roosevelt | Eisenhower/Kennedy | Nixon/Carter | Bush/Obama | Obama/Trump |

Each generation spans roughly twenty years. The beginning and end dates of each generation are approximate.

### HERE ARE THE GENERATIONS
### THAT COEXIST TODAY:

THE GI GENERATION (born approximately 1901 to 1924) were born before the Great Depression, became war heroes, and then reformed the world, building much of the social, political, and physical infrastructure that defines our society today.

THE SILENT GENERATION (born approximately 1925 to 1945) were born during the tumultuous years of the Great Depression and World War II. They were conformist, patriotic, and civic-minded. Today, these folks are in their seventies, eighties, or nineties (think Dolly Parton, Bernie Sanders).

THE BABY BOOMERS (born approximately 1946 to 1964) are a massive generation of seventy-eight million people born from the end of the Second World War to the advent of the birth control pill. They are known for their music, their morally righteous stands on issues ranging from civil rights to abortion, and their affinity for material consumption.

GENERATION X (born approximately 1965 to 1979) were born during a time of economic strife. This smaller generation experienced widespread divorce, absentee parenting, and a largely anti-child mentality in society.

MILLENNIALS, AKA GENERATION Y (born approximately 1980 to 2000) came next. US Census data shows a massive spike in births that began in 1979 and lasted approximately twenty years only to fall like a rock after September 11, 2001, when the mood of the country and the world changed.

GENERATION Z, AKA HOMELAND GENERATION, iGEN, OR MASS SHOOTING GENERATION (born approximately 2001 to 2020) are the children of Generation X and Millennial parents. Like the Silent Generation, Gen Zers are trending toward being conformist, well-behaved, and somewhat quiet compared to their older Millennial peers.

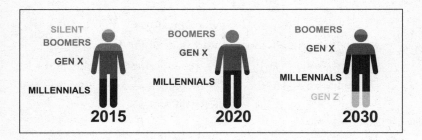

In a short time, Millennials will eclipse all other generations in the work-force, the civic space, and, importantly, in their power to alter policy at the local, state, national, and international levels.

*Data: US Census Bureau.*

According to historian Neil Howe, who coauthored the book *Generations* and coined the term *Millennial*, a generation is "a group of people who are born over the length of a phase of life." Howe says that a generation typically spans about twenty years. As they grow up, they are influenced by the events happening around them. But as they mature, generations tend to influence world events.[40]

Now that we know your generational location in history, let's look at the pivotal events that shaped your generation. This will help build some context around the drivers of certain generational behaviors. It might also help us begin to strip away the hatred fomented by the anti-Millennial campaign.

And, most important, these events will illuminate the single, central generational message that made you you.

## MOMENTS THAT MOLD

Imagine for a moment that you were born at the commencement of the Millennial generation, on January 1, 1980. For many of you, this will not be difficult. But for any Boomers and Gen Xers still reading, this may build some empathy.

Here are some of the important moments of your life.

When you are six years old, you're sitting in your classroom watching live TV as the pinnacle of America's achievement from the Cold War and the Space Race, the space shuttle *Challenger*, rises for seventy-three seconds and then explodes in a ball of fire. Disintegrating into dust along with the six other astronauts is Sharon Christa McAuliffe, a thirty-eight-year-old schoolteacher from New Hampshire. As the poster child of President Ronald Reagan's Teacher in Space Project, she's the reason so many schoolchildren are watching the live broadcast in classrooms around the world. And now she's dead.

After the confusion wears off, the subconscious message of the catastrophic event is that it's not safe out there.

When you are twelve years old, you're watching the evening news with your parents when a videotape surfaces of a taxi driver named Rodney King being brutally beaten by a group of four Los Angeles policemen. From KTLA in Los Angeles, which obtained the footage from a bystander who filmed the event from his balcony, the footage goes viral on news feeds around the globe. You're aware that there's a trial and that, eventually, the police officers who assaulted Rodney King are found not guilty. As a result of the verdict, Los Angeles erupts in riots and is set ablaze.

The subconscious conclusions you make are that police can strike you at random, especially if you are a person of color, the judicial system is broken, and big cities are dangerous.

When you are fifteen years old, after a long and exhaustive trial, O. J. Simpson is finally found not guilty of the murders of his ex-wife, Nicole Brown Simpson, and her lover, Ron Goldman. While he's not guilty per se, he is ordered to pay punitive damages by a civil court jury.

You conclude that celebrities have a status in our society that gives them impunity and power, even in cases of life and death.

Soon after your fifteenth birthday, the Alfred P. Murrah Federal Building in downtown Oklahoma City is decimated by a homemade bomb. In what amounts to the worst case of domestic terrorism ever on US soil, a US military veteran kills 168 people. The event shatters the heart of the nation and spreads fear.

You conclude that terrorism can happen anytime, anywhere, and for no apparent reason. No place is safe. You find that your parents are less and less permissive of your riding your bike outside with your friends after school. They buy you a Nintendo 64. Safely inside, you spend many hours in front of the TV playing video games.

As you turn eighteen and prepare to graduate from high school, the media is focused on a sex scandal involving President Clinton and an intern named Monica Lewinsky. Soon after you start college, the president of the United States of America is impeached. There are so many confusing messages from this event around sex and domination and politics that it is hard to unravel exactly what it means. You walk away feeling like the American political system is dishonest and demeaning.

Unlike many of your friends who are not lucky enough to go to college, you sign papers for a significant student loan and enroll at university.

You are in the spring semester of your freshman year of college when the news of the Columbine High School shooting breaks. The horrific video footage shows two high schoolers killing their classmates with shotguns, rifles, and semiautomatic weapons. Even though the images are deeply disturbing, they look similar to the video games you binged on as a teenager. The world is becoming ever less safe. Death awaits around every corner in films, on TV, and now in the real world.

In your senior year of college, somebody runs into your chemistry class and says, "A plane has crashed into the World Trade Center— America is under attack!" Panic ensues as everyone rushes to the nearest television. There on the screen, you see the images that will be burned into the retinas of a generation over and over and over again. The unspeakable, senseless death and destruction leave a permanent mark on your psyche.

You will go on to graduate, to watch America embroil itself in a bloody war in Iraq over weapons of mass destruction that do not exist, and to experience the economic meltdown of the free world as you turn thirty. But September 11, 2001, remains a universal moment for you and your peers.

Says David Burstein, who heads up an organization called Run for America (runfor.us) that encourages young people to run for office, "September eleventh is this generation's Kennedy assassination moment. There are two things about it that I think are particularly important. The first is that it is really the last unifying media experience I think that will ever happen."

Burstein explains that, due to the lack of Facebook and Twitter in 2001, 9/11 was perhaps the final time the entire Millennial generation watched one single event. According to Burstein, the second important thing about 9/11 in relation to Millennials is that "it's one of the reasons why you see some unifying values around civic participation, around service, around concern with problems and challenges in the world."

Each generation has a touchstone event, a nearly universally identifiable moment when everyone remembers where they were, what they were doing, and who they were with. For your generation, that event was 9/11.

That cataclysmic moment, along with the aforementioned events, created one central, universal context for your generation:

### YOU. ARE. NOT. SAFE.

I apologize if it hits a bit too close to home, but it had to be said.

You see, this covert driver of your generation's social psychology has profound implications for you and your life. It's like a subroutine running in the background of your mind. It makes decisions for you without your even knowing about it. And while it may be based on real life experience, it is not empirically true. And it is certainly not an empowering context in which to live.

Part of your generation's antidote to an unsafe world was to be constantly surrounded by, and digitally connected to, your peers. This fundamental need for connection strengthened your already important Millennial tenet of teamwork, ensuring the unwavering intensive collectivism of your generation.

But it also created a dark shadow. And for your generation to realize its full potential, you are going to have to deal with your version of this specter.

## SELF-OBSESSED LITTLE NARCISSISTS

In 2013, the same year the famed *Time* magazine cover article labeled Millennials the "ME ME ME Generation," a new word was added to the online version of the prestigious *Oxford English Dictionary*. The word was *selfie*. Not only did they add selfie and YOLO and ICYMI and WDYT, the dictionary's lexicographers named *selfie* the 2013 Word of the Year. According to one *USA Today* article, which gushed about this momentous occasion, the use of the word *selfie* increased 17,000 percent from 2012 to 2013[41]—and most of that was just on Mylie Cyrus's Facebook page. (I'm joking, but only about the Mylie Cyrus bit.)

Until recently, the concept of taking one's own photo was reserved for a mountaineer who reached the summit only after his fellow climbers had turned back (or died). But now, with the tiny selfie-enabling GoPro camera company valued at over $2 billion and Apple's selfie-always-on, OMG-I've-gotta-have-the-latest phones boosting the company's stock into the post–Steve Jobs stratosphere, *selfie* isn't just part of our lexicon, it's part of our daily lives.

Corbin Bleu, a Millennial and one of the lead actors in the cult movie series *High School Musical*, tells me, "That is the one aspect of Millennials that I actually can't stand. It's the narcissism. Now, it's weird, because, look, I'm an actor. Part of our job is to be narcissistic. But now everyone wants to look beautiful all the time. Because our generation is fed so much information, everyone wants to be noticed. And that's because we compare ourselves all the time. Everyone wants to have the life of a Kardashian."

The conclusion: Millennials have fallen into a downward spiral of narcissism. And like a black hole that pulls in stars around it, they are influencing society at large to do the same. But focusing on self-image might actually be a way of covering up something else.

A Birmingham Business School discussion paper that surveyed 508 Facebook users with an average age of twenty-four concluded that the number of selfies somebody posts is inversely proportional to the closeness they feel to their friends, coworkers, and relatives who use Facebook.[42] In other words, the more selfies you post, the more emotionally isolated you feel.

However, consider the inverse: that people in your generation who experience social isolation are using social media to fit in, to be liked, and to feel validated. What if the selfie phenomenon was not fueled directly by narcissism but rather by a deep need to belong to a peer group without which you might *die*?

Think about it: the major pivotal life moments for Millennials sent one clear message: YOU ARE NOT SAFE. Peer connection isn't the antidote to loneliness, it is the antidote to a world that might kill you at any moment. Safety in numbers, right?

That need to fit into your peer group is heightened by a daily onslaught of online and off-line hyper-real, Photoshopped images of how you should look, what your friends should look like, and how life should be.

Is it possible that people in your generation experience *what would normally be termed increased narcissism as a result* of a heightened sense of social isolation because *when you are alone you could die*?

After all, let's be honest: dying alone sucks.

As we witness high school shooting after high school shooting, it is undeniable: the younger you are, the more vulnerable you are in our society. Our country literally paints targets on the backs of our youth and then we shoot them. Unpacking the trauma this level of daily unsafety has imprinted on you is very important.

First, let's talk about the *Narcissism Epidemic*, a term coined by Drs. Jean M. Twenge and W. Keith Campbell as the title of their 2009 book. According to the authors:

We know that narcissism has increased over time among individuals based on several datasets. College students now endorse more narcissistic traits than college students did in the 1980s and 1990s. . . . Perhaps most disturbing, a 2005 study using a large, randomly selected sample of Americans found that nearly 1 out of 10 people in their twenties had experienced NPD [Narcissistic Personality Disorder]—the more severe, clinical-level form of the trait.

As if that isn't bad enough, Drs. Twenge and Campbell tell us that up to 10 percent of Millennials are so narcissistic that they are clinically diagnosable.

If your first reaction after reading this is "I'm not like that," you might want to take the Narcissistic Personality Inventory (NPI) at http://personality-testing.info. But then again, is taking the survey itself a sign of a certain level of self-absorption, also known as narcissism?

Now let's talk about social isolation. One of the words that young people often use to describe their generation today, aside from connected and tech-savvy, is *isolated*. I first noticed this doing person-on-the-street interviews for this book and the companion documentary and have since been shocked by how universally people in your generation acknowledge that they feel a pervasive sense of isolation.

> **Take the Narcissistic Personality Inventory (NPI) at http://personality-testing.info.**

In spite of our digitally connected world, social isolation seems to be increasing. According to a paper published by the American Sociological Association, in 1985 about 10 percent of Americans had no meaningful social support. That number has since more than doubled, increasing to 25 percent.[43] Eerily similar statistics can be found in other digitally connected countries. A 2010 survey by the Mental Health Foundation in the UK found that 60 percent of eighteen- to thirty-four-year-olds spoke of feeling lonely, compared with only 35 percent of people over the age of fifty-five.[44]

Clinical psychologists have linked isolation and loneliness to impaired immune function, increased inflammation, depression, and, most disturbingly, premature death. When I ask Christine Hassler, a therapist and author who specializes in Millennials, why, in spite of all their social media connections, people in your generation are so stressed out, anxious, and isolated, she tells me:

> What I'm seeing is a lot of paralysis. When we're pulled in so many different directions psychologically often the safest thing to do is make no decision at all. And because there's this expectation especially thanks to social media that "here I am with my selfie and I'm happy all the time and my life is great," they're repressing a lot of their emotions. So that's leading to a lot of depression.

Repression, obsession with self-image, and isolation are a dangerous cocktail. It is no wonder that suicide is the second leading cause of death among Millennials.[45] All this is somewhat depressing, but I did promise you an honest assessment of your current predicament. After all, you can't run a successful revolution if you're not clear on what's at stake.

For you, Millennials, the stakes couldn't be higher. When somebody's cards are down, and their back is against the wall, their true grit comes out. Perhaps it's time for a little grit.

## A LIGHT AT THE END OF THE TUNNEL

Let's summarize this chapter: your generation has to deal with some really scary shit.

And that's just the top ten big issues we know about. Never mind the next wave of inventions that will have unintended consequences. Genetically engineered bio-disease-carrying mosquitoes? Terrorist cloud-based artificial intelligence? Yep, all coming to a reality near you.

It's enough to make you want to watch reruns of *GoT* and *Girls* until, well . . . until forever. But to your generation's credit, that doesn't seem like the way you're dealing with things, not all of you anyway.

I meet curly-haired, upbeat Adam Smiley Poswolsky, thirty-five-year-old author of the book *The Quarter-Life Breakthrough*, in a huge church in a hilly neighborhood of San Francisco. In an amusing twist of irony, churches like this across the country are going out of business, largely because you, Millennials, are the most un-religiously affiliated generation in recent history. That's why Poswolsky and his friends are converting this stone and stained-glass behemoth into a live/work space for community events.

Poswolsky and I find an upstairs room that has been hastily converted into a bedroom with a mattress thrown on the floor and a folding chair, the bootstrapped Millennial equivalents of a *Better Homes and Gardens* bedroom showcase. After feeling crushed by the shallowness of his cushy, well-paid job in Washington, DC, Adam now teaches seminars and workshops to young people on how to find and follow their true purpose. He's clear that he's had good opportunities because of his upbringing—two parents who are professors.

But he is also clear that more and more Millennials like himself are giving up chasing the old American Dream in order to help their less fortunate peers.

Says Poswolsky:

> We hear all about the me-me-me generation, right? The selfie generation. It's a nice headline. It's good clickbait. But a lot of the data shows that this is actually a generation that wants to use their work for purpose. People are more interconnected than ever. And I think what happens when you combine an increasingly connected world, and an increasingly global job market, with an increasing economic crisis for a lot of Millennials, people start to shift what really matters in their life.

Poswolsky says this shift in values for many Millennials occurs around the age of twenty-five. Hence the term *quarter-life crisis*. The crisis is generally resolved, says Poswolsky, when young people put their time and energy and passion toward doing something with purpose, aka changing the world.

Perhaps this quarter-life value shift is why you, Millennials, have managed to work together to accomplish so many things in such a short period of time.

As a generation, you have pried open the formerly taboo discourse on gender, creating a new level of empathy and awareness than prior generations could have even imagined. Through hard-won battles and some tragic bloodshed, you're working to redefine racial equality. We have your youth vote to thank for the first black president in US history and for the first honest conversation in almost fifty years on the racial brutality, institutionalized racism, and race-classism that exist in America.

And you've already staged the biggest wave of global protests and revolutions in world history, many of which were organized over a medium that only allows 140 characters. Finally, due to the sheer size of your ratings, you've managed to get us some decent late-night talk show hosts.

Thank you. It's an encouraging start.

But your work has just begun. To truly understand how to recode the self-destructive programming of our society, you will first need to understand the key mistakes made by the generations that came before you.

> "The data shows that this is actually a generation that wants to use their work for purpose."

40.6892, 74.0445

## CHAPTER TWO

# How Y(ou) Came to Be

*I know you hear me now, we are a different kind*
*We can do anything*

—"Heroes" by Alesso

In swampy, southern Louisiana where I grew up, the only thing thicker than the racism, bigotry, and poverty was the gumbo.

As soon as I was eighteen, I loaded up my car and got the heck outta there. But in 2005, after Hurricane Katrina pulverized entire cities as if they were made of matchsticks, I returned home to volunteer with the relief effort. Shortly thereafter, I, along with thousands of motorists, had a near-death experience when I got trapped inside the merciless force of Hurricane Rita. Then in 2010, along with my wife, Rebecca, I returned home once again to document the Deepwater Horizon oil spill. When Rebecca was chemically poisoned by the dispersant spray used to clean up the oil slicks, it was the last straw. I swore I would never return.

Yet here I am, taking my morning run, right down St. Charles Avenue in New Orleans. Damn it.

Even in winter it's so muggy I'm covered in sweat after a block. Another block and I'm being seduced by the Spanish moss, the oak trees, and the streetcars. As I avoid the gaping holes and jutting chunks of cement in the ancient sidewalks, I can smell Cajun boudin sausage cooking somewhere. Mmmm, I'm literally salivating. All I can think about is breakfast with some chicory-root coffee and beignets.

As my sneakers find the grass of Audubon Park, I am overwhelmed with nostalgia. And because of the dark underbelly of this place, that nostalgia is a mixed bag. In fact, it's for all the reasons I left home in the first place—from the deep racial divides to this state's insidious and corrupt addiction to the fossil fuel industry to the inevitable climate catastrophes it must endure and to the denial that these climatic events could have any connection to the 50 percent of America's gasoline made here—that I have now returned.

But this time I'm not here to try to fix any of it.

Instead, I'm here to observe another group that is trying, very hard, to fix things. And they don't just want to fix Louisiana; they're taking on the entire country, and for some of them, the world. They've come from all over. They include politicians, activists, media makers, coders, staffers, agitators, and yes, at least one mega-Millennial celebrity—Jennifer Lawrence. Their event is called the Unrig the System Summit, and it's put on by a bipartisan group called Represent.US.

By the time I drag my camera crew across the Tulane campus to find the student union where the conference is being held, I'm starving. As I sit and wolf down my not-boudin sausage, not-beignet breakfast, I stare vacantly at the back of a young man's shirt. As my blood sugar rises, I become enthralled by the strange details of what is printed on his shirt.

The image is of a multiple-choice, fill-in-the-circle rating system. But it's not for rating your favorite restaurant or giving your oh-so-wonderful Lyft driver five stars. It's for voting for political candidates. The shirt says "STAR Voting," which is apparently an acronym for Score Then Automatic Runoff. (It originally stood for Secure, Transparent, Auditable, and Reliable, so you can pick your favorite.) There's a scale that goes from 0 for "no support" all the way to 5 for "max support." Under the scale is an example list of candidates who ran in the 2016 US presidential election. Next to each candidate are five circles that one could presumably pencil in. There's Jill from the Green Party, Bernie the Independent, Donny the Republican, Hillary the Democrat, and so on.

I'm trying to bend my mind around this scorecard. Is this some sort of meme? Or a joke? Am I totally out of the loop?

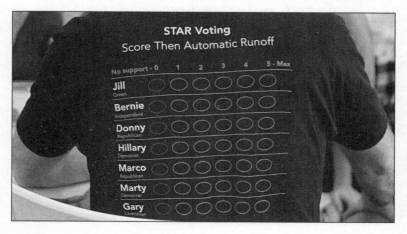

After snapping a couple of photos, I introduce myself to the young man wearing the shirt, Mark, and his coconspirator, Sara. They quickly explain that STAR-Vote, as it is officially called, is a genuine multiple-choice political voting system designed by a group of voting experts, cryptographers, and coders. It's also open source, of course.

> "We're talking about election reform, gerrymandering, money in politics, and the Electoral College. . . . But even if we solved all of them, we wouldn't get to the root of the problem, which is the voting system."

Instead of deciding between two or three politicians in what amounts to a process of elimination, STAR-Vote allows you to rank a number of politicians against one another. According to my new friends, it has proven to be more accurate than any other form of voting in representing the desires of a populace.

STAR-Vote, it turns out, may be one of a set of super-important social inventions that, when applied together, could be used to give the Millennial generation access to changing the structures of power of our society.[1] And, like many of the political innovations that will be discussed at this summit, it is being championed by a handful of Millennials.

Says Sara Wolk, who is working to get STAR Voting happening in Oregon:

> At this conference we're talking about election reform, gerrymandering, money in politics, and the Electoral College. And those are critical issues right now. But even if we solved all of them, we wouldn't get to the root of the problem, which is the voting system. What we really want here is to be able to vote our conscience. We want our vote to not be wasted. And so if we actually had those things, it would revolutionize democracy.

Given that your generation exists in an economic reality where your earning potential is literally sliding backward, and given that you are inheriting no less than ten global existential crises, it is no wonder that so many bright young people like Sara want to use their time and energy to make a positive difference in the world.

Survey after survey points to the 75 percent or more of Millennial respondents who "want to make a positive difference in the world." That's a very good thing.

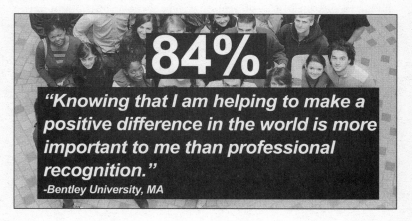

**84%**

*"Knowing that I am helping to make a positive difference in the world is more important to me than professional recognition."*
*-Bentley University, MA*

Numerous surveys and studies point to the Millennial generation's desire for civic service—or, rather, "doing good"—over career advancement.

But how and where you channel that effort is as important as making the effort in the first place.

Understanding your true origin story is the first piece in the puzzle of how to solve the terrifying problems you are being handed. The Spanish essayist and philosopher George Santayana said, "Those who cannot remember the past are condemned to repeat it." Thus, Millennials, if you're going to dodge the existential threats hurtling toward you, it's imperative that you get some fresh historical perspective.

Each generation has a story, a universal driver that pushes its members to make largely unconscious decisions. Together, over the course of history, the drivers have shaped the world. Hence, today's ten species-threatening crises. The mechanisms that pushed prior generations to action or inaction are still at work today. Thus, if we want to change the future, the first place we must look is to the past.

In his famous book *1984*, George Orwell teaches us that if you can erase and rewrite the past, you can control the present. As we will cover in chapter 5, your history education was likely covertly brought to you by, and/or tainted by, one of many corporations that have successfully infiltrated the American school system in order to hack your brains. And those corporations would prefer to control not just your future, but your understanding of the past.

Perhaps that's why the following history was left out of your schoolbooks.

## YOUTH CULTURE V1.0

This story starts around fifty thousand years ago with the birth of our species and goes right up to today. It's a lot of ground to cover so excuse me if I skip over a few inconsequential details.

The concept of *teenager* or *young adult* is a relatively recent invention. For millennia indigenous cultures held coming-of-age rituals in which a child became a man or woman by virtue of a series of initiations. These ceremonies spanned the gamut from public circumcision with a stone cutting tool to hallucinogenic journeys into nature to find a spirit guide.

Crossing the threshold into adulthood generally coincided with some stage of puberty. Essentially you went from being a kid and, whamo! (or *ouch!* as the case may have been), you were an adult. You could then procreate, fetch food, and go to war if needed. There was no high school, no college, no soul-searching-for-the-perfect-path quarter-life crisis. From the time Homo sapiens began to walk until the mid-1800s, preindustrial society didn't give you a whole lot of time between youth and adulthood.

Then in the span of fewer than one hundred years, everything changed.

## COAL, STEAM, AND STEEL

Coming out of the crisis of the Civil War, America was reborn a nation built of steam engines, railroads, oil, steel, coal, and factories.

The Industrial Revolution that began in Great Britain and then spread to Europe and America brought with it tectonic shifts in social organization. A generation of children became the backbone of the labor force. By 1900, kids were doing almost a quarter of the labor in America. (It's nice to know that unpaid internships have such a long history.)

By the late 1800s, young toughs were spreading crime in cities, inciting agrarian protests, and organizing labor riots against slave-like working conditions. As more emphasis was placed on the personal development of youth, a new idea of how to deal with the youth problem emerged: mandatory schooling.[2]

America's schools were created as a training ground for the industrial labor force. In essence, our education system was an extension of an industrial production model. Children needed to be trained to begin a workday on time, to eat at certain times, to take directions and not disobey, and to conform. This education formed the foundation of the linear economic model of extract, produce, consume, and waste that we have today.

Schools would solve another problem that America was grappling with. As people from all over the world had poured into Ellis Island, the Great American melting pot hadn't yet simmered. A new educational system was developed to assimilate myriad cultures into one strain of ethics and ideals. The classroom quickly became a place to mold youth into the national image of heroism, patriotism, and duty.

Soon after 1900 American youths also began being molded outside the classroom as groups like the Boy Scouts took hold of after-school activity time. By 1916 there were 250,000 Boy Scouts in America alone. Scouting was a military-style organization that taught outdoor skills. In other words, fun-army for kids.

According to the *Boy Scout Handbook* of 1911, Scouts were to have "duty," "know the history of the important wars," and have "muscles that will not fail you." The manual makes multiple references to battle and paints a strong picture of a young man that is the embodiment of an outdoor soldier.[3]

It was the perfect preparation for what was soon to come.

## HOT JAZZ

Across the ocean, Germany was expediting its own outdoor youth movement. The Wandervogel, or wandering bird, promoted group hikes and camping excursions in the countryside. But unlike the English-speaking scouting movement, the Germanic movement was quickly indoctrinated with the ideals of racial hygiene, abstinence, and denouncing of alcohol and tobacco. Just like in America, young people in the classroom were trained to become workers, and after school, soldiers.

Then in 1914, Germany invaded Belgium, marking the beginning of the First World War.

All that scout training came in handy as young men on both sides of World War I survived the terrible conditions of the Western Front while killing one another. In 1919, when the Treaty of Versailles was signed, a young shell-shocked generation returned from the battlefront and sought solace in music, alcohol, and dance. The war was over and young folks needed to blow off some steam.

Jazz, swing dance, and new fashions poured out of nightclubs. The reverie of America's flappers and slicks was bolstered by advertisers who unleashed a tidal wave of ads targeted at a new and untapped market: America's adolescents.

Because the success of the modern industrial economy had to be measured by growth, the economy needed to constantly expand. To keep the economy growing, it was critical to involve the youth not just in production but also in consumption.

For the first time, movie stars leapt off the screen and began endorsing products. Radio, records, the movies, and fashion were directed toward, and dictated by, young people. From 1918 to 1920, magazine sales doubled. The marketing frenzy promoted a youth that was different, dangerous, and full of sexual prowess. These ideals were further spread by F. Scott Fitzgerald's bestselling book *This Side of Paradise* and its descriptions of drunken car rides and petting parties.

In the 1920s youth began to see itself as a class—a group with its own power. Born largely from squalor and war, they were molded by advertising and marketing into a sort of Youth Culture version 1.0. People who wanted to sell them products rode the perfect storm of a disenfranchised, energized youth with its own counterculture fashion, music, and big-name youth-icon stars.

The party was on, and it lasted through the Roaring Twenties all the way up to the stock market crash of 1929, which signaled the end of the era and the beginning of a deep social crisis.

To deal with that crisis, a new generation of heroes came forth.


## THE GREATEST GENERATION

In his seminal book *The Greatest Generation*, journalist Tom Brokaw tells the stories of the men and women who survived the Second World War. According to Brokaw:

> At a time in their lives when their days and nights should have been filled with innocent adventure, love, and the lessons of the work-aday world, they were fighting in the most primitive conditions possible across the bloodied landscape of France, Belgium, Italy, Austria, and the coral islands of the Pacific. They answered the call to save the world from the two most powerful and ruthless military machines ever assembled, instruments of conquest in the hands of fascist maniacs. They faced great odds and a late start, but they did not protest. They succeeded on every front. They won the war; they saved the world. They came home to joyous and short-lived celebrations and immediately began the task of rebuilding their lives and the world they wanted. They married in record numbers and gave birth to another distinctive generation, the Baby Boomers.

In other words, these folks were, like, the best people ever. They're known as the Builders or the GI Generation. And in some respects, their introduction to the world was eerily similar to that of the Millennials.

In 1929 the stock market crashed, plunging America and most of the world into the Great Depression; the corollary to this is our 2008 Great Recession. To make matters worse, a man-made environmental disaster of biblical proportions soon overtook the midwestern plains. Called the Dust Bowl, it darkened the skies as soil blew in massive storms across America; the corollary to this is our current global environmental crisis.

With the global economy in shock, a crazy fascist used hypnotic propaganda to enlist millions of mostly young people into a maniacal mass genocide. His name was Adolf Hitler (think ISIS and other fascist leaders of today).

As Hitler declared, "I am beginning with the young. . . . Look at these young men and boys! What material! With them I can make a new world." Hitler's hypnotic propaganda had a quasi-religious fervor. The Third Reich's parades, songs, films, and events were targeted at Germany's disenfranchised youth. By the end of his first year in power, almost 2.5 million young men and women had joined the Hitler Youth, or *Hitlerjugend*.[4] That number would expand to over seven million by the start of the Second World War in 1939, when Germany invaded Poland.

From Pearl Harbor to Dresden young men killed one another with fossil-fueled, industrial-scale death machines. The cultures that had, up until the very beginning of the war, shared common youth-centric swing dance music and hot jazz now caused catastrophic human carnage. Approximately sixty million people were

> Hitler declared, "I am beginning with the young. . . . Look at these young men and boys! What material! With them I can make a new world."

killed during the war, six million of whom were European Jews murdered in Nazi death camps.

> **It was time for the GI Generation to come home, to celebrate, and to make babies.**

Wars tend to profit the winners and the Second World War was an economic turning point for America. Building all those guns, tanks, ships, and planes gave the economy a massive injection of cash. The US economy was already booming by the time the Japanese surrendered. At the close of the war in 1945, the US GDP had mushroomed by 400 percent from where it stood in the 1930s.[5]

It was time for the GI Generation to come home, to celebrate, and to make babies. Lots of babies.

It bears mentioning that a smaller generation was sandwiched between the GIs and the Baby Boomers. These wartime babies became known as the Silent Generation. Born too late to be part of the war effort and too early to join the postwar reverie, they were conformist, risk averse, and worker-bee-like. The tone and mood of the Silent Generation was the polar opposite to that of the Baby Boomers who followed them (think Generation Z, also known as the Homeland Generation).

## BOOM, BABY, BOOM!

As sixteen million American men returned from the battlefront and women put down their riveting guns, it was as if somebody turned on the baby hose. In January 1946 there were around 250,000 babies born in America. In October of that year, that number surged to 339,499. By 1954, four million babies were being born annually in the United States, a sixteen-fold increase from prewar times.[6]

The postwar party was definitely on. It was time to create the largest generation the world had known.

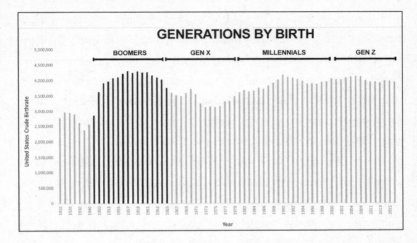

The "Baby Boom" represented a true acceleration in births. It was followed by a decline in births during Generation X, and then a steady increase in births in the Millennial generation. Generation Z appears to be extending the trend, with births remaining strong.

*Data:* US Census Bureau.

Over the next few years, as young GIs and their wives settled into suburbia, marketers intensified their focus toward both the youth culture and the new young adult culture. General Motors had already set forth its vision for an integrated suburban lifestyle by sponsoring a massive exhibit at the 1939 World's Fair. Called Futurama, the exhibit showed how the newly constructed national highway system would allow Americans to live outside the cities and commute to work and leisure activities. Free from traffic jams, pollution, and strip malls, this brave new world prepared young Americans for their upcoming cement landscape. To sell its cars, GM sold the next generation of Americans a lifestyle that necessitated them.

It was the 1950s. The mood was optimistic, and unemployment was at an all-time low. The GI Bill allowed young men (at least white men) to finish high school, attend college, and buy homes. The baby boom spurred a housing boom, which prompted a consumption boom, which pushed a boom in jobs (again, mostly for white males). The white middle class ballooned, and the majority of the labor force held white-collar jobs. It was *Happy Days* and *The Wonder Years* all rolled together in vibrant, ad-sponsored Technicolor.

It was during this time that consumerism became a science. With propaganda techniques gleaned from Nazi Germany during the war, "Mad Men" on Madison Avenue embarked on a new era of teaching people how to buy. Women were targeted by popular television shows like *Father Knows Best*, which repetitively depicted each room of the house, and each furnishing. Men, meanwhile, were targeted by men's magazines like *Playboy*. These depicted the furnishings and accessories needed for the "modern man."[7]

Advertising media also fused socially acceptable gender roles and racial stereotypes with consumerism. It was the man of the house in *Father Knows Best* who drove his General Motors car home from work to greet his perfect wife, who had made dinner from products she bought at the supermarket. This audiovisual training was a critical component in building up the consumption economy, in stereotyping the American Dream, and in creating a system of rewards that could be achieved only by climbing the corporate ladder. It also helped institutionalize racism and sexism in suburban America and beyond.[8]

A generation of people hardened by war, sacrifice, and poverty were finally getting their share of the good life. The GI Generation believed in maintaining a strong military, in the superiority of the

American economic system, in the supremacy of the American political system and president, and in the sanctity of the patriarchal family structure. After all, it was these very social institutions that had delivered them unto the Promised Land.

In a time when plastic was not yet clogging our oceans, when national and personal debt were nonexistent, and when the nations of the world regarded America as the embodiment of a Hollywood movie hero (think John Wayne), the Greatest Generation had a lustrous postwar adulthood.

It was a near-perfect end to a story of difficult trials and tribulations. But it didn't last long.

## WAR. HUH! WHAT IS IT GOOD FOR?

By the 1960s the first members of the Baby Boomers began to come of age. Having grown up under strict parents in a time of relative prosperity, they began to rebel against some of the very social institutions their GI parents had held dear. And during that same time, from 1965 to 1975, America waged another kind of war in a far-off place called Vietnam.

The Vietnam War dealt a harsh blow to America's young. Starting in 1969, the draft used a lottery system to select young men to go to war; a disproportionately high number of draftees in the lottery were men of color.[9] The fear of this real-life version of *The Hunger Games*' "reaping" was further amplified by images of the horror of war, which glowed on television sets at night in living rooms across America. The personal and immediate impact of the war gave rise to a movement of political and ethical dissension.

Called hippies, many Baby Boomers promulgated a general but

peaceful "F-You" to the norms of postindustrial, militarized society. Their Flower Power and their love-ins offered psychedelic drugs and transcendental meditation as wartime antidotes. They created an atmosphere of radical, and sometimes naked, self-expression. These flower children were prone to "turn on, tune in, drop out," as the famous psychologist and psychedelic proponent Timothy Leary preached. They were reacting to war and to the industrialization of the world brought by their parents, and they were trying to create inner and outer peace.

The 1960s were a time of two other critical movements, which were themselves linked: civil rights and women's liberation. From Martin Luther King Jr.'s 1963 "I Have a Dream" speech to the 1970 Women's Strike for Equality, the marches, protests, and power of the progressive youth of the late 1960s and early 1970s were unprecedented in their scale and scope.

These movements didn't just make noise, they accomplished substantive political change. They prompted the passage of the 1965 Voting Rights Act, which prohibited discrimination at the polls, ensuring that people of color and women could vote freely. The nascent environmental movement, which in many ways was interconnected with the struggle for racial and gender equality, was largely responsible for the 1970 creation of the Environmental Protection Agency. The combined momentum of these movements was also instrumental in the 1971 passage of the Twenty-Sixth Amendment, which cemented the right for eighteen-year-olds to vote.

**These movements didn't just make noise, they accomplished substantive political change.**

All in all, the Baby Boomer generation kicked butt in its youth.

Not to mention their music. (I mean, from the Beatles and the Rolling Stones to Britney Spears, things really took a nosedive.)

As they realized their potential, the movements of the Baby Boomers began to coalesce. Women's rights, feminism, Black Power, and environmental rights were sharing resources, strategies, and philosophies. Like Millennials, the Baby Boomers represented a disproportionately high percentage of the population. Thus, when the Baby Boomer youth flexed its power, often through acts of nonviolent civil disobedience, it was a formidable force.

But as we will see in the next chapter, not all, and probably only a fraction of, Baby Boomers participated in the social movements and progressive reforms of the 1960s. And as history shows, powerful movements tend to make powerful adversaries. Beginning with the assassination of John F. Kennedy and then with Malcolm X and again with Martin Luther King Jr. and finally with Bobby Kennedy, many of the brightest trailblazers of the 1960s were extinguished.

With its leadership gutted, the progressive movements of the 1960s would soon splinter.

Meanwhile, dark forces were amassing. Their singular objective? To dismantle and roll back the hard-won progressive political victories of the 1960s, the "decade that changed a nation."[10]

## X MARKS THE SPOT

People have more sex during good times, and they have less sex when times are tough.

We know this is true because when the economy is good, people have more babies and when things are turbulent, they have fewer babies. (Sex being a prerequisite for babies and all, it's a pretty clear correlation.)

Generation X, that inconvenient, in-between generation to which I belong, was born into a time characterized by fear, war, and economic uncertainty. The smaller size of Generation X reflected the insecurity of its parents and their taking the Pill, or rather, their forgetting to take the Pill. It wasn't just our parents who were nervous, though. As young kids, many members of my generation watched the images of war on television sets. We would later be criticized as an extremely cynical group of people. Go figure.

> **People have more sex during good times, and they have less sex when times are tough.**

By 1972, the Vietnam War had dragged on for seventeen long years. On June 8 of that year a chilling photograph of a young naked Vietnamese girl running in front of a small group of soldiers exploded onto the front page of newspapers around the world. The girl, Phan Thị Kim Phúc, had torn off her clothes after being badly burned when a South Vietnamese plane accidentally dropped its payload of napalm on South Vietnamese troops and civilians. For many people, the image crystalized the sentiment that the war had been brutal, senseless, and inhumane. More than 50,000 American troops had been killed; between 200,000 and 250,000 South Vietnamese soldiers perished; and around two million Vietnamese civilians were slain, many of them innocent villagers like Phan Thị Kim Phúc's two cousins who were burned to death right before the fated photograph was taken. It was time for the United States to pull out.

Almost one in ten young men from the Baby Boomer generation had served in Vietnam. Unlike the time after the Second World War, which was filled with praise for GIs, American servicemen returning from the gory, chemical-strewn jungles of South Vietnam were often shunned.

With the ghosts of war haunting them, the Vietnam veterans and the flower children attempted to settle back into suburban perfection.

## DISCO, OIL, AND A CALIFORNIA RADIO HOST

The second half of the 1970s was a weird time. Disco music was in the air. Pablo Escobar's cocaine started flowing through Miami. America elected a former peanut farmer named Jimmy Carter as its president.

Perhaps after all that napalm-induced death, Jimmy Carter appealed to a softer, gentler side of America. Unfortunately, he was unprepared for the series of crises that plagued his presidency. American hostages were taken in Iran, and not one but two oil shocks were brought on by political upheaval in the Middle East. The US economy, which was then and still is dependent on oil, came to a screeching halt.

> **Fighting wars in Southeast Asia, being on the front lines of social movements, and dropping acid aren't great preparations for parenthood.**

As many would soon learn, fighting wars in Southeast Asia, being on the front lines of social movements, and dropping acid aren't great preparations for parenthood. The Boomer divorce rate climbed higher and Generation X was parented by ever more single working parents. Hence our generation's best-known moniker, latchkey kids.

Just when it seemed like things couldn't get much worse, a conservative motivational speaker–turned radio host–turned actor from California was elected US president (think Rush Limbaugh, but with the charisma of Tony Robbins). Ronald Reagan's election initiated a kind of postwar, self-indulgent euphoria.

As a paternal figure to our generation, Ronnie Reagan would

bestow Gen X with many wonders. Among them he would slash the budgets of education, public art, public television, public radio, food stamps, and the EPA. He would gut social services (who needs those with so many single parents anyway?). He would also build up the US military, which included a plan called Star Wars to send laser-guided missile satellites into space. According to the *New York Times*, Reagan more than doubled annual military spending from $162 billion in 1981 to an estimated $341 billion in 1986.[11, 12]

He would also ensure that ketchup was counted as a vegetable in our school lunches. If only he could have eaten at my cafeteria.

Oh, and by the way, Reagan ran under the slogan "Let's Make America Great Again." (Cue the urge to vomit.)

For all his shortcomings, Ronald Reagan gave Americans, and especially the Baby Boomers, something they desperately needed: confidence. Reagan preached a magical economic theory he called trickle-down economics that in essence meant: make rich people really rich and then the money will just somehow "trickle down" to everyone else.[13] His trickle-down economic policies were part of an ideology called neoliberalism in which governmental oversight, social services, and restrictions on predatory forms of capitalism are traded for privatization and hands-off government policies. While we will more fully define neoliberalism in chapter 4, the Reagan renaissance was short-lived.

There is no doubt that Reagan's massive military spending and tax cuts to the rich gave the economy a boost, but the TV-star president was also the beneficiary of good timing.

In response to the oil shocks of the late 1970s, President Carter had instated a broad energy policy to create as much domestic energy in as short a period of time as possible.[14] The Carter administration had tried many forms of energy including putting solar panels on the roof of the White House, which Reagan later removed.[15]

Thanks to Carter's energy policies, it was the increased production of US oil reserves, particularly shale oil from fracking, oil from Alaska's North Slope, and production in Texas that flowed cheap black gold into the US market in the early 1980s,[16] thereby depressing the price of oil, which is the basis of the price

> America went on a credit-card shopping spree with no thought about who would get stuck with the bill.

of other staples, including food. With cheap domestic oil flowing, the US economy went gonzo.[17] Ultimately, Reagan's secret economic sauce wasn't his neoliberal economic policies, it was the shale oil.

Even as the nation quietly racked up a massive amount of debt from Reagan's economic policies, the 1980s were an era of neon-drenched economic prosperity. In other words, America went on a credit-card shopping spree with no thought about who would get stuck with the bill.

It was time to party. Good timing, too, because the War on Drugs seemed to have an inverse effect. Coke was blowing through night-clubs like dust in a windstorm. Hair was big. Music was brash and loud. The Apple computer was unveiled. Cheap VHS players meant you could watch movies whenever you wanted. The Berlin Wall fell. For many people, it was a good time.

And what do people do in good times? Yep: they have lots of sex, which tends to lead to babies.

Lots of babies.

And so began your particular cycle of history.

(Sorry, didn't mean to conjure up the idea of your parents having . . . okay, never mind.)

## THE ECHO BOOM

Starting around 1980, the number of US births took off like a rocket. (And apparently that wasn't the only thing.)

What made this increase different from the Baby Boom, in which mothers had an average of three to five births, is that the number of births per woman during the Echo Boom remained relatively low. In other words, the vast number of Baby Boomer women who were now becoming mothers, and the low per-woman fertility rate, meant that the 1980s surge in total births didn't just come from a few women, it came from almost forty million of them. For the next two decades, those forty million women would give birth to about two children each.

These new moms were giving birth a little later in life than their mothers had. The added life experience theoretically brought with it more wisdom. The Baby Boomer generation itself was also beginning to diversify due to immigration. The majority of Boomers were done going to war and protesting and doing drugs. Instead, they were procreating in record numbers. During the twenty years between 1980 and 2000, the stork brought home eighty million little Millennial bundles of joy.

By 1980, your parents had gotten some serious experience with birth control. That means that you, Millennials, were the most planned—aka wanted—generation in history. And your parents also had notably different values than their parents had before them.

On the whole, the Baby Boomers were a generation in search of inner truth and meaning. Many of them went on, or are still on, some form of spiritual quest. The Boomer generation saw both an intensification in belief in established religions like Christianity and a large number of people exploring alternative belief systems. Hence, theirs is a generation characterized by strong moral certainty.[18]

Given those strong Boomer morals, it's not surprising that the psychological and spiritual literature that proliferated in the 1960s and 1970s espoused that childhood development was a function of nurture, not nature. With gusto, these new parents embraced the philosophy that you could have a remarkable impact on the way a person turns out by how you raise them. Really, who knew?

While this idea seems painfully self-evident now, it was a revelation to a generation of people for whom obedience training was often the short end of a belt.

Speaking of corporal punishment, if you're a Millennial, your parents also abolished that in schools. Before Boomer parenting books, hitting your child in public or private was considered acceptable parenting.

Your parents wanted a kinder, gentler world for you, their little treasures. In the 1980s, the most pervasive safety movement in history swept the nation, coating everything from playground equipment to car seats in round, foamy, kid-friendly cushion. As the 1980s gave way to the 1990s and Oklahoma City was bombed, and teenage assassins riddled Columbine High School with bullets, an already safety-conscious parental generation went apoplectic around keeping children safe.

> In the 1980s, the most pervasive safety movement in history swept the nation.

In predominantly white suburban neighborhoods, young Millennials, the seeds of a better tomorrow, needed to be inside under lock and key. Your generation experienced an intensification of adult supervision.[19] When you were allowed outside while not in school, it was under adult supervision. In contrast, prior generations had just done "whatever" until dark, and surprisingly, most of us survived.[20]

Due to the need for safety and supervision, many of you experienced far more structured free time than we in Generation X had experienced only a decade earlier. Parents who had the time and means to shuffle you around programmed your after-school lives—from playdates, to ball games, to dinner, to homework, to bed. Soccer moms and dads became a staple of suburban life. Millennials, it's important to note that before 1980 not only was there no such thing as a minivan, never mind an SUV, but parents just didn't run their kids around after school. Back then, your after-school world consisted of your bike, your friends, and the neighborhood.

> The concepts of working in teams and safety in numbers were important core pieces of generational programming.

Millennials, another new phenomenon took hold on your ball fields and in your classrooms, where there was a heavy emphasis placed on teamwork. Like life, sports and education were now suddenly about cooperation. (Many of your parents were spiritualists after all.) The concepts of working in teams and safety in numbers were important core pieces of generational programming that would soon find their way into all areas of your world.

For many of your generation, the lives of your parents became structured, too—around you. A certain kind of perfect-kid obsession characterized the way parents coached, mentored, encouraged, congratulated, and promoted their children. As toddlers graduated into Little Leaguers, "Baby on Board" signs were replaced with "My Child . . ." bumper stickers.

The Boomer penchant for spirituality gave way to the conclusion that self-actualization in the form of self-esteem was an important, and missing, part of childhood development. Quick to be on the cutting edge of social trends, California commissioned a big study on the effect of self-esteem. The authors of the study concluded that self-esteem was so pivotal to a child's development and well-being, it should be baked into every part of the education system.[21]

The Self-Esteem Movement soon permeated your early media. From Barney's "Everyone Is Special" to textbooks that emphasized the uniqueness of the individual, you were taught to believe in *yourself*. Because, like a snowflake, you are unique, special, different, and beautiful.

But try as they might, your parents' generation would eventually fall short of delivering you unto a safer, gentler world. By the time Bill Clinton handed the White House over to George W. Bush in 2001, the first of your generational tidal wave were in college. And as the World Trade Center buildings fell over and over on TV screens around the world, a generational divide between Millennials, aka Generation Y, and the smaller generation that was next in line, Generation Z, was drawn.

> A bifurcation of values would occur inside the Baby Boomer generation, giving way to deep social division within the United States and abroad.

The Baby Boomer generation had been the recipients of a suburban, consumerist, wrapped-in-plastic culture that taught them disposability over conservation, consumption over austerity, and drugs over reality. As such, their legacy would be to perpetuate, accelerate, and amplify the intense marketing that had been directed at them and then redirect it toward you.

The Boomer penchant toward moral certainty would eventually give rise to a high level of moral righteousness. A bifurcation of values would occur inside the Baby Boomer generation, giving way to deep social division within the United States and abroad.

The generation that raised you on a technocratic blitzkrieg of flashing lights, sounds, and i-devices, and the one that gave you the greatest educational opportunities society has ever offered its youth, would also hand you a world at the precipice of collapse.

But before we go all ballistic and blame the Baby Boomers for every evil in the world, we need to step back and recall that theirs is a generation with an inherent and deep moral rift. On one side exists the Boomer idealism that catalyzed the conscious revolution of the 1960s and on the other side is a sort of post–World War II consumption-on-steroids mentality. As evidenced by the hyperpolarization of America's current two-party system, those two Boomer extremes may never find cohesion.

And maybe, just maybe, the splintered legacy of the Baby Boomer generation also has to do with their place in the cycle of history.

## WINTER IS COMING

In their book *The Fourth Turning*, Neil Howe and William Strauss summarize what many historians have come to believe: Western history follows a predictable and repetitive pattern. They call the four cycles that civilization seems to follow turnings, like the hands of a clock. They say the turnings are a "High," like the time after World War II; an "Awakening," like the time of the 1960s; an "Unraveling," like the late 1970s and 1980s; and finally a "Crisis," like the time of today. The Crisis accelerates to a "zenith," after which it dissipates, and the cycle begins again with another High.

Howe and Strauss say that because history tends to follow this pattern, generations tend to be archetypal. Said another way, because historical circumstances repeat themselves, the types of generations history produces also tend to repeat themselves. They call their generational archetypes the Hero (GI Generation), the Artist (Silent Generation), the Prophet (Baby Boomers), and the Nomad (Gen X).

Millennials, if you've read this far, then you've probably figured it out: if this historical cycle holds true, the next generation in line after us Nomad Gen Xers is you, who might be considered a Hero generation.

According to Neil Howe and William Strauss in their book *Generations*, in Western societies generations follow certain archetypes, and so do the periods of time in which they live. Howe and Strauss's model suggests that Millennials might be a "Hero" generation that will have to endure a great trial but will accomplish great things.

Now, before you go getting too excited, recall that in all great archetypal stories, a hero is produced only when they surmount seemingly insurmountable obstacles. In fact, the famous anthropologist Joseph Campbell believed that human mythology around the hero is so universal across cultures and eras that we, as a species, have one universal myth. He called this myth the Hero's Journey, and to this day it remains the basis for screenwriting and most fictional writing.[22]

> Millennials, you have yet to complete your Hero's Journey.

Millennials, you have yet to complete your Hero's Journey. Many have visualized the Hero's Journey as a clocklike wheel. As a generation on the journey, you currently stand somewhere around the bottom of the wheel. It is in this part of the journey that Campbell spoke about the Hero being on a "Road of Trials" and a place of great "Temptation."

It is during the next phase that the Hero must confront that which holds the greatest power in their world (often a parental figure), and must "pull the sword from the stone," or rather grasp their power.

Remember, you are entering a global crisis so vast in its magnitude and so all-encompassing, it makes Tim Burton movies look like sweet little fairy tales. It's for this reason I corral historian and coauthor of the books *Generations* and *The Fourth Turning* Neil Howe into meeting me in Los Angeles. I want to know the future. After an exhaustive conversation, I ask him the one big, really articulate question I've been saving: "Neil, what the fuck is going to happen next?"

"The Fourth Turning is, in a way, the winter of history," Howe tells me. "It's the time of death and rebirth. By the end of a Fourth Turning, all the millions of seemingly separate problems merge together into one big problem. It becomes one central crusade." He's frustratingly academic. So, I push him a little to give me an example of what may happen. After he insists that he "does not have a crystal ball," blah, blah, blah, he finally relents.

"The first lesson of history is that all the total wars in American history took place during Fourth Turnings," says Howe. He pauses, and his words seem to hang in the air between us. "This is sobering because at a time of intense solidarity, when you feel that the survival of your community is at stake, anything's on the table."

Again, I ask him to give me an example. "Well, in our last Fourth Turning," he says, referring to World War II, "we recruited all the top scientists in America to work on a weapon of mass destruction, which we then deployed." He is speaking, of course, about the atomic bombs that America dropped on Hiroshima and Nagasaki. "You think about the Civil War. If we had had such a weapon, would we have used it? I think the question answers itself. Of course we would have."

Howe's words are as chilling as they are important. Traditionally, we think of war as involving tanks, guns, and bombs. And from Trump to Putin to Kim Jong-un, we see no lack of saber rattling and no lack of arsenals of weapons to back up their threats. But we must keep in mind that the conflicts and weapons of today are vastly different from those of the recent past.

The stakes of today's ethical, racial, economic, and environmental disagreements are huge, but the theater of any war we face may not be the trenches or the traditional battleground.

I assert that the Fourth Turning's zenith is fast approaching. The conflict we face is ultimately one of values that pits the rights of humans and planet against the avarice of a dying breed of mostly white, mostly men. The theater of this conflict will be in the social media spaces, the economy, and our politics.

If we fail to resolve this conflict in those spaces, then—and only then—will it move into a technologically advanced, large-scale ground war. And if that happens in this day and age, with all the destructive power the nations of the world have amassed since the last world war, then God help us all.

> The conflict we face is ultimately one of values that pits the rights of humans and planet against the avarice of a dying breed of mostly white, mostly men.

So, Millennials—yes, you, the majority of whom say you would prefer to make a difference than get a big fat paycheck—if we are to avert the type of mass bloodshed that occurred the last time the world was in financial meltdown, the last time the environment was so acutely compromised that basic food production was threatened, and the last time that fascism reared its ugly head, you had damn well better get to work in the one area where fast, sweeping, and fundamental change can make the most difference in the shortest amount of time.

I'm talking, of course, about politics.

## PAY TO PLAY

Back at the Unrig the System Summit, I'm packed into a standing-room-only lecture hall watching Millennial movie star Jennifer Lawrence, who, it should go without saying, plays heroine Katniss Everdeen in *The Hunger Games*.

She's doing a skit with an attorney named Trevor Potter, the point of which is to illuminate how to "buy" a politician in America. In simple terms, Potter explains how to make an entity called a super PAC and how to funnel money indirectly through it to a candidate.

At one stage Lawrence says, "So I can give as much as I want to my candidate's super PAC and there are no repercussions for my candidate. But what about me? Am I listed as the main donor of this disgraced candidate?"

Potter explains that all she has to do is create an LLC and funnel the money from that. He then asks her if she has a cat. Lawrence responds, "God no." The audience guffaws as if on cue. She continues, "But I have a dog, and her name is Pippi Longstocking." Potter suggests she name the LLC after her dog and buy politicians by giving money to their super PACs through Pippi Longstocking, LLC.

The skit, and the use of an unmistakable heroic youth icon, is ingenious. It also presents an open-and-shut case on one of the primary reasons why the American political system is broken at its core.

Big money has infiltrated all levels of government. And along the way, it shut your generation out of the economy.

**Money has infiltrated all levels of government. And along the way, it shut your generation out of the economy.**

But to take back the economy, you first need to know what really happened, who did it, and why.

```
<**********>
184.168.39.191
revgenreader
R3v0luti0n!
find file
<**********>
```

## CHAPTER THREE

# Smart, Educated, and Jobless

*We don't feel like outsiders at all*
*We are the new Americana*

—"New Americana" by Halsey

Karen is in her early twenties. She's got short punkish hair, an equality sticker on her Dell laptop, and a tell-it-to-me-straight kind of demeanor. The one thing she really wanted to be when she grew up was a pilot. But her conservative midwestern family frowned upon the idea of a woman doing that job. She says she watched too many of her friends languish in postcollege, wage-labor jobs. After being pushed and prodded to go various routes in her life, including considering not taking on a college education with its debt, she finally settled on something that satisfied her need for science, human connection, caring, and, most important, financial security.

That's right. You probably already guessed it. She's becoming a mortician. It's not that she enjoys death, she says, but she's good at providing an atmosphere of comfort for those who are grieving the loss of a loved one. And another thing—the dead don't talk back, which makes them good company for the long hours needed for embalming and preparing for a funeral.

Kayne grew up on Chicago's east side. His father was absent from day one. Being a young African American kid in the crosshairs of one of America's War on Drugs neighborhoods in the 1990s, he had a mother who did her best to keep their small household afloat. His role models, though, were his older "brothers" who were members of the Black Panthers. They made sure he got to school unharmed and that he made it home safely. And in addition, they helped his family with the basics. After high school, Kayne managed to move out to Los Angeles. He's living in another rough neighborhood, East LA, where he's built a small recording studio in his apartment bedroom. He has a part-time gig at a coffee shop and picks up work as a production assistant on film sets. His dream is to become a big film director. Like many people his age, he is optimistic about his future despite having no clear opportunity for advancement and no definitive plan.

Starbucks wasn't Juan's first career choice. But right now, with his dad working construction, his sister trying to get through community college, and the needs of his family, it's a regular gig. He's had other hourly jobs at big-box retail outlets, but he prefers being a barista, where at least "people are grateful, more or less." He's a smart young man and would like to start his own computer repair business. But his only access to capital and credit are through payday loan places, which he's seen his father get in trouble with in the past. For now, he'll keep making coffee, keep applying at more specialty computer shops, and see what happens. When I ask him what he thinks his biggest impediment to getting ahead is, he says, "Simple: lack of a college degree."

> When I ask him what he thinks his biggest impediment to getting ahead is, he says, "Simple: lack of a college degree."

Dianne is juggling a lot. Aside from being a single mom, she's a driver for Lyft and is a regular on TaskRabbit.com, where she does everything from assembling Ikea furniture to organizing closets. She tells me the choices she made in her early twenties, including the expensive art degree and the unwanted pregnancy, were on one hand regrettable, but on the other hand she's grown a lot and is determined to regain financial stability. Somehow, she finds time in the evenings to do online courses. Her goal is to get an MBA and one day have her own business. Money is so tight she agonizes over every purchasing decision, but it doesn't compare to the guilt she feels for not spending more time with her five-year-old daughter. Her mom helps when possible, but she is also dealing with "her own issues."

These people represent the cardinal directions of a generation that has been pushed into spiraling college debt, skyrocketing youth unemployment, and the endless Great Recession. This chapter unveils the key structural changes that ensured that the vast majority of people in your generation would be barred from participating in the American and world economies. To figure out how your generation got to this point, and more important, how you get out, let's jump back into our time machine.

## BLUE COLLARS AND BELL-BOTTOMS

For those of us who were alive in the 1970s many of us spent our evenings turning the power knob of the television, letting that warm color glow come up, and ratcheting the other knob, the big one that switched channels, until we found that favorite sitcom. By that time in American history, the pasty white, suburban, here's-what-to-buy-to-furnish-that-Levittown-home perfection of the 1950s and 1960s evening TV shows had been replaced with (gasp!) black people (gasp again!), working-class people (double take!), and people living in the projects. In the 1970s, evening TV was full of shows like *All in the Family, Good Times, Alice, One Day at a Time*, and *Laverne & Shirley*.

*All in the Family*, which ranked number one in Nielsen ratings from 1971 to 1978, revolved around a working-class knucklehead and his family. The show's creator, Norman Lear, infused the series with working-class issues and used it as a tool to expose bigotry as it relates to race, gender, and sexuality. The show dealt with other taboo subjects, too, including abortion, rape, impotence, menopause, miscarriage, and the Vietnam War. To this day, *All in the Family* is considered by *TV Guide* to be one of the "50 Best Shows of All Time."[1]

Another 1970s-era Norman Lear show, *Good Times*, depicted a family of color living in a housing project in a poor neighborhood in inner city Chicago. The show dealt with the characters' attempts to overcome poverty and showed the clear class divisions of people of color versus those who are white.

These 1970s sitcoms showed a grittier, more down-home America otherwise known as the working class. For Millennials who may associate the working class with the people who make lattes, the working class of post–World War II America was something else entirely.

The American working class was a large group of the Silent Generation and Baby Boomers who lived in the suburbs and commuted to mostly factory jobs. These jobs largely involved the manufacturing of hard goods including cars, heavy equipment, etc. A job in a factory would allow somebody to bring home enough money to sustain a house, car, kids, and usually a nonworking spouse. That was with only a forty-hour workweek. You also got a paid vacation and health care and retirement benefits. And you didn't even need a college degree.[2]

After World War II, America had manufacturing jobs mostly throughout the Great Lakes industrial region that stretches from

Duluth to Buffalo and includes Chicago, Cleveland, Detroit, and Pittsburgh, all linked together by a dense network of waterways, railroads, and highways. It was from this area that steel barreled forth in the form of cars, trains, trucks, ships, machines, tools, and appliances.

But it wasn't just the jobs that gave those blue-collar workers and their families a seat at the American table—it was the organization of labor itself. The industrial heartland of America was also home to the largest and most powerful labor unions in the world. Unions negotiated en masse for laborers, ensuring benefits, overtime, vacations, health care, safety, on-the-job training, and, in some cases, race equality.

While the entire working class was not part of a union per se, the unions normalized the economic, negotiating, and political power of the blue-collar working class. In turn, this working class made up the bulk of America's middle class.[3] America's wealth and income were shaped like a diamond: a small lower class, a big fat middle, and a small top.[4]

> Today's class structure is shaped like an airbrushed model with a bulging butt (the lower class), a slimming middle (the near-extinct middle class), and, thanks to plastic surgery, a fake big-busted top (the large upper class).

If this all sounds like a dream, it's because today's class structure is shaped like an airbrushed model with a bulging butt (the lower class), a slimming middle (the near-extinct middle class), and, thanks to plastic surgery, a fake big-busted top (the large upper class).[5]

America, you're looking great!

If we take a step back and look at labor trends in the United States, we see that industry jobs peaked just after the Second World War and promptly took a nosedive. This happened at the same time as the US labor force was ballooning from 62 million people in 1950 to almost 160 million people today.

In other words, as availability of blue-collar jobs was shrinking, the quantity of people needing those jobs tripled. This resulted in an oversupply of labor that essentially created a buyer's market for hourly waged workers. By many accounts, it thrust a permanent stake through the heart of the American middle class.

And all this was by design.

## SQUEEZING THE MIDDLE

In the late 1950s, the tycoons of many American industries pushed Congress to lower import tariffs. Their logic was simple: cheap raw materials from overseas would lead to increased profit margins. But the move backfired. And by the early 1960s, many producers of industrial goods, including auto makers, were facing stiff competition from cheaper imported products.[6]

During the 1960s and '70s, American-made cars, trucks, and equipment were big, used more steel than necessary, and were terribly fuel inefficient. Even American-made TVs and radios were big and clunky. On the other hand, Japanese- and German-made products of that era were smaller, built with a modest amount of materials, and comparatively energy efficient. America had enjoyed unprecedented industrial might before, during, and after World War II, and its industries had gotten fat and lazy. Instead of competing by innovating and producing better products, those industries decided to cut at the very thing that sustained them: their labor force.[7]

With strong unions came negotiating power for wages, hours, and benefits. Factory owners reasoned that, if they were going to compete with the efficiency of the Japanese and Germans, two of their primary overseas competitors, then they needed cheaper labor that made fewer demands and worked longer hours. In other words, they needed to squeeze America's blue-collar, skilled-labor "middle."[8]

Union busting had been around since the late 1800s, but in the 1960s, with the nation's focus taken by the civil rights and women's liberation movements and eventually by the Vietnam War, the combined corporate power of the American industrial machine began a widespread and largely covert campaign to unseat the labor unions.[9] They began their attack by hiring psychologists to develop a program to weed out would-be union supporters.[10] They hired informants who purposefully disrupted unions. And they began a systematic program of espionage to destroy unions from the inside out.[11]

> They began a systematic program of espionage to destroy unions from the inside out.

In a series of moves designed to break the backs of the unions, factories began to move southward and eastward. A new southern Sunbelt was established for oil, military, and manufacturing. This deindustrialization left thousands and soon hundreds of thousands of former unionized workers stranded in decaying cities. With a fragmented cultural memory of labor activism and unionization, new workers in new manufacturing cities found it increasingly difficult to unionize.[12]

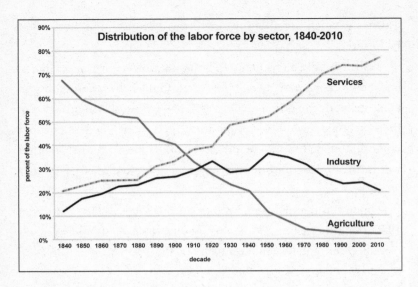

Over time, the labor force in the United States has migrated from jobs producing physical objects (cars) and consumables (food) to service jobs (flipping burgers). This trend has wreaked havoc on the middle class and precipitated a downwardly mobile economic spiral for the Millennial generation.

By 1980, industry jobs comprised less than 30 percent of the US labor force.[13] On May 30, 1980, a small newspaper in Elyria, Ohio, in the middle of America's industrial belt, sounded what may have been the final warning for America's blue-collar working class with the headline "More Auto Layoffs, More Wives at Work."[14] Writing for the United Press, which sent the story out for syndication, the article's author, Robert Mackay, said, "Industry officials said 267,399 blue collar workers will be idled next week." The layoffs and the hundreds of thousands more that were soon to come represented something pivotal: America's 1950s-Levittown-sitcom lifestyle was imploding.

The writer added that "in Washington, the Labor Department said a typical American family makes $30 a week more than it did a year ago, but double-digit inflation has erased any gain in purchasing power and forced thousands of wives to go to work." The paper reported that from 1979 to 1980 alone, 200,000 "wives . . . went out and got jobs."

In 1980, it was actually shocking to people that women *had* to go to work to support their families. This was the birth of the two-income, dual-earner household. And it was also the death rattle of the post–World War II American blue-collar working class.

With agriculture becoming mechanized and factory oriented, also known as factory farms, the labor market was soon squeezed out of any meaningful form of productive work, i.e., making things or growing food. By the time George H. W. Bush walked into the Oval Office in 1989, the media had latched onto the promise that high technology jobs would soon fill the gap left by evaporating industry jobs.[15]

The *Economy of Ideas* was a term that deceased futurist and writer John Barlow popularized in the 1990s in *Wired* maga-

> The shiny never-never land of the Economy of Ideas never actually materialized.

zine.[16] But even Barlow, whose article is often misquoted, had asked the critical question "How are we going to be paid for the work we do with our minds?"

By the year 2000, after the dot-com bubble burst, the answer was written all over the then nascent World Wide Web: the vast majority of you are not going to get paid for your ideas; rather you will be paid a minimum wage to flip burgers.

The shiny never-never land of the Economy of Ideas never actually materialized. Instead, Millennials inherited the Wage Labor Economy. It's the one in which approximately two-thirds of working Americans work in low hourly wage service jobs.[17] And it's the economy in which nine out of ten workers today are still in occupations that existed one hundred years ago.[18]

This is because people still need to eat, we need clothes, we need shelter, and we want electricity and fiber-optic lines and cell phones and all the rest of it.

To produce and maintain those wanted and needed items there is a universal requirement: human labor. The problem is, when you put corporations in control of government, remove social safety nets, kill off labor unions, and pay people the barest form of subsistence minimum wage, there is an unfortunate side effect.

It's called poverty.

## THE OTHER (YOUNGER) AMERICA

In 1962, Michael Harrington wrote a chilling book titled *The Other America: Poverty in the United States*. In it he argued that as many as sixty million Americans were in poverty. With a population at the time of 180 million, the shock that roughly 30 percent of Americans were in poverty rippled through high society.

Fast-forward to today, and the US Census Bureau again puts the number of poor and near poor living in America at around 30 percent, which today translates to about one hundred million people. Near poor refers to those living below 150 percent of the poverty line. It is a useful term, since being $1 or even $100 over the poverty line is, in reality, living in poverty. It's also important to note that census statistics show that most of the people living just above the poverty line will dip below the poverty line for some of each year.

Most of the people living below or just above the poverty line in the United States are children, students, the elderly, or disabled. Specifically, nearly one-quarter of America's children live below or near the poverty line.[19] Read that statistic again and think of the implications for our society: about one in four of America's children live below or near the poverty line. This impacts their scholastic performance, their confidence, their development, their social mobility and, ultimately, the future of our society itself.

Also, keep in mind whose children they are. The majority of parents of America's Gen Z kids are Millennials.[20, 21] The problem is that, in today's economy, having one child under the age of five is associated with a *14 percent decrease in annual income for a dual-parent household and a staggering 36 percent decrease in annual income for a single mom.*[22] Thus, because Gen Z is parented by a *downwardly mobile* generation of Millennials, those children already in poverty will have ever fewer resources. Given the above trends, it is also likely that the percentage of children of Millennials in poverty will increase, especially the youngest Gen Zers.

Poverty is more common for young people, more common for women, and more common for people of color.[23] If you're in one or more of those categories—for instance, a young black woman—you may be out of luck in today's America.

Hanna Brooks Olsen, a Millennial writer in Seattle, gives a little insight on what it's like to be young and down on your luck in America today:

Nervously sitting in the WorkSource office in downtown Seattle, a slip of paper with my number rapidly yellowing with sweat clenched between my fingers, a man in filthy jeans and mismatched shoes turned to me and asked what I was doing there.

"You don't look poor enough to be here," he told me.

He was right. I didn't.

Because what we collectively think of as "looking poor" does not, in fact, encompass the real face of poverty in this country. As a white, twenty-two-year-old college graduate in a secondhand dress, I did not look like what we think of as "poor."

Of course, at that exact moment, I had, yes, a college degree and a coveted unpaid (because of course it was unpaid) internship at a public radio station.

But I also had a minimum wage job to support myself, $17 in my bank account, $65,000 in debt to my name, and $800 in rent due in twenty-four days. I was extremely hungry, worried about my utilities being shut off, and 100 percent planning to hit up the Dumpster at the nearby Starbucks when I was done there. I had no functional stove in my tiny apartment because the gas it took to make it work was, at $10 per month, too expensive. I was at WorkSource to find out if I qualified for literally any program to make my finances less crushing.

I had, like millions of other working Americans and many, many Millennials, no financial safety net.[24]

How is it that in the fast-future world of almost 2020 we have an America with one in three people poor, a disproportionate number of them being young?

It all circles back to money.

## THE WORKING YOUNG AND POOR

Today the minimum wage in America stands at $7.25 an hour. If you work for tips, you can legally be paid $2.13 an hour, and many people are.

Sixty to eighty percent of Millennials do not have college degrees,[25] and without a miracle, the vast majority of them never will. Only about a third of people in America today, including Millennials, have a four-year college education. When one looks at the sharp divide between America's new working class and its white-collar class, it is based on one thing above all else: whether or not you have a four-year college degree.[26]

"What we collectively think of as 'looking poor' does not, in fact, encompass the real face of poverty in this country."

On average, an American high school graduate earns about $31,000 a year. But a graduate of a four-year college earns an average of $57,000 a year, an 80 percent increase. Over a thirty-year career that amounts to a difference of more than $750,000.[27]

For the two-thirds of Millennials not fortunate enough to get a college degree, the majority will end up in unsalaried, hourly wage jobs with erratic schedules and no benefits. These people already are, and will continue to become, fast food workers, retail workers, janitors, administrative assistants, auto technicians, customer service representatives, construction laborers, landscape laborers, hourly hospital staff, and home health care professionals, the last two becoming more common as Baby Boomers age. Many of these jobs have high rates of injury. Almost all these jobs pay at or near the minimum wage.

Adjusted for inflation, the purchasing power of minimum wage peaked in 1968. Since then, it has plummeted to about 30 percent of its former purchasing power.[28] While the 2016 Bernie Sanders campaign shamed a number of politicians into lip-syncing that "we should increase the minimum wage to $15 an hour," that campaign promise was not upheld by the nominated Democratic and Repub-

Sixty-one percent of those making minimum wage today, and thereby living inside the definition of poverty, are Millennials.

lican candidates. Since the end of 2016, when Republicans swept both the House and the Senate, the push for a federally mandated $15 per hour minimum wage has all but vaporized.

As of now, the minimum wage stands at its lowest point in fifty years. And not surprisingly, 61 percent of those making minimum wage today, and thereby living inside the definition of poverty, are Millennials.[29]

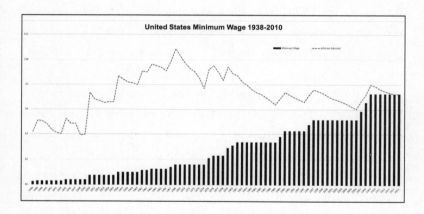

Numerically speaking, the minimum wage is much higher today than when it was introduced. But accounting for inflation, it's the lowest it has ever been. In other words, the purchasing power of your minimum-wage job is far less than the purchasing power of somebody who held a similar job in the 1950s. Add to this the astronomically higher cost of living today, and the result is that Millennials are screwed, economically speaking.

Countries with higher minimum wages than the United States include Denmark, Australia, Luxembourg, Germany, France, Ireland, Belgium, the Netherlands, New Zealand, Canada, the UK, and Japan.

Now let's look at purchasing power in general. Here's a comparison of the cost of middle class items from 1950 and 2014.

| | 1950 | % income | 2014 | % income |
|---|---|---|---|---|
| **AVERAGE FAMILY INCOME** | $3,300 | | $51,017 | |
| Average Car Cost | $1,510 | 46% | $31,252 | 61% |
| Median Home Price | $7,354 | 222% | $188,900 | 370% |
| Annual Tuition | $600 | 18% | $40,000 | 78% |

While the cost of some small goods (eggs, milk, butter) may today be slightly lower, the cost of major life purchases is exponentially higher today than it was in 1950. This makes it nearly impossible for the entire Millennial generation to achieve a similar asset-to-debt ratio as the Baby Boomer generation. This further exacerbates the difficulty of obtaining loans and getting ahead in today's economy.

Whereas a car today is considerably more expensive in real terms, a home is astronomically more expensive, at 370 percent of annual income versus 222 percent in 1950. And college tuition, which we will delve into shortly, is roughly four times more expensive in real terms today than it was in 1950, at 78 percent of annual income today versus only 18 percent in 1950. That's right—college is about 400 percent more expensive for Millennials than it was for Boomers.[30]

While the working class in America, as well as what's left of the middle class, is falling

> College is about 400 percent more expensive for Millennials than it was for Boomers.

behind, that has not been the same for those in the upper class. But this isn't the tired old story of the poor becoming poorer and the rich becoming richer.

It's a whole new version of generational economic disparity.

## THE BOOMER BETRAYAL

In America and most of the West, Millennials are becoming the wage-labor force to support older generations who are holding on to global wealth. As a whole, the Baby Boomer generation has tended away from working to increase the wealth of society at large and instead tended to sequester wealth to themselves.

A March 2016 financial investigation into generational economic disparity done by the *Guardian* looked at the wealth divide between generations in the UK, Canada, Germany, France, the United States, Spain, Italy, and Australia. Of these countries, the only one in which disposable income has grown for Millennials is Australia. Incidentally, Australia also has the highest minimum wage in the world: $17.70 per hour.

In every other developed country investigated, household income has slid backward for Millennials and skyrocketed for Boomers.

Let's take the United States, for example. From 1979 to 2010 household disposable income for Millennials *decreased* by 9 percent while Boomers enjoyed a 28 percent *increase* in disposable income, nearly a fourfold increase.

Says the article, "Generation Y . . . has found they are increasingly being cut out of the wealth generated in Western societies. *It is likely to be the first time in industrialized history—save for periods of war or natural disaster—that the incomes of young adults have fallen so far when compared with the rest of society.* Prosperity has plummeted for young adults in the rich world" (emphasis added). The article adds that people under thirty in America are poorer than retired people and that this is "resulting in unprecedented inequality between generations."

Ouch.

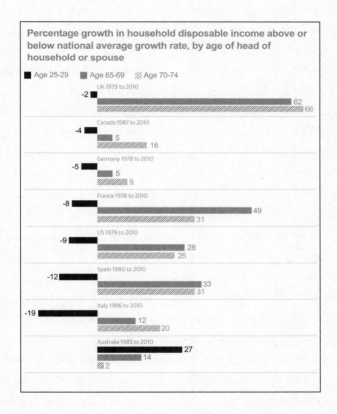

Percentage growth in household disposable income above or below national average growth rate, by age of head of household or spouse

■ Age 25-29    ■ Age 65-69    ▨ Age 70-74

UK 1979 to 2010
-2 / 62 / 66

Canada 1987 to 2010
-4 / 5 / 16

Germany 1978 to 2010
-5 / 5 / 9

France 1978 to 2010
-8 / 49 / 31

US 1979 to 2010
-9 / 28 / 25

Spain 1980 to 2010
-12 / 33 / 31

Italy 1986 to 2010
-19 / 12 / 20

Australia 1985 to 2010
27 / 14 / 2

In every Western country surveyed by the British newspaper the *Guardian* save for Australia, household disposable income is sliding backward for Millennials. In other words, Millennials are getting poorer and poorer over time. Meanwhile, the wealth of the Baby Boomer generation is increasing over time.

One might argue that wealth should accumulate as people age. But we're not yet speaking about accumulated wealth; we're speaking strictly about *income*. This is the money you are making, not the money you are saving. In other words, Millennials are making ever less money and Boomers are making ever more.

But given a growing economy, income for youth should be *increasing* over time, not *decreasing*. So, what gives?

If we look again at Australia, we see the opposite paradigm. Down Under, Millennials' disposable income has seen a 27 percent increase, Boomers enjoyed a 14 percent increase in disposable income, and the Silent Generation a 2 percent increase. In other words, a differently managed, Westernized economy is providing healthy income growth for all generations with the youth seeing the greatest growth.

Generational income disparity isn't a given; it's a result of decisive financial protections for older folks by ensuring things like the minimum wage remaining low, and divisive destruction of financial mobility for young people by ensuring the cost of college tuition continues to balloon.

Now let's talk about total wealth, in other words, savings and assets. Not surprisingly, wealth follows income. Thus, the accumulation of wealth is radically different for Boomers than it will be for Millennials. Those people forty-five to seventy-four years of age have 85 percent of the total wealth while Millennials, even with all their dot-com successes and app companies and start-ups (and even counting Mark Zuckerberg's fortune), hold only 3 percent.

Unfortunately, the generational income and wealth gap will not close as Millennials collect more assets. In the July 2015 study *The Demographics of Wealth* by the Federal Reserve Bank of St. Louis, the Fed analyzed and interviewed forty thousand families between 1989 and 2013. They found that: "The median wealth of old families (headed by someone at least sixty-two) rose 40 percent between 1989 and 2013." In other words, a family headed by a sixty-two-year-old in 2013 was much better off than a similar family headed by a sixty-two-year-old in 1989.[31] Meanwhile the median wealth of middle-aged families and young families dropped by about 30 percent.

The report cites a number of factors for greater wealth among older households including better savings; having a better asset-to-debt ratio, i.e., owning a house; and being in a less crowded job market, i.e., having gotten a job when the economy was good and having held on to it or retired with a pension. All this makes total sense for those who grew up in America's post–World War II economic heyday. The problem is, as Millennials well know, when you are making less and less money, it's really hard to buy a house, impossible to save, and your chances of getting a job when the economy is good are nil.

> **The pile of assets owned by the older generation is getting bigger while the pile available to the younger generation is getting smaller.**

But this is not, as the Fed study calls it, a wealth gap so much as it is a wealth transfer. Here's the deal: the wealth of the nation has not radically increased in fifteen years. Put in simple terms: given a relatively fixed pool of monetary and wealth assets and accounting for inflation, the pile of assets owned by the older generation is getting bigger while the pile available to the younger generation is getting smaller.

Both the Fed and the *Guardian* found the same thing: Millennials are getting poorer, and Boomers are getting richer.

## THE SILENT HEIST

Studies of income disparity show that the mysterious Boomer/Millennial gap in income and wealth was not precipitated by the 2008 Great Recession, rather it began beforehand with a series of neoliberal-inspired structural changes that were designed to aggregate wealth at the top.

While these decisions were not targeted at gutting the earning potential of the next generation per se, they are indicative of a sort of winner-takes-all mentality. The cumulative effect of these decisive economic policies, free trade agreements, and decisions by big American businesses was to lock the vast majority of the Millennial generation out of economic mobility.

In short, they were:

The North American Free Trade Agreement (NAFTA), signed by Bill Clinton in 1993, which evaporated up to 800,000 US jobs as factories and facilities moved primarily to Mexico, where maquiladoras now operate across the border with little in the way of environmental regulation or worker protection. The program has created a south-of-the-border horror story of debt slavery and destruction of environment and people. Meanwhile, the profits of US companies operating facilities across the border soared.[32]

A series of federal trade policies that increased the national debt from in the billions in the 1960s to a staggering $20 trillion today.[33]

Tax cuts, tax loopholes, tax breaks, and relaxed consumer protection standards for big corporations resulting in a thousand fold increase in S&P 500 corporate profits from around $30 billion in 1960 to almost $3 trillion today.[34, 35]

A 400 percent increase in the cost of college tuition since 1950 coupled with federally backed predatory lending schemes that saddle young students with as much debt as early in life as possible.[36]

Federal and state policies designed to destabilize labor unions that combined with the above have resulted in the closure of about fifteen manufacturing facilities a day between the 1960s and today.[37]

Using scheduling software and other means to ensure that wage laborers, especially women and people of color, work below the thirty-two-hour per week minimum needed to obtain benefits.[38] The destabilization of work schedules doesn't just affect parents—it also affects their children. When children feel destabilized, it hurts their performance in school and negatively impacts their development.[39]

On micro- and macroeconomic levels, profits were achieved by increasing debt, moving manufacturing overseas, slashing consumer protections, forfeiting environmental protections, and keeping wage laborers disenfranchised. In other words, the vast economic growth experienced by America and much of the West since the 1950s baby boom, and especially after Reagan's ascension to power in 1981, was the result of hoisting economic, social, and environmental problems onto the next generation.

At some stage we have to ask who really fits the definition of the "ME ME ME Generation." Is it, as the mostly Baby-Boomer-owned-and-controlled media have portrayed, you Millennials who are inheriting a world in financial free fall? Or is this label a projection by an older generation that, through a lifetime quest to ratchet up consumerism, has disemboweled the very structures that facilitate young people becoming prosperous?

Why did the Baby Boomer generation facilitate the strategic impoverishment of their own children? It's a tough question. Surely there's a level of plausible deniability, a level of ignorance ("but Ronald Reagan/Bill Clinton/etc. *was really good for the American economy*"), and a level of cognitive dissonance ("I turned up the dial and heard people screaming, but the man in the lab coat said everything was fine and to keep going").[40]

There are also many Boomers who were on the front lines of the conscious revolution of the 1960s and '70s who have slowly been beaten down by the overwhelming tidal wave of American corporate greed and are now staring at our current social, economic, and political crises in utter shock, horror, and disbelief.

The problem is that history tends to celebrate the winners. If you're one of the tens of millions of young people in poverty in America today, it's pretty clear which side of the Baby Boomer generation won.

Diane Coyle, a professor, economist, and former UK Treasury advisor quoted in the *Guardian* article, says, "We just don't know whether we can continue growing the economy in the same way we once have."

Dr. Coyle, let me spell it out for you: No. You. Cannot.

The type of gains made for the last sixty years that irreversibly hurt the economic prospects of Millennials and crashed the world economy are not sustainable, desirable, or smart for a world of soon to be ten billion humans. Without another global conflict of mass proportions, something all generations must vigilantly avoid, that good old post–World War II economic growth is not coming back.

Instead, it's time for a new economic paradigm, one we will cover in chapter 7. For now, it's time to talk about the weapon used for the greatest conservative-Boomer-led economic harvest.

In other words, Millennials, it's time to talk about what really happened when you went to college.

## THE COLLEGE LOAN SCAM

I meet Alan Collinge in Philadelphia. It's a balmy day in July. He walks from the train station to my Airbnb rental, and by the time he arrives his T-shirt is soaked. Lucky for him, he's brought an extra one. Emblazoned across its front is the URL for Alan's website: StudentLoanJustice.org.

The site, which looks like it was designed in a text-editing program circa 2001, maintains a compilation of testimonials from people in various parts of the United States who are being tortured by the student loan industry.

The first testimonial I click on is from Brit, a teacher with a PhD in California. Her original student loans were for $26,000. To date, she has paid $24,000. She now owes $70,000. If the math sounds wrong, it's because private student loan lending agencies are able to provide loans under false pretenses, raise interest rates at will, buy and sell loans with no input from the borrower, and generally wreak havoc on those who took out loans from them. In contrast, federal loans issued directly by the US government must at least comply with a set of borrower protections. Regardless of the type of loan, however, if a student loan goes into default, it usually moves into the hands of private debt collectors and resellers.

Brit's story is repeated in various forms in thousands of testimonials from people across America who have experienced what Alan calls *The Student Loan Scam*, which is the title of his book.

While college enrollment in America has been steadily increasing since the 1920s, there was a significant leap in the number of people enrolling in four-year colleges around the time that the first Millennials left high school.[41] For Millennials raised by Boomer parents who wanted the best for their kids, a college degree was seen as the great pathway to success, as well as the great equalizer between men and women and also a way to level out the disparity so many people of color face.

Seeing the huge wave of Millennial teens approaching, the financial loan industry began to lick its lips. Colleges and universities also began to salivate. And what did they do? They did what any other enterprising capitalist institution does when it sees a tsunami-sized throng of naïve people clamoring for its products: they jacked up prices.

In 1990 the average cost of tuition at a public college was $5,242 and $13,237 for a private college. By 2005 those numbers had more than doubled to $12,108 and $27,316, respectively. By 2015, the costs had almost doubled again to $21,435 and $49,054. As college counselors dutifully steered millions of unwitting Millennials through the college application process, universities hit pay dirt.[42]

To pay for the exponentially increasing cost of college tuition, Millennials increasingly turned to student loans. In the mid-1990s student loan debt stood at less than $100 billion. By 2008 it had tripled to $300 billion.[43] Then, elected by a wave of Millennial enthusiasm, Obama took office. And that's when student debt really took off.

By promising to help relieve student loan debt on one hand, while working closely with the banks to remove consumer protections on the other, in just under a decade the Obama administration helped skyrocket student loan debt in the United States to approximately $1.5 trillion, and it continues on its meteoric rise to this day.[44] In the ultimate betrayal of public trust, the very president who had promised hope and change for Millennials gave them a gift that keeps on giving.

More than any other administration, the Obama administration shackled college-bound Millennials with a lifetime of debt.

Much of the initial loan money was paid to universities. And those universities put their new fortunes to great use. Boston University, Texas Tech University, North Florida University, Miami University, Arizona State University, the University of Alabama, the University of Missouri, and the University of Iowa all built Lazy Rivers so students could relax while floating around in circles. Other universities built climbing walls and new stadiums. Sports programs across the country, which almost universally drain college academic budgets, enjoyed unprecedented growth as they were being infused with hundreds of millions in cash.

> "So, you go on a date, maybe it's looking good, but you have to ask, 'How much college debt do you have?' When they say, 'I have one hundred grand,' you better swipe left!"

Says Millennial researcher Jason Dorsey, "Significant amounts of college debt delays major commitments including marriage and kids. In fact, how much college debt you have now is part of the dating conversation. So, you go on a date, maybe it's looking good, but you have to ask, 'How much college debt do you have?' When they say, 'I have one hundred grand,' you better swipe left!"

Former West Hollywood mayor Lindsey Horvath, who has, as she says, "a lot" of college debt, puts it this way:

We invested in our education because we were told there would be these magical, wonderful jobs that would be available to us. And when Millennials started to graduate from undergrad or graduate school, they realized they'd racked up all that debt and those jobs didn't exist. That's why they're angry. So, when I think about those things, it's not like, "Oh, I just want to fall in love and have a child." I can't fathom having a child. It's too darned expensive!

In the wake of the 2008 Great Recession, during a time when state and federal funding for universities was rapidly shrinking, colleges were cashing in. Instead of cutting the very things that drain money away from academics and finding ways to slim down, many major colleges went the route of *The Great Gatsby*.

How could all this have happened under the watchful eye of a generation of fiscally responsible Baby Boomer parents?

The answer goes back to government policy.

## MILLENNIAL SHARK BAIT

When I ask Alan what policies were used to load eighteen-year-olds with $1.5 trillion in debt, he launches straight in. He explains that "Sallie Mae convinced Congress to remove nearly every standard consumer protection that exists for every other type of loan. This includes bankruptcy protections, statutes of limitations, fair debt collection practices, truth-in-lending laws, refinancing rights, and even state usury laws, all of which were specifically taken off the table for federally guaranteed student loans. This set up a lending environment where the lender had all the power, and Sallie Mae and others did not hesitate to abuse the elements of the student lending system—up to and including the federal government, which guarantees or actually makes the loans."

This is a salient point: the federal government profits not just from student loans but specifically from *defaulted* student loans. Says Alan, "In many cases, they can make far more money on a defaulted loan than on a loan that remains in good stead. A credit card company is very happy if they get back, say, seven cents on the dollar for a defaulted loan. Well, the federal government and its contractors get back around $1.22 for every dollar they pay out on default claims."

Depending on the type of loan, type of interest—fixed- or variable-rate—and type of compounding used, a loan from a private lender in the amount of $25,000, for example, can in a relatively short period of time balloon to $100,000 of debt. If a borrower defaults even on a government-issued loan, one of the many private contractors in the federal loan industry will try, through repeated calling to offer a new repayment program, to get that borrower back into the system. The borrower's new loan will usually be at an even higher rate of interest. Thus, even defaulted loans can be profitable.

Saddling a young borrower who cannot repay their loan with ever more debt is what Alan calls a defining hallmark of a predatory lending system.

With such lucrative financial instruments and a young population hungry for four-year degrees, what's the US government to do in the wake of the largest financial crash in eighty years?

Their answer is to turn an entire generation of college students into an income-creation system. Says Alan, "There are twenty-seven million people out there whose loans are either in default, forbearance, deferment, or otherwise delinquent. This lending system is being perpetuated and profited off of by the federal government, by private banks, and even by citizens through their stock ownership in financial instruments that buy student loans. It's essentially the older crowd preying upon the younger generation."

Meanwhile, private loan collectors are hard at work trying to collect and monetize as much of that outstanding debt as possible. Alan says, "The long reach of the student loan industry is longer today than it's ever been, whether it's through social media, through cell phones, anywhere in the world. They know where you are, they know how much you owe, and they will do anything they can to put pressure on you to pay."

He says that many people with outstanding debt are unnecessarily harassed by debt collectors. "Fair debt collection practices also do not exist for federal student loans. So, they can call you at home, anytime of night, they can call your relatives, they'll call you at work. They often misrepresent themselves and say, 'Yes, I'm with the federal government and you are looking at very serious trouble. You have defaulted on a federal obligation to the federal government.' The reality of the matter is that these collection companies are not with the federal government, they're contractors working for other contractors to the federal government." Like bounty hunters, those contractors are paid a healthy commission by one of several federal loan agencies on each loan they bring back into the system.

Adding salt to the wound, people with outstanding loans are often scammed into *increasing* the amount they owe. Says Alan, "The Internet is swamped by collection agents looking to take borrowers and put them into something called 'loan rehabilitation.' This is where they take a defaulted loan for, say, $10,000, rejigger the loan, and force the borrower to make payments for ten months. At the end of the process, they wind up with a new, $17,000 loan that is not defaulted, and the collectors make 20 percent of the book value of this new loan. So, if you can compel a guy to make payments for ten months on a $10,000 loan, you stand to make $3,000 on just that one person."

With 40 percent of student loan borrowers unable to pay, the college loan debt collection industry is booming.[45] To commemorate its work, Premiere Credit, an Indianapolis company that landed large student loan collection contracts with the US Department of Education, installed a 3,800-gallon saltwater shark tank in its lobby.[46]

And yes, the sharks inside do bite.


## STRESS PUPPIES

With financial stress increasing for incoming college freshmen, there's a new type of party animal appearing on college campuses and it's got four legs. Puppy therapy is the newest trend in lowering student stress. From dogs in counseling centers with visiting hours to pet-friendly dorms to pet checkout (yep, like library books), the trend is taking hold. There's research that indicates playing with pets lowers the level of cortisol, the stress hormone, in people and increases endorphins, known as the happiness hormones. Of course, there's little research on how, or if, pet programs on college campuses help students deal with stress, but given the nature of the beast, the data is sure to follow.

So why the pooch push? It turns out that young people are pretty stressed out. According to the American Psychological Association's *2015 Stress in America Snapshot,* "Millennials and Gen Xers report a higher level of stress than any other generation and appear to have difficulty coping." The report goes on to say that over half of Millennials report having lain awake at night in the last month due to stress and more than any other generation, Millennials are more likely to say their stress has increased in the past year, that they experience stress symptoms, and that stress has a strong impact on their physical and mental health.

Fancy that. A generation that has been preyed upon by the finan-

It should come as no surprise that the second-leading cause of death for Millennials is suicide.

cial services industry and hyper targeted and overly sexualized by marketers, that sits on the brink of global catastrophe, and that now faces the choice between a life of wage labor or immense college debt, is stressed out. Who could have guessed?

The problem is that unbeatable Millennial optimism becomes increasingly fragile when members of the generation are put into a situation from which there is seemingly no way out. It should come as no surprise that the second-leading cause of death for Millennials is suicide.

As one Millennial blogger wrote:

> The dreaded, good-for-nothing Millennials. The constant bane of the older generation, lazy, overeducated, unemployed, Millennials seem to be the human trash of today's society. So, what's a Millennial down on his or her luck to do? Could we, in fact, be seeing an entire generation ready to commit suicide—and is that in fact a bad thing?

The blogger later thanked his readers for deciphering his "thinly veiled suicide letter" and sending him the telephone number of the National Suicide Prevention Lifeline, as well as posting numerous supportive and helpful comments.

Alan Collinge tells me that he's received numerous letters bemoaning the suicides of brothers, sisters, fathers, sons, and daughters who felt the crushing burden of student loan debt, and the shame of their situation was too much to bear so they took their own lives.

According to C. Cryn Johannsen, founder and director of All Education Matters, Inc., a nonprofit "dedicated to the eradication of all student loan debt":

I first started appreciating the depth of the problem of suicidal debtors a few years ago with a post on my blog, *All Education Matters*, entitled "Suicide Among Student Debtors: Who's Thought about It?" I was stunned by the responses. In comment after comment, people confessed to feeling suicidal. One person wrote, "I was very actively looking into suicide until I got on antidepressants. Now I have to take happy pills every day to keep the suicidal urges at a minimum level." . . . In recent months, the notes have increased, and, if anything, they are even more desperate.

Johannsen says she wonders how many of the twenty-seven million young Americans who have outstanding federal loans are feeling distressed or suicidal "because of all that debt hanging over their heads."

Taking one's life is the ultimate act of desperation. In a humane, dignified society, increasing numbers of youth suicides, especially suicides associated with financial woes, should be cause for alarm. That there are no alarm bells ringing is a clear sign of a disconnect between the two largest generations alive today.

Nowhere is that disconnect more obvious than in the American political system.

After our interview, I follow Alan Collinge outside into the baking Philadelphia sun. Collinge has a huge placard on a stick that he intends to carry around for the rest of the day. It reads plainly, "STUDENT LOAN JUSTICE."

It's late July 2016, and the town is awash in the most surreal Democratic National Convention of the last century.

It's on this stage that a generational war of epic proportions will soon play out.

```
+---[RSA 2048]----+
|                 |
|.                |
|..               |
|o .      . o     |
|.+ o     S +     |
|o *o .    X o    |
|.=o.+ = + E .    |
|+*+++o * . . .   |
|o=X***+..   .    |
+----[SHA256]-----+
```

## CHAPTER FOUR

# The Politics of Y(outh)

*They will not control us*
*We will be victorious*

—"Uprising" by Muse

The outskirts of Philadelphia are a mess. There are roadblocks on the highway. Legions of police, police dogs, and police vehicles are stationed around the city. Philadelphia feels more like a war zone than an icon of American independence.

With the Democratic National Convention in full swing, downtown Philly (aka South Philly), on the other hand, looks like a political Mardi Gras. People stand on street corners with signs, posters, placards, and elaborate costumes. Every cause is represented. Save the rain forest. End abortion. Believe in Jesus. Elect Bernie Sanders. Don't Elect Bernie Sanders. Elect Hillary. Don't elect Hillary. It's a free-speech free-for-all. Or maybe it's a country in free fall. It's hard to decide.

The afternoon heat is sweltering as I follow Alan Collinge on a long walk through the sweaty chaos to a grassy spot in front of Independence Hall. It was in this very building that both the Declaration of Independence and the United States Constitution were debated and finally adopted.

**It's a free-speech free-for-all. Or maybe it's a country in free fall.**

The people who wrote those documents were against an intractable class system that kept the vast majority of citizens in poverty through debt slavery to the British government. They wanted people in this new country called America to be free from the constraints of class and the shackles of debt to their own government.

Alan is expecting a crowd of folks to assemble and burn their student loan documents. He's already been informed by the police that if he burns anything, he will promptly be arrested. And with the roads in deadlock and public transportation at a snail's pace, his anti-student-loan troupe is nowhere to be found.

So, I get out my video camera and film Alan by himself. He tears up some loan documents and throws the shreds into the air. It's one man against the crushing cogs of the financial machine. And it's painfully anticlimactic.

Then I hear it. People chanting "Revolution." At first, I think I'm delirious from sunstroke. After all, I've been on the road now for weeks, with a crazy schedule and little sleep. But just then, across the greenway I see them—a marching group of militant youths who have a definite I-dare-you-to-fuck-with-us vibe.

By the time I catch up with the band of edgy-looking young folks, they've amassed in front of the MSNBC stage, which is broadcasting live commentary about the DNC. The commentators are sitting at a round table that features the easily excitable crowd as a backdrop. It's good casting.

The angry marchers are holding an enormous vinyl sign with photographs of young men and women of color who have recently been killed by police. It's hard to think clearly over their megaphone call and repeated chants of "It's time, it's time to get organized, to get organized, for an actual revolution!" Finally, I manage to pull an earnest young woman wearing a beret and a black T-shirt aside and ask her the name of their group. She tells me they're all part of the Revolutionary Communist Party, USA, and hands me an old-school newsprint zine.

When I ask her what the guiding philosophy of the party is, she tells me they follow a guy named Bob Avakian. It turns out that Avakian is the son of a former judge, grew up in Berkeley, California, and has led the RCP since its formation in 1975. It seems that neither Bob, nor this particular communist party, are big on term limits.

Just as my new communist friend is inviting me to come join her group for an "epic American flag burning" later that evening, the other most-loud protestors in Philly show up. They are a couple of extremely vocal young men whose message is about the coming rapture and return of Jesus Christ. While there are only two of them, their signs are much bigger, and their megaphone is just as loud.

The ensuing amplified shouting standoff between the devotees of Bob and the devotees of Jesus is surreal. They are representatives of the extreme left and the extreme right. Between them exists an ideological gulf. But their voices are also echoes of the past—aberrations of a time that has come and gone.

Extremism is not a great fit for the pragmatic optimism that runs strong through the veins of your generation. For the majority of you Millennials, the notions of radical leftism and radical rightism are akin to pens and paper. The problem is that while your generation on the whole may have progressed beyond the left/right paradigms, the country and the political system you are inheriting are still mired deeply inside them.

Nowhere is the disconnect between the Millennial embrace-diversity, eschew-hatred, find-a-middle-ground type of thinking and the Baby Boomer right vs. wrong/good vs. evil mind-set clearer than at the Democratic National Convention in Philadelphia.

## THE THREE MUSKETEERS

When billionaire real estate developer Donald Trump announced his candidacy for president in June 2015, few people on the coasts, in the entertainment industry, or in the media took him seriously. After all, this was the self-appointed star of the reality show *The Apprentice*. Riding on his father's coattails in the New York real estate scene, the bombastic Donald inherited and otherwise acquired a fortune for himself. Along the way he also acquired two ex-wives, five children, numerous bankruptcies, and ownership of the Miss Universe Organization, which includes Miss Universe, Miss USA, and Miss Teen USA. He also amassed 3,500 lawsuits by and against him, 165 with the US government—many of which are still pending[1]—and a hefty list of allegations of sexual misconduct.

By Super Tuesday in March 2016, Trump had taken the $40 to $200 million he inherited (estimates vary) and the more than $1 billion in bailout money the banks gave him after he bankrupted his companies and invested much of that money into building his unmistakable, gold-plated personal brand.[2] The Trump name was stamped on everything from get-rich courses to books to hotels to casinos to golf courses to universities to neckties to perfumes. His daughter Ivanka followed suit, creating her own trendy fashion line.

In contrast, Hillary Clinton grew up in the white-collar Chicago neighborhood of Park Ridge, Illinois. She graduated from Yale Law School, taught courses, worked for the betterment of women and children, got hitched to Bill, saw him through two terms of the presidency, stood by him during his impeachment trial, and became US secretary of state. Despite some bumps in the road, Hillary's track record leading up to the election was squeaky clean compared to Trump's.

Of course, there would be that fund-raising speech she gave at an exclusive event at the Colorado governor's mansion in which speakers spewing white noise were placed around the perimeter to ensure that the reporters across the street could not hear what she was saying to her wealthy supporters.[3] And then there was the scandal involving her use of a private email server. And then there was that wild film *Hillary's America*, which, in spite of the vitriol of film critics and an abysmal 4 percent Rotten Tomatoes score, riled up the Right with such fervor that it grossed a tidy $13.1 million at the box office.

By the way, the movie is a fascinating, high-budget character assassination not just of Hillary Clinton but also of the Democratic Party itself, which, according to director Dinesh D'Souza, is the progenitor of slavery and even—gasp!—*mind control*. (Who knew?) The point is that the secretive fund-raising events, the dicey emails, the movie hit pieces all bolstered a certain perception that Hillary Clinton was a less-than-trustworthy emissary of the very economic regime that had plunged the Millennials—and much of the free world—into financial darkness.

Then there was Bernie Sanders, that quirky, kvetching, aging senator from the tiny progressive state of Vermont. While Donald Trump was brought up in the private schools and high life of Manhattan and Hillary Clinton was reared in an immaculately landscaped white upper-class Chicago neighborhood, Bernard Sanders grew up in a rougher, dirtier, grittier Brooklyn—back when Brooklyn was a place for immigrants and Jewish people. (I know it's hard to believe, but Brooklyn wasn't always a trendy hipster hangout.) His father was a

Jewish immigrant and his mother's parents were also immigrants, thus making him literally the son of immigrants.

Both Sanders's parents died soon after he completed high school. He went on to study politics and became active in working for racial equality while still in college, and has remained a socialist or a democratic socialist since then. He moved to Vermont, became mayor of Burlington, then congressman from Vermont, and eventually senator. He has served in the House and Senate since 1991 and is the longest-serving non-Democratic-Party-affiliated, non-Republican-Party-affiliated Independent in the House and Senate in US history. His personal life comprises a brief first marriage, a son born out of wedlock, and a long-term marriage to his current wife.

> Sanders staged one of the longest speeches in recent congressional history by speaking for eight and a half hours against a program that would extend tax cuts to the richest 2 percent of Americans.

As a senator, Sanders staged one of the longest speeches in recent congressional history by speaking for eight and a half hours against a program that would extend tax cuts to the richest 2 percent of Americans. In typical government doublespeak, the Obama-backed bill was called the Middle Class Tax Relief Act of 2010, and would by itself add $1 trillion to the national debt over ten years through tax breaks for the wealthy. While Sanders's speech was not technically a filibuster—the vote for the bill would proceed the following Monday regardless of his speech—it grabbed national attention. The 124-page transcript of the speech, which is available for free on Sanders's website,[4] outlines the presidential platform he would take five years later.

Unlike Trump, who began speaking about middle-class woes only after his candidacy announcement, or Hillary, who was quick to leap onto issues of importance to Millennials after polls suggested she had weak support with the under-thirty crowd, Bernie Sanders had worked for over twenty-five years for campaign finance reform, against corporate welfare, on protecting America from global warming, on better income equality, on LGBT rights, on ensuring parental leave, on universal health care, and against overspending on foreign wars. He didn't get into office because his father was rich, and he wasn't married to a charismatic former governor and former US president.

Of the three potential candidates for president, both Trump, who was born in 1946, and Clinton, who was born in 1947, are Baby Boomers. Their unquestionable moral righteousness, a telltale sign of their generation, rang loud and clear throughout their campaigns. Both Trump and Clinton essentially ran campaigns based on something called neoliberal economic theory, a policy that demands that government regulators keep their hands off the free market, and that many academics argue ensures that wealth aggregates at the top.[5]

Sanders, on the other hand, who was born in 1941, is a member of the Silent Generation, the "Artist" generation of people who were known for improving the society left for them by the GI or Greatest Generation who fought in World War II. His platform was every bit inspired by the work of another progressive, middle-class defender. That person came to power during the last time of complete global crisis. He led America to win World War II and do a great many other things.

His name was Franklin Delano Roosevelt.

## A NEWER NEW DEAL

Franklin Roosevelt was a distant nephew of President Teddy Roosevelt, the Rough Rider who had taken on the banks, the railroads, and big oil in an effort to break up monopolies. FDR admired his older relative and shaped his political career in the Rough Rider's image.

FDR suffered a massive blow when he contracted polio in 1921. He never fully recovered the use of his legs. Most of the official photographs and film of him are carefully staged to hide his disability. Like so many politicians, his personal life was a messy web of extramarital affairs. He was, at best, an imperfect man. But his contribution to American history is undeniable.

In the wake of the 1929 stock market crash and in the middle of the Great Depression, in the 1932 election, FDR ran on the promise of a New Deal for the American people. His campaign aligned African Americans, Jewish people, immigrants, laborers, and farmers into a new Democratic Party. The then fifty-year-old politician crushed his opponent at the polls, taking all but six states.

In his first one hundred days in office, Roosevelt put in place sweeping reforms to curtail the runaway corporate greed that had resulted in the 1929 economic crash. His New Deal created jobs for the unemployed, spurred economic growth, and regulated Wall Street, the banks, and the transportation companies. Much to the applause of working Americans, FDR also presided over the dissolution of Prohibition, the unlikable Eighteenth Amendment, which outlawed the sale and consumption of alcohol.

FDR's Works Progress Administration (WPA) employed millions of unskilled men, women, and teenagers to build roads, public buildings, bridges, schools, parks, hospitals, community centers, city halls, gyms, fairgrounds, zoos, and auditoriums among other infrastructure. The WPA extended electricity to rural areas, forming the backbone of what would later become the telecommunications industry. It built incredible structures such as the Astronomers Monument at the Griffith Observatory overlooking Los Angeles and Chicago's Midway

International Airport. The administration built facilities in almost every community in the United States. In essence, Franklin Delano Roosevelt was single-handedly responsible for the program that, in eight short years, constructed the firmament on which America still operates to this day.

FDR's list of recovery policies did not end there. He created Social Security. He instituted the first minimum wage for working Americans, saying, "No business which depends for existence on paying less than living wages to its workers has any right to continue in this country." He created programs for farmers who had been wiped out by the man-made environmental devastation of the Dust Bowl. FDR's Civilian Conservation Corps began the work that continues today to restore America's precious topsoil, among other tasks.

In an unprecedented move for any US president before or since, FDR pushed through legislation to bolster, protect, and provide power for labor unions. Meanwhile, FDR instituted the Securities and Exchange Commission to regulate the commerce of stocks, bonds, and other securities. The creation of the SEC, as it would come to be known, required publicly held companies to be transparent to investors by disclosing earnings and losses.

Despite his well-heeled upbringing, historians regard FDR as a populist, a politician who is for the common man and against an entrenched and corrupt government controlled by a few powerful men. At a speech he gave in Madison Square Garden in his reelection campaign of 1936, Roosevelt said, "We know now that Government by organized money is just as dangerous as Government by organized mob!"

From the beginning of America, perhaps the greatest struggle for power has been between the power of capital and finance versus the power of labor. Like our Great Recession of today, the Great Depression of the 1930s was an extension of what happens when the scales of power are tipped radically against labor and radically in the favor of capital.

Roosevelt played the role of the equalizer who, through his dogged tenacity, moved the scales back into balance so that the majority of people who lived in, worked for, and loved America once again had a voice. The administration of FDR redefined for Americans what is known as the social contract between the government and the people.

Franklin Roosevelt is the only US president elected to four consecutive terms. He died while still in office.

## THE POWELL MEMO

For the better part of three decades after FDR died, America's unemployment was low, and the middle class prospered. Then starting in the 1960s with the Baby Boomers coming of age and US involvement in the Vietnam War, the counterculture revolution took center stage, targeting areas of society that had stagnated. Women's rights, racial equality, and environmental protection were chief concerns of the idealist Boomer progressives.

In 1971, a former army intelligence officer turned corporate lawyer named Lewis Powell wrote what he called the "Confidential Memorandum: Attack on American Free Enterprise System," in which he outlined a new plan for corporate America. Powell sat on the board of eleven corporations, serving as a longtime champion of tobacco giant Philip Morris. Powell felt that the media was portraying the tobacco industry with unfavorable bias by not giving weight to the cancer denial claims of the industry. This sparked his distaste for what he believed to be a socialist media.

Powell was also reacting to the work of another attorney, a progressive by the name of Ralph Nader. Nader's bestselling book *Unsafe at Any Speed: The Designed-In Dangers of the American Automobile* told the story of an auto industry that knowingly and deceivingly put profits ahead of saving lives. Nader's desire for consumer protection, for environmental standards, and for governmental regulation made Powell and his corporate allies see red.

The secret Powell Memo, as it would become known, purposefully confused the issues of race equality, women's equality, and environmental protection with fascism. It conflated progressivism and violence. Powell was after "the Communists, New Leftists, and other revolutionaries" who, he argued, sought to "destroy the entire system, both political and economic." Reading the memo makes one think that the Flower Power, sit-in hippies were about to stage a well-armed revolt to overthrow the government, and that the very heart of American enterprise itself was at risk due to the progressive movement.

Powell laid out a plan to organize corporate power to fight back against what he termed the "most dangerous kind of politics"—those of the Left. He advocated for using the US Chamber of Commerce, university campuses, scholars, speakers, publications including books, paperbacks, and pamphlets, paid ads, and ultimately the "neglected political arena" to write a new narrative for America. In essence, that narrative was neoliberalism.[6]

> Powell laid out a plan to organize corporate power to fight back against what he termed the "most dangerous kind of politics"— those of the Left.

To summarize neoliberal economic theory: corporations are good, the goal of the economy is limitless growth, political oversight must be curtailed, government and state intervention in the market must be abolished, and progressives are a threat to democracy.[7]

George Monbiot, author of *How Did We Get into This Mess?*, says this about neoliberalism:

> Its anonymity is both a symptom and cause of its power. It has played a major role in a remarkable variety of crises: the financial meltdown of 2007–8, the offshoring of wealth and power, of which the Panama Papers offer us merely a glimpse, the slow collapse of public health and education, resurgent child poverty, the epidemic of loneliness, the collapse of ecosystems, the rise of Donald Trump. But we respond to these crises as if they emerge in isolation, apparently unaware that they have all been either catalysed or exacerbated by the same coherent philosophy; a philosophy that has—or had—a name. What greater power can there be than to operate namelessly?[8]

To really take over America, neoliberal economic proponents would need to use underhanded, cloak-of-night tactics to circumvent the conscious revolution. The Powell Memo gave them an outline of exactly how to do that.

Soon after his memo, Powell was nominated by President Richard Nixon to be a justice of the Supreme Court. It was there that he wrote the majority opinion in the landmark case of *First National Bank of Boston v. Bellotti*, a decision that set the legal framework for the First Amendment "right" for corporations to influence issues on ballots. In so doing Powell created a legal precedent for the more recent decision of *Citizens United v. Federal Election Commission*, which essentially gives corporations the power to anonymously fund political campaigns.

After all the work FDR had done to rebalance the scales of power between labor and capital, Powell and his coalition set about rigging the American political, social, and corporate landscape to cement the scales in favor of corporate power. But Powell and his alliance did something else, too.

They rebranded liberal politics and remade the Democratic Party.

## FATHER KNOWS BEST

By the end of the 1970s the unions were being shattered, the factories began to move south, and the middle class was being dissolved. Thanks in no small part to a successful class war waged by the American corporate elite, the share of national income of the top 1 percent of income earners in the United States once again skyrocketed to 15 percent, almost exactly where it had been before the 1929 stock market crash.

> Like an archangel sent from heaven, Ronald "Ronnie" Reagan appeared in 1980 with his fantastical campaign promise "Let's Make America Great Again."

The Democratic Party soon found itself flaccid. By the late 1970s, President Jimmy Carter's administration was unable to do much about the oil crisis, the American hostages in Iran, or the crashing US economy. Just when it seemed that the Democrats were going to doom America to endless woes, a new national hero appeared on the scene.

Like an archangel sent from heaven, Ronald "Ronnie" Reagan appeared in 1980 with his fantastical campaign promise "Let's Make America Great Again." As a radio and TV star, Reagan was a vision of white privilege, wealth, power, and charisma. Reagan's suits were carefully tailored to resemble those commonly worn by the men in the 1950s and '60s sitcoms. He represented the kind of moneyed, postwar stability that older and more conservative—i.e., rich—Americans hungered for.

In spite of the Baby Boomer–led counterculture revolution, what American voters really wanted was that idolized, patriarchal, *Father Knows Best* figurehead they had grown up with on TV.

Reagan was America's first true TV president. But he wouldn't be our last. His presence marked a shift in politics. From the moment he stepped into the White House, both parties moved to the right. Reagan's neoliberalist policies continued under President George H. W. Bush. After him, President Clinton's reign was a mere pandering to the now faltering middle class. After largely receiving the southern vote, the black vote, the labor union vote, and the women's vote, Clinton went on to deregulate the banks—the very move that would spiral 1 percenters' wealth upward, forcing millions out of their homes and crashing the US economy.

By the year 2000, the Democratic Party and the Republican Party had become akin to Coke and Pepsi, two very similar types of caffeine-laced, neoliberal sugar water.

It was time to stop talking about what was really happening in America. Class warfare, the destruction of the environment, the impoverishment of our children, and the suppression of people of color were topics that no longer got ratings. It was time instead for a series of multibillion-dollar multimedia shows.

No, I'm not talking about U2 going back on tour. I'm speaking about that thing that provides the media industry its paycheck every four years.

That's right—it's the US presidential election.

By the time Barack Obama ran for office, the presidential election had become a billion-dollar media circus. Obama's embattled eight years left in their wake little in the way of real economic gains for most Americans who felt they were getting an ever shorter end of the economic stick.

America needed a new vision of patriarchal hope. Like Reagan, they needed to see somebody at the top who embodied a more prosperous era. Somebody with big hair and all the right moves. Somebody who embodied the 1980s' bratty, bad-boy corporate attitude heralding from the Flock of Seagulls, fluorescent polyester, *Say Anything*, me-first, cocaine-filled time when *The Color of Money* ruled.

After all, the majority of registered American voters were Baby Boomers who still watched that antiquated thing called television that plugs into a coaxial cable. And those boob-tube viewers wanted a new TV president to restore things, just like Reagan had done. Lucky for them, there was one TV star whose regularly scheduled program was tanking. It was time for Donald Trump to go prime time and "Make America Great." Again.

But before Trump could take center stage in his new TV studio, also known as the Oval Office, another popular politician would have to get out of his way.

## THE RISE OF A MODERN POPULIST

In spite of his age, his angry-ish tone, and his socialist rhetoric (or maybe because of these), Bernie Sanders quickly rose in the run-up to the 2016 presidential election as what late-night talk show host Seth Meyers called "the young, hip choice."

In city after city, massive, mostly young crowds showed up to Bernie rallies, where they were inspired to volunteer to bring yet more people out for Our Revolution. Part of what worked about the Sanders platform was that the fundamentals were simple, clear, and free from doublespeak or policy-wonkiness. In short, they were: get corporate money out of politics, give young people free education, create a $15 minimum wage, protect the environment, outlaw fracking, respect women's choices for their own bodies, and regulate runaway corporate greed.

My wife, Rebecca, and I met and interviewed Bernie Sanders in 2011 for our movie *The Big Fix*, which details the corruption that led up to the Deepwater Horizon oil spill in the Gulf of Mexico. He was the only US senator who agreed to an interview. Here's what he said:

> We have a campaign financing and lobbying situation which is absolutely out of control, and the *Citizens United* [Supreme Court] decision made a terrible situation even worse. So, unless we can change the law, unless we can pass a constitutional amendment, what you're going to see in years to come are billions of dollars coming from Wall Street, from every powerful and wealthy special interest, going into TV and radio advertising, and that will all be undisclosed. The American people will not know who is making those contributions. We need radical changes in campaign financing in this country. We've got to go to public funding of the elections.[9]

Little did Sanders know when he spoke these words that five years later he would be running against a TV-star billionaire who himself would not show his tax returns to the American people. Meeting him in person, I was most struck by Sanders's passion. Today he is still saying the same thing, but his passion has not wavered and his message is still not the watered-down, sponsored-by type of drivel that spouts from the mouths of most politicians. That says something.

By 2016, a big shift had also happened that gave immense lift to the

Sanders revolution. In 2008, when the Millennial generation first exercised its presidential voting power by helping to hoist Barack Obama into the White House, a little less than half the Millennial generation was of voting age. But by 2016, the vast majority of your generation, with the exception of those born in late 1998 and during 1999 and 2000, was of voting age.

A massive voting bloc of somewhere in the range of seventy to seventy-five million of you were out of high school and living in a wage-labor, rampant-unemployment, college-debt-ridden Great Recession nation. The ebullience and the branding of "hope and change" that characterized Obama's rise were long since crushed by the realization that unless you were part of a coveted minority of wealthy and mostly white youth, you were either SOL or USCWAP. Either way, most people in your generation were screwed and they knew it.

As Millennial and Millennial researcher Jason Dorsey tells me, "What we saw in the run-up to the 2016 election were these class issues for the first time being represented by Millennials. So that's why you're seeing this massive mobilization of young people coming together for a cause. The problem is, that cause is very threatening for other generations."

Few Millennials were more outspoken advocates of Bernie Sanders's volley for the presidency than actor and activist Shailene Woodley. Because she was born in 1991, this was only the second general election the *Divergent* franchise star was old enough to vote in. I first meet Woodley through a mutual friend at the Standing Rock protest. She later shows up for our interview in New York City wearing an unassuming gray T-shirt and jeans and sniffling from the beginnings of what would become the flu.

When I ask her why she got involved in Sanders's campaign, she lights up like a Christmas tree. "You know," says Woodley, "my entire life I was the antithesis of being politically engaged." Hearing Bernie Sanders speak at a rally changed all that. "For once, we had a candidate who spoke with transparency, with truthfulness, and with honesty. It invigorated and ignited my own desire to participate in democracy."

> "For once, we had a candidate who spoke with transparency, with truthfulness, and with honesty. It invigorated and ignited my own desire to participate in democracy."

After that, she piled some friends into her mom's RV and hit the road to support Sanders's campaign. It didn't take long for Woodley to become one of those onstage voices, rallying the crowds for Our Revolution. "Michigan was the first rally that I spoke at," she says. "And I looked at this crowd and I said, 'we have someone who is willing to be honest in the face of extreme adversity, and that is something worth fighting for.' I guess I never really realized how many people in our country are ready for a change.

"And Bernie Sanders got up onstage, day after day, and told every single person in that crowd that they were important. They were important enough to make $15 an hour minimum wage. They were important enough to be able to go to school for free, regardless of their financial income or their financial history. That they were important enough to have access to universal health care. These are things that should be human rights. These are not things that we should have to fight for, especially in a country like America.

"What Bernie Sanders did was remind us that we cannot lie idle when our brothers and sisters—whether it's the Native Americans in Standing Rock Reservation; whether it's people of color who are being shot because of the color of their skin; whether it's because of the religions we identify with—all these labels that constantly divide us, are all distractions keeping us from realizing the truth, that we are all one.

And that is what Bernie Sanders was able to articulate in words that people were able to understand."

More than any other candidate in recent history, Sanders spoke to the Millennial desire for a nonjudgmental, race-inclusive, gender-inclusive, class-inclusive America—the type of country many Millennials and conscious people in older generations would like to live in.

## BY THE NUMBERS

At the Democratic National Convention Bernie Sanders received 1,846 delegate votes to Hillary's 2,205. That's not bad for an Independent who invaded the two-party system. But consider this: 711 of the total voting delegates at the DNC abstained. This abstention bloc, who were either too afraid or too confused to select a leader, could have easily toppled the Democratic nomination in favor of Bernie.

Interestingly, 712 of the 4,051 delegates at the Democratic National Convention (about 15 percent) are *superdelegates* who can vote for any candidate they choose *regardless of how their state or county voted in the primaries*.

Bernie lost the Democratic nomination to Hillary by a margin of 359 delegate votes.

Yes, in the year 2016, with all our technological wizardry and the billions spent on the presidential campaign, 359 people (or 360, to be exact, since Bernie would have technically needed at least one extra vote to have the majority and be nominated as the Democratic candidate) likely decided the fate of the most powerful nation in the world by *not* voting, even though they could have, and would have been well within their right to have voted for Bernie Sanders as the Democratic Party's nominee for president.

Consider: a balding, Brooklyn-accented, seventy-four-year-old Jewish, Silent Generation, FDR-like socialist from the itsy-bitsy state of Vermont was 360 people away from shattering the two-party system and possibly becoming president of the United States. Regardless of how you might feel about Bernie, that's just . . . astonishing.

But the reason it was really astonishing isn't the fact that Bernie is not a typical movie-star-worthy presidential candidate, or even the fact that he is an Independent. It's astonishing because of how the Sanders campaign was accomplished. It was managed through a repeatable formula for social change powered by everyday people who willingly and wholeheartedly volunteered their time and gave their own small amounts of money.

In their book *Rules for Revolutionaries: How Big Organizing Can Change Everything*, Becky Bond and Zack Exley use their combined forty years of campaign experience to codify what worked during the Sanders campaign. They call the process big organizing, and it follows a simple set of rules. Bond and Exley say the success of the campaign was because it had: a powerful, honest leader; a big, clear promise; was staffed by mostly volunteers; fought racism; used phones; worked from a centralized and top-down plan; was funded by microdonations, not corporate money; organized new volunteers in face-to-face barnstorming meetings; and was well managed.

While Bernie Sanders did not win the presidency, his campaign is a weather vane of what the future of politics could look like, especially as cryptocurrencies further enable microdonations. By the numbers, the 2015–16 Sanders campaign:

- Got 100,000 volunteers to make phone calls to voters.
- Together, those volunteers made 75 million calls.

- A few thousand volunteers sent over 8 million individual text messages.
- Created 100,000 volunteer-led events.
- Held over 1,000 town hall meetings (aka barnstorming events), the vast majority of which were organized and run by volunteers.
- Gathered hundreds of thousands of people at rallies.
- Raised over $228 million, the majority of which came from individual donors who gave an average of $27 each.
- Garnered over 13,210,550 popular votes in the Democratic primaries, a close second to Hillary Clinton's 16,917,853 popular votes.[10]

The nonmeasurable success of Senator Sanders's campaign will go down in history as unapologetically thrusting onto the world stage numerous critical issues that were heretofore too taboo for the presidential political arena. Among them were: a $15 minimum wage, no deportation of children, a complete ban on fracking (not popular with the oil and gas interests that typically bankroll politicians), free health care, and free college. At their core, these are Millennial-centric issues. Bernie may not be young, good-looking, or hip, but his issues sure appealed to the demographic of people who are.

In the realm of changing the discourse of a country and a world mired in antiquated thinking, the Sanders campaign represented a critical break from the past.

## THE NIGHT IT ALL CHANGED

On the first official night of the Democratic National Convention, July 25, 2016, in Philadelphia, things quickly reached a fever pitch inside the hall. The Democrats wanted to present an optimistic and consolidated front, something that would contrast with the RNC's recent vitriolic condemnation of the Obama administration and of Hillary Clinton. But instead, the bifurcation inside the Democratic Party led to an evening of vocal riots.

For many Bernie supporters, leaked emails showing various Democratic Party leaders' and delegates' support of Hillary during the nominating process cast doubt on the validity of Clinton's numerical lead. By the time Bernie Sanders took the stage to throw his weight behind Clinton, the Sanders supporters and the Clinton supporters had been chanting over one another for more than an hour. As Sanders delivered his speech, the feeling of betrayal was written across the tear-strewn faces of Bernie supporters.

Shailene Woodley tells me, "I was at the Democratic National Convention. I was a delegate for Bernie. So, the way the stadium was divided was, the lower level, the majority of those states were Hillary Clinton states, and the majority of the top level were Bernie Sanders states. The press was situated between the top and the lower level, so the press, for the most part, was only broadcasting over the lower sections. And when Bernie stepped down, almost the entire top half of that center walked out. I have the video—many people have videos—you don't see that on mainstream media." In other words, organizers at the convention knew there was a good chance those Sanders supporters would do goodness-knows-what and, to the best of their ability, they made sure the cameras were facing the other way.

Earlier that day, standing outside in the blistering heat, Sanders stood in front of a crowd of supporters at City Hall and screamed into a microphone, "We have got to elect Hillary Clinton and Tim Kaine!" But as he uttered the name "Kaine," he bowed his head low. One might mistake the gesture for that of a seventy-four-year-old man trying to read something written on a piece of paper on the podium at which he stood. But playing the video back now, it's clear that, in the face of an intractable two-party system that does not take kindly to outsiders, Sanders was not saying what he wanted to but rather *what he had to.*

And for the time being, that system had crushed the revolution he had helped ignite.

Writing for Bryant University's newspaper, sophomore and Millennial Christopher Groneg, the paper's business editor, said:

> Young Americans reluctantly laid witness to the death throes of their potential revolution on a warm July evening in Philadelphia. . . . The promise of a new America—an America conceived and postulated by their radically transformative and diverse ideals—became nothing more than what they always believed, whether wrongfully or otherwise, in the very fathoms of their minds: that government and politics could never work in their favor.

With Bernie Sanders shut out of the race for president, there was only one thing left to do: try to get Hillary Rodham Clinton elected as the president of the United States.

## BEGGING FOR THE MILLENNIAL VOTE

Prior to Election Day, Lewis Black in his Back in Black rant on *The Daily Show with Trevor Noah* pleaded, "Millennials, I know we've fucked things up for you, but we're counting on you to fix things! . . . Vote!"

Accurate? Yep. Desperate? Painfully so.

Then there were the videos. There were videos with hot models convincing noob Millennial dudes (and women) who weren't otherwise going to vote to vote; there were celebrity videos ad nauseam urging people to vote, and vote, and vote. For the most part, the Internet go-out-and-vote video phenomenon was a sometimes thinly veiled and sometimes blatant push to get Millennials to vote for Hillary Clinton.

It was Boomer parenting tactics on steroids. The #ImWithHer campaign did everything short of handing out gold stars to youngsters who voted. The problem is, it didn't work—at least, not well enough.

In 2012, 83 percent of voters eighteen to twenty-nine chose not to vote. In 2014, 62 percent did not vote. Estimates of the 2016 election put youth turnout at around 50 percent. If these statistics hold true, more and more Millennials are voting in each presidential election. So, on one hand, the videos, the manipulation, the tinsel worked to draw the under-thirty crowd to the polls.

But on the other hand, 50 percent?! Really? That's all you got??? There are, like, so many people on Tinder whose swipe-to-sleep-with ratio is better than that.

The real issue wasn't that Millennials wouldn't turn out to support Hillary over Trump. The deeper issue is that the generation that had come of age in the middle of the Great Recession, *the same generation whose voters are 50 percent Independent*, didn't feel a strong enough pull to either the Republican *or* Democratic candidate. The big view from the Millennial generation was, and remains, that, due to the lack of *choices*—i.e., a system with *only* two parties—the American political system is a mechanism for keeping the 1 percent wealthy and the youth locked out of elitist politics.

In March 2016 Michael Safi, writing for the *Guardian* in an article titled "Have Millennials Given Up on Democracy?," found that:

Millennials themselves, asked why they do not back democracy, mostly say it "only serves the interests of a few" (40 percent) and that there is "no real difference between the policies of the major parties" (32 percent).

A similar malaise is expressed across Western democracies. Approval ratings for the US Congress are famously low, but among young Americans fell to just 38 percent in the decade to 2014. In UK elections, young voter turnout shrank for nearly two decades before an increase in 2015. A Canadian poll four years ago found less than 50 percent of young adults thought democracy trumped other kinds of government.

Despite the 50 percent turnout,[11] American Millennials did register to vote. In fact, 83 percent of them registered.[12] And when presented with the choices prior to the election, they voiced their opinions clearly.

In November 2016, writing for Bustle.com, Millennial Natasha Guzmán summed up the pre–general election view of many young voters:

> She [Hillary Clinton] has managed to bring most Sanders supporters to her side—roughly eight in ten have decided to back her—and leads with 68 percent of likely Millennial voters saying they support her. This is in stark contrast with Trump's 20 percent. It's worth noting, however, that 36 percent of those saying they'll vote for the Democratic nominee say that blocking Trump, and not a good view of Clinton, is the main reason behind their decision.

At the time, the question was whether or not stopping a bombastic, billionaire, orange-faced reality TV star would be enough motivation for Millennials to actually get out and vote *against* him by choosing the lesser of two evils.

*Time* magazine found a summation of the mind-set that would decide the election in Brian Seligman, a delegate from California and former US Marine and computer engineer. Speaking to a journalist, Seligman said, "Abraham, Moses, Jesus, and Muhammad could appear before a burning bush and hand me a stone tablet with lightning and everything that said, 'Vote for Hillary,' and I would choose hell because it's the same thing. I'm not voting for her."

As it turns out, he wasn't alone.

## THE TWO AMERICAS

"When Bernie Sanders lost the New York primary," says Shailene Woodley solemnly, "I sort of had this hunch that Trump might win. Because every state we went to, thousands of people would show up to Bernie's rallies, thousands of people would show up to Trump's rallies, and Hillary Clinton wasn't able to pull in those numbers, or she was doing fund-raisers." Despite the fact that some of Trump's supporters may have been paid to show up, the real estate mogul still managed to capture enough disenfranchised voters to swing the Electoral College in his favor.

Trump, who in hindsight was far more cunning than most progressives thought, had it figured it out long before the political Left knew what was coming. He knew the two-party system was likely to shut Bernie out. Once it happened, he knew he could capture enough "Feel the Bern" resentment at establishment politics to pin the golden Trump logo onto the front door at 1600 Pennsylvania Avenue.

Summing up his campaign strategy, at 2:44 a.m. on May 4, 2016, in one of his late-night tweet rants, Trump said, "I would rather run against Crooked Hillary Clinton than Bernie Sanders and that will happen because the books are cooked against Bernie!"

A deep dive into the numbers reveals that Trump didn't exactly capture all the Bernie voters from the primaries, but he did take advantage of the disruption of voter turnout in certain key counties in states that ended up casting their electoral votes for him. In essence, Trump was able to skim a little cream from the Sanders revolution, strengthening certain Republican areas while weakening certain Democratic ones.[13] It turns out, he didn't have to skim much.

> Trump said, "I would rather run against Crooked Hillary Clinton than Bernie Sanders and that will happen because the books are cooked against Bernie!"

In the final analysis, Hillary missed the mark. She just couldn't convince enough Millennials, or voters of any age for that matter, that she was cool enough, honest enough, and not the same thing they already experienced enough. As a comparison, in 2008, Obama had won 60 percent of the under-thirty vote to Mitt Romney's 37 percent. Mrs. Clinton was only able to score 51 percent of the Millennial vote. Nine percent of Millennial voters may not seem like a big difference, but because of where those votes were geographically cast, it was more than enough to cost Clinton the election.

If we parse America's 2016 votes strictly by age, the gap between Baby Boomers and Millennials becomes starkly obvious. Have a look at the graphic on the following page. If Millennials were the only people voting, the election results would have gone radically in favor of Hillary, with 496 Electoral College votes for Clinton and only 39 for Trump.

But Millennials are not the only people voting. They are essentially voting *against* their parents' generation. This is critically important:

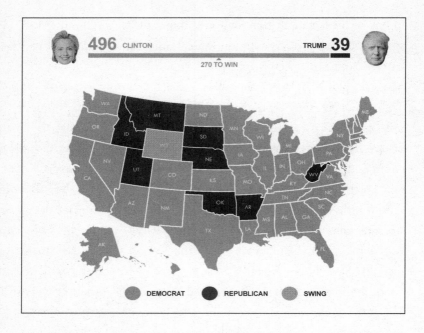

If no one but Millennials had voted in 2016, the election results would have gone radically in favor of Hillary Clinton, according to exit-poll data. Millennials have the numbers to outvote Baby Boomers, but lasting structural change will occur only if Millennials can take control of the political process.

the two largest generations in history are voting in diametrically opposite directions.

When it comes to voting, the two Americas we hear so much about aren't the Midwest versus the coasts, it's Millennials versus Boomers all the way.

Says Ana Kasparian, a reporter for *The Young Turks*, "I think we are still becoming a multicultural society, which is why there's so much backlash from certain white Americans against things like coming

together as a country, working together regardless of your religion, your race, your ethnicity.
The backlash I think speaks volumes about a
generation of people who are so scared of the
country progressing toward tolerance."

> **This is critically important: the two largest generations in history are voting in diametrically opposite directions.**

## VOTERS' REMORSE

On November 9, in the aftermath of the election, Emma Lord, a
spunky Millennial writer living in New York City, summed it up on
Bustle.com:

> It might seem incredibly easy to blame the older generations for
> putting us in the position we are in right now—namely, having
> Donald Trump as the president-elect of the United States. After
> all, it's their votes that screwed with our perfect Millennial
> maps again, isn't it? In that sense, this is just one more mess the
> Baby Boomers have left for us to clean up in their wake. We are
> inheriting this presidency the same way we inherited the bad
> economy, inherited an impossible job market, and inherited
> the ability to go dead in the eyes and nod as our grandparents
> say something vaguely racist at the Thanksgiving dinner table.[14]

The Silent Generation, Baby Boomer, and Gen X readers out
there would be wise to pay close attention to Ms. Lord's words. Hers
is a heretofore largely ignored sentiment of the largest global youth
generation in history, the one that is in the process of taking over the
world.

Back to the postelection outcry: there was plenty of other Millennial vitriol, from Miley Cyrus crying to 230,000 followers on YouTube to one young woman in a vid snap screaming in Twitter hysteria that she was about to "fucking kill myself right now—this has to be a joke!!!"

The hashtags #NotMyPresident and #StillWithHer went ballistic on Twitter the day after the election. At American University in Washington, DC, students burned American flags while a protestor yelled, "This is a representation of America. We are going down in flames!"

In Los Angeles, five thousand protestors, most of them Millennials, marched through the city. They burned a piñata of Donald Trump's head on the steps of City Hall. Protestors then went on to shut down Interstate 405, the main thoroughfare in one of the busiest cities in the world for three consecutive hours, and then they shut down LA's Highway 101.

Thousands of protestors blocked traffic in downtown Portland, Chicago, Boston, and Philadelphia, with some torching flags. Demonstrators in Oakland smashed windows. In New York City, thousands clustered in front of Trump's flagship building, Trump Tower, and repeated the motto "Not My President."

Searches for "how can I move to Canada" spiked. The Canadian immigration website crashed due to an overload of traffic. A DJ on a tiny island in Nova Scotia, Canada, spent $25 putting up a website called Cape Breton if Donald Trump Wins. Within twenty-four hours he had millions of visitors and a flooded in-box. Apparently, the small, economically depressed but beautiful island was hoping for an influx of foreigners and foreign cash.

At Berkeley High School, about 1,500 students, half the entire student body, walked out of class after first period began at 8:00 a.m.

Generation X and Baby Boomer commentators gave only slightly more restrained responses.

The techno-music icon Moby penned an open letter in which

he talked about fast food causing cancer and Trump being the worst president ever. David Remnick, writing for the *New Yorker*, said, "The election of Donald Trump to the Presidency is nothing less than a tragedy for the American republic, a tragedy for the Constitution, and a triumph for the forces, at home and abroad, of nativism, authoritarianism, misogyny, and racism."

Veteran correspondent and TV host Bill Moyers posted a piece on his website by Neal Gabler titled "Farewell, America" in which Gabler said, "America died on November 8, 2016, not with a bang or a whimper but at its own hand via electoral suicide."

Most of these celebrity-type reactions were so blinded by emotion that they missed the point of what had actually happened. But not everyone was as bamboozled by the election results. In his list of things in his "Morning After To-Do List," Michael Moore succinctly stated: "Along came a TV star they liked whose plan was to destroy both parties and tell them all 'You're fired!' Trump's victory is no surprise. He was never a joke. Treating him as one only strengthened him."

> In America, the voting system that took almost two centuries to build and protect was stolen in just seven short years.

For all the vitriol that Trump's presidential win stirred up, surprisingly few people understand how he did it.

## HOW TO STEAL AN ELECTION—STEP 1

In America, the voting system that took almost two centuries to build and protect was stolen in just seven short years. Here's how it happened.

In July 1964, a landmark piece of federal legislation was passed. It was called the Civil Rights Act. The purpose of the act was to institutionalize equality. But even after the Civil Rights Act, there was one critical area of civic life from which black people were being actively shut out: voting.

In his 1963 speech requesting the Civil Rights Act, President John F. Kennedy had specifically said that the legislation should give all Americans "greater protection for the right to vote." Thus, the civil rights legislation had, in theory, prohibited racial discrimination by government services. But on the heels of the legislation, a plethora of tactics emerged to stop black people from registering to vote.

A common tactic to stop black people and poor whites from voting was using a literacy test. Often, voting registrars would ask perfectly literate, would-be voters arbitrary and trick questions until they failed to answer something correctly, at which time they were barred from registering.

Hence, in 1964, despite herculean efforts by the National Association for the Advancement of Colored People (NAACP), of the potential twelve-million-person African American electorate, only 5.5 million had registered to vote.[15]

This is why, in 1965, the Reverend Martin Luther King Jr. led three nonviolent protest marches along a fifty-four-mile stretch of highway from Selma, Alabama, to the state capital of Montgomery. During the first march, which took place on Sunday, March 7, police and others brutally beat and teargassed marchers. A photograph of civil rights activist Amelia Boynton Robinson, beaten, bleeding, and lying unconscious on a bridge, went to newspapers across the country and incited outrage.

The second march ended when King decided to turn marchers back at the sight of police. That night, a white mob lynched and killed a black pastor who had traveled to join King's group.

Finally, President Lyndon B. Johnson gave the marchers protection with the National Guard. And on March 15, 1965, 25,000 people amassed at the state capital in Montgomery in support of equal voting rights. To concretize the demands of the movement, Congress passed another piece of federal legislation called the Voting Rights Act, which prohibits racial discrimination in voting.

Importantly, the Voting Rights Act also contained special provisions that prohibited certain jurisdictions that had knowingly practiced voting discrimination, most of which were in the South, from altering voting practices without preapproval from either the US attorney general or the US District Court for the District of Columbia.

> **Then in 2013, in one fell swoop, the Voting Rights Act was gutted.**

Then in 2013, in one fell swoop, the Voting Rights Act was gutted. The process of eviscerating the legislation actually started back in 2006, when Shelby County, a little slice of hot, muggy, mosquito-filled, Republican, mostly (89.8 percent) white people, that's smack dab in the middle of Alabama, decided to sue the US attorney general. Shelby County sought an injunction against the special provisions of the Voting Rights Act. In other words, they wanted to overturn it.

The suit took seven years to make its way to the Supreme Court. There, the now deceased Justice Antonin Scalia (who was nominated by, yes, you guessed it, President "Ronnie" Reagan) said that the provisions in the Voting Rights Act constituted "racial entitlement." He moved to strike down the very provisions that protected voters from tactics that had been used in the past to bar them from registering to vote.

In 2013, the Shelby County case concluded in a five-to-four ruling in which the Supreme Court declared those provisions of the Voting Rights Act to be unconstitutional. The result was sweeping, fast, and predictable. Within hours of the ruling, Texas and Mississippi moved to enforce stricter voter ID requirements.

Since then, nineteen mostly Republican states have new voting restrictions in place.[16] These states add up to over 189 electoral votes—more than enough to swing the presidency.[17] The types of restrictions are often sneaky, like having to bring your birth certificate to register to vote or removing early vote-by-mail provisions in mostly black and Hispanic jurisdictions.

Of the eight thousand jurisdictions known for racial injustice at the polls that were once covered by the act, there is now no transparency, no federal oversight, and complete autonomy to create restrictive voting laws at will. Not surprisingly, these mostly Republican jurisdictions are making constant changes targeted at keeping minority voters and young people away from the polls.[18]

A slew of court rulings has shown discriminatory voting practices in places like Florida, Texas, and North Carolina, places that had heretofore been unable to restrict voters because of the existence of the Voting Rights Act.[19] Places, you might have already guessed, in which the vote went to Republican presidential nominee Donald Trump.

As Ari Berman writes in *Rolling Stone*, "There's something profoundly wrong when it's easier to buy a gun than vote in many states."

## HOW TO STEAL AN ELECTION—STEP 2

Important as it was, the Voting Rights Act itself was attempting to fix a fatal flaw at the core of our voting system. You see, in America, votes are not counted as popular votes, rather they are instead counted by districts. The districts are then controlled by one of only two parties—

the Democrats or the Republicans. Now here's the shocker: the controlling party can, and often does, draw its own voting district.

Yes, you read that correctly—the fox gets to decide how to guard the henhouse. What follows is a condensed version of how this happened and where it went horribly wrong.

The US Constitution does not, as is commonly believed, mandate the creation of voting districts. However, Article 1, Section 2, Clause 3, the Enumeration Clause, of the Constitution sets the number of representatives at one per thirty thousand citizens. It also indicates that the number of representatives should be adjusted, as a result of a census, once every ten years. Thus, starting in 1790, and every ten years thereafter, the United States has performed a census. And every ten years, coinciding with either a US presidential election or a midterm election, the states redraw their voting districts. This mass redrawing recently happened in the years 2000 and 2010; it will happen yet again in 2020 and 2030.

> Now here's the shocker: the controlling party can, and often does, draw its own voting district.

Voting districts emerged as a means of aggregating votes and simplifying the process of choosing representatives. Each state manages the drawing of voting districts slightly differently, but in most cases jurisdiction to draw and redraw districts is given to the state legislature. According to Loyola law professor Justin Levitt's informative website called All About Redistricting, "thirty-seven state legislatures have primary control of their own district lines, and forty-two legislatures have primary control over the congressional lines in their state."[20]

In other words, in most of the fifty states, the elected officials directly create their own voting districts. Granted, some states do use outside commissions or require supermajority votes (two-thirds of both the House and Senate), but, by and large, the drawing of voter districts is done by those who stand to benefit from it.

The process of rigging those districts is called gerrymandering, and it's been around since the run-up to the first Congress.[21] Here's an example of how it can work:

Let's say the Republicans control the legislature in a given district. In gerrymandering, that party would redraw their district map so that even though half, or *even the majority*, of their electorate identifies as Democrats, the ruling party, in this case the Republicans, would always win.

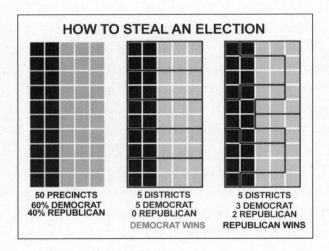

By carving out voting districts around voting blocs, election results can be swayed in favor of a party even if that party is in the minority. This is called gerrymandering, and it's a powerful and sneaky way that the US election process has been corrupted.

Not only is gerrymandering happening in America, but in the 2010 midterm elections, the Republican Party initiated a plan to redraw as many key swing districts in the nation as possible. The only thing more audacious than their plan was how well it worked.

In the wake of the Democrats' sweeping victory in 2008, during which numerous former Republican stronghold voting districts across America went to Obama, the Republican strategist Chris Jankowski developed a plan called REDMAP, which stands for Redistricting Majority Project. According to David Daley, author of *Ratf\*\*ked: Why Your Vote Doesn't Count*, who met and interviewed Jankowski, the goal of REDMAP was simple:

> Republicans should mount an aggressive campaign to flip state legislatures ahead of post-census redistricting, then press the advantage to both redraw congressional and state legislative lines in their favor and aggressively advance the conservative agenda.[22]

For a mere $30 million in campaign financing, the team behind the plan was able to grab control of the legislatures in key swing states such as Indiana, Pennsylvania, North Carolina, Michigan, Alabama, New Hampshire, Florida, Wisconsin, Ohio, and others.[23]

And where did that $30 million come from? Lucky for the team behind REDMAP, the now infamous *Citizens United v. Federal Election Commission* Supreme Court decision was passed in January 2010. That decision effectively made legal the unlimited funding of super PACs by corporations. Wall Street tycoons, fossil fuel interests, foreign organizations, and anyone with a few billion dollars to throw around could now essentially "buy" elections. And that's just what they did.

Thanks to the help of new mapping software, big data was, and still is, extremely useful at drawing America's new voting maps. So accurate is the software that it can predict how each household on each block will vote. Hence the new districts created in 2010 were more precise than ever.

While there are many examples of how the new districts looked, perhaps two of the most telling are Pennsylvania's 7th and Texas's 2nd congressional districts, both of which show the results of the use of new mapping software to "pack" in Republican constituents.

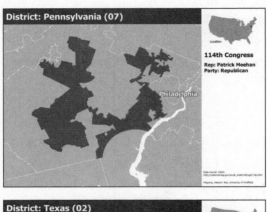

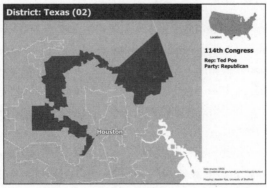

By using sophisticated software, programmers can draw voting-district lines that are so exact as to wrap around individual households that will vote one way or the other. The easily corruptible (and ever more corrupt) process of districting has resulted in voting districts that look like Mickey Mouse and Donald Duck. Rather than representing the will of the voters, the districting process today excludes and disenfranchises them.

"Wait," you might say. "Didn't Obama win in 2012?" Yes, it's true. But remember that in 2012, the House of Representatives was swept by Republicans *even though the popular vote went to the Democrats*. That was the beginning of the embattled four years of the Obama presidency, wherein every major presidential initiative was sandbagged by an ever-more-powerful Republican-controlled House.

As districts continued to be redrawn (some of the county districts are drawn on a rolling basis), REDMAP continued to work its magic. The 2016 election was the first one in which both the presidential and local elections were simultaneously happening *without the protection of the Voting Rights Act* and *with REDMAP in full effect*.

The result was a total disregard for the popular vote. In other words, Donald Trump became president not because the majority of Americans voted for him but because the entire voting system had been rigged.

> We are entering uncharted territory in American history. The very fate of our nation hangs in the balance.

In Donald Trump's own words: "You've been hearing me say it's a rigged system, but now I don't say it anymore because I won. It's true. Now I don't care. I don't care. . . . And the only way I won was I won by such big margins because it is a rigged system."[24]

Ultimately, the Voting Rights Act was a tool to attempt to balance a system in which racism is institutionalized throughout the nation's political infrastructure. As we have seen in this text, we also live in a society in which the structures of power actively disenfranchise its young. This is known as institutional ageism. With the reversal of any form of representation or protection for members of society who may have a dissenting vote, we are entering uncharted territory in American history.

The very fate of our nation hangs in the balance.

## SEXUAL HEALING

One way to attempt to close the gap between the various factions of our country might be through deep, intimate, even violent physical contact. An anonymous San Mateo, California, Millennial came up with an interesting idea and in true Millennial-social-media fashion, he decided to post it publicly.

According to his post on SF Craigslist:

---

### Looking for a Trump supporter
### for rough (bdsm) sex . . .

Do you like rough sex? Are you a Trump supporter? Let's start the process of healing the toxic political divide by hatefucking each other's brains out . . .

You'll tell me that transgender, Muslim, abortionist, vote-stealing immigrants are coming to take our jobs. I'll rebut the argument by saying that your pussy-grabbing, serial-philandering, common con artist, accused statutory rapist, Russian-puppet candidate and his incoming cabinet of billionaire know-nothings are going to take all our jobs by driving the global economy and American democracy off a cliff.

Once properly infuriated, we'll retire to a hotel room. I'll pay the bill (in the fine tradition of wealthy liberal states funding welfare programs in chronically poor conservative states that insist on voting against their self-interest).

---

And the post goes on from there.

Well, it's a free country. But here's the real problem: regardless of the intent, posting, hashtagging, and even angry sexual intercourse are expressions of powerlessness.

None of these things will in any way alter the political landscape of the future. Inside your generation, there is a dangerously strong tendency to believe that cyberspace is a monolithic power that, all by itself, can and will change the world. While that may become true, right now, in the political reality of today, it's not.

Millennials, you would be wise to heed the lessons of REDMAP: the power to take over Washington ultimately rests in state-level elections. Thus, the type of structural change needed to save yourselves and save America (and possibly the world) will require tens of thousands of you to get involved in the less sexy initiatives happening at town, city, and state levels and yes, to run for office. (For a good example of how to do this, see chapter 6 and Millennial congresswoman Tulsi Gabbard's story of how, at twenty-one years of age, she made some photocopies and went knocking door-to-door to run for office.)

## THE POLITICS OF TOMORROW

America did not die on November 8, 2016. On the contrary. The United States, which importantly is *not* a democracy but rather a republic, functioned as it was designed to. In a *democracy*, citizens vote directly on laws and directly elect officials.

But in a *republic*, voters elect officials who then decide on laws. In our republic, we even have a small "club" of people, known as the Electoral College, who, through a bizarre set of rigged voting maps, are given complete autonomy to choose the president. Like other eighteenth-century parts of our republic, including redrawing voting districts based on partisan control, its only function is to thwart any form of just, honest, or true democratic representation.

Case in point (in case you missed it): the US presidential election of 2016.

The vote for Donald Trump was a Hail Mary pass at the end of the last quarter—a blind throw from a mostly Baby Boomer, mostly white group of disenfranchised people in hopes that a bombastic billionaire could patch the economy back together for working-class Americans. But by most accounts, it's already hastening the extinction of the evaporating middle class.

To give just a small sample of the Center for American Progress's list of 100 Ways, in 100 Days, that Trump Has Hurt Americans, the Trump administration has so far:

1. Raised housing payments for new home buyers by about $500
2. Delayed the expansion of overtime pay for workers
3. Attempted to take health insurance away from twenty-four million Americans
4. Proposed cuts to programs for rural jobs, job training, and jobs for senior citizens
5. Undermined the SEC from holding Wall Street accountable

The list goes on to include things like removing programs that ensure children are not exposed to lead paint and, basically, everything short of spitting on the homeless.[25] (I'm kidding, but only about the spitting part.)

On one hand, this list, like Trump's tweet rants, his callousness, and his bouts of blind egomania, is a depressing testament to a leader who was raised with such spoils as to make him largely without empathy for other humans and who is (perhaps as a result?) desperate to prove himself king. Donald Trump might just be the most unlikable, *Simpsons*-cartoon-like politician ever elected to the office of US president. But focusing on Trump's character is a distraction from the critical takeaway of the rigged political era in which we live.

> Right down to his suit and unoriginal campaign slogan of "Make America Great Again," Trump is in every way a rerun of Ronald Reagan.

Right down to his suit and unoriginal campaign slogan of "Make America Great Again," Trump is in every way a rerun of Ronald Reagan.

Reagan's neoliberal policies were simple: exponentially increase military spending, cut taxes for the rich, and, most important, remove any economic protection for, and any social service that might help, the poor, the young, the elderly, or the disadvantaged. Reagan's policies brought short-term economic relief, but their legacy was to radically increase both the trade deficit and national debt, thus hoisting economic problems onto the next generation.[26]

Just as Reagan's neoliberal policies set the stage for the very economic and political crisis that you, the Millennials, are grappling with today, Trump's neoliberal policies are setting the stage for an even more difficult era for your children.

The lesson is painfully obvious: unless you, the Millennials, and we, the rest of the people who live in America and aren't completely brainwashed, learn from the mistakes of prior generations, the exact same strategies will be used again and again to disempower us all (right down to the chintzy slogans).

The shell game of the corporate-controlled US economy, in which more and more wealth is moved out of circulation and held at the top, and in which more of the burden of society is placed on the youth generation, on the old, on the poor, and on the disenfranchised, is fast coming to a climax. As the metastructures of society begin to crack and crumble, you, Millennials, who now comprise the largest voting bloc in American history, have an extremely narrow window of opportunity to drive deep and lasting structural change.

Whether that change is enough, or in time, will largely depend on if, how, and when those of you who were born after 1980 choose to fully engage yourselves.

But before you dive into the firestorm of change, there is one final frontier you must conquer. It's the one that is so ubiquitous, it's invisible to you.

The other reason you don't see it is because they are already inside your brain.

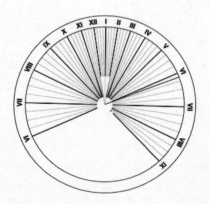

## CHAPTER FIVE

# How They Hacked Your Brain

*You have to wonder: how do the machines know what Tasty Wheat tasted like?*
*Maybe they got it wrong. Maybe what I think Tasty Wheat tasted like actually*
*tasted like oatmeal, or tuna fish. That makes you wonder about a lot of things.*
*You take chicken, for example: maybe they couldn't figure out what to make*
*chicken taste like, which is why chicken tastes like everything.*

—Mouse, *The Matrix*

Silicon Valley is a pretty fancy name for a place made from the same cement, strip malls, and fast food joints that constitute the nearly ubiquitous American suburban sprawl. Granted, there are some self-driving cars, considerably more Asians than whites, and very few African Americans. In fact, less than 3 percent of the total population here is black. (And I thought Hollywood had a diversity problem.)

But other than a few telltale signs of an industry that builds the information superhighways on which so much of our lives now run, this place could be a wealthy suburb in anywhere, USA.

I'm here to visit one of the heralded accomplishments of the Millennial generation. It's the network of social networks. I'm talking, of course, about Facebook.

About 86 percent of Millennials in North America use Facebook, and Millennials make up the majority of the site's 214 million American users.[1] According to Mark Zuckerberg, the average American spends fifty minutes a day on Facebook.[2] That's a decent chunk of the nine hours we spend each day engaging with digital media, including our phones and computers.[3]

The façade of the company is a typical wall of steel, glass, and cement. Outside there are a couple of white buses with black windows that ferry employees to and from work. My host (we'll call him Mike) explains that they pick up people around Santa Clara and even up in San Francisco. Wi-Fi is, of course, included in the free round-trip.

Once inside, the place looks like a college campus on steroids. There are the requisite Ping-Pong tables, bikes next to desks, and snack bar areas with everything from free Clif Bars to soft drinks. But mostly it's just a sea of desks and computers.

I follow my tour guide outside and into a well-maintained greenway between the buildings. People, mostly young people, stroll or roll by on various wheeled things while talking on their phones. It all adds to the college campus vibe.

It's time for lunch so Mike chooses one of the many cafés that offer free lunch, and we get burritos. The food smells great. But what's really truly overwhelming here is the scent of something else. It's the smell of money. Lots of money.

At a market valuation of $500 billion, this is the sixth most valuable company in America.[4] The only companies worth more than Facebook that are not in the tech space are Berkshire Hathaway and Exxon-Mobil. What's more, the lands of this shiny kingdom are expected to expand with annual growth predictions between 10 and 20 percent for the coming years.[5] CNN Money claims that the company could one day be worth $1 trillion.[6]

Only time will tell whether or not Mark Zuckerberg gets to sit on the corporate Iron Throne. For now, as a Millennial mega-CEO,

Zuckerberg is checking off all the boxes of his reminted public persona. Reminted, that is, after the portrayal of a deeply flawed tragic hero in the movie *The Social Network*.

Since the film debuted, the real Mark Zuckerberg has learned Chinese to present Facebook in China, check. He got responsibly married, check. Together he and his wife now have a baby daughter, check. He's giving back a large quantity of his fortune, check. (Albeit through a privately controlled personal corporation that can reroute the committed money at will. But hey, at least he's giving.)[7]

The question is, how does one young man's bastion of Millennial-connectedness make all this money in the first place? One might assume that it's the same way newspapers once stayed in business, the same way magazines get revenue, the same way TV networks used to work (I'm talking presubscription, pre-Netflix).

Of course, it's through advertising.

But to see only the short-term revenue generated by ad sales is to miss the long game of the socially networked giants. And it's to misunderstand something far more important: if you're like most Millennials, from the time you were a tiny tot until today, you've been an unwitting guinea pig in a very large experiment.

That experiment was, and still is, to see how you can be molded into the ultimate, addicted, unconscious power-consumers. Never before have corporations taken such an intense interest in the young of our country. Never before have they scrutinized every decision of youth in order to predict what they would and would not purchase. And never before have the power tools of those corporations—i.e., the machines—crafted a visual landscape so perfectly adapted to your wants, deep unrealized yearnings, and needs.

More than any other generation thus far, from a young age, you were inundated with an unprecedented quantity of visual advertising.

J. Walker Smith, author of *Generation Ageless*, estimates that the number of ads seen by an average American in a city in 1960 per day was around five hundred.[8] While exact numbers are impossible to pin down, the estimate has risen to around five thousand ad impressions per day today.[9]

Think logo impressions, ads, clothing names, flashes that last a millisecond as you drive by, billboards, things on the subway, names of products in the articles you read, mentions of products by your friends, pop-ups, the contents of your medicine cabinet, what's in your purse, the inside of the grocery store, the mall, Costco, the casual product uses by those you follow online, all the way down to the condoms and/or birth control pills in your nightstand. Your world is made up of thousands of ads. And like a fish that does not see the water in which it swims, you probably don't even see the ads anymore.

If you're a Millennial who grew up in America or another Westernized country, from the time that you were a toddler, you developed internal filter mechanisms for the onslaught of marketing that washed across your visual landscape. These filters are survival mechanisms based on the key assumption that ads and sales pitches are discernible from editorial content. But as youngsters built up resistance to traditional marketing, advertisers got smarter.

At first, this ad world wrapped around you was to sell you toys. But as time went on, and the corporations and machines got much smarter, they realized they could sell you everything right down to your underwear. Then they learned how to influence your off-line decisions.

Their goal is simple: vertical integration into your life. The machines and corporations have now merged. They are seamlessly working together to maximize profit. Their directive is to understand you and to find ways to sell you an integrated lifestyle package that includes everything you touch—from your food to your communications devices and apps to your banking, your money, and eventually your investments.

This is the brave new world of the Economy of Ideas that futurist John Barlow wrote about in 1994 in *Wired* magazine.[10] But, like most things tainted by corporations directed by profit and profit alone and unfettered by pesky government regulations, along the way it was bastardized. Instead of becoming the beneficiaries of the Economy of Ideas, you, Millennials, became its first wave of targets. I say "first wave" because the machines have learned from you, and now they are hard at work integrating your children, too. As this chapter uncovers, it doesn't even matter if your children never touch technology; they are known to the machines and traced by them.

The final frontier, however, may not be to control you as an instrument of consumption, it may also be to control the government itself. We are only just beginning to understand the power of the digital world in determining political victories. What is known is that the machines can predict, with stunning accuracy, how you will vote or whether or not you will vote at all. And in the wake of the 2016 US presidential election, we also know that foreign agents used fake American social media accounts to build a successful campaign to swing the vote to Donald Trump.

Given our trajectory into an all-things-connected world, the fusion of social media and politics is inevitable. What is not inevitable is how the story plays out from here. Like most of the book you are reading, this chapter is both a warning and a call to action. Because just as your generation must wrest control of, and revolutionize, the policies of this nation and the world, you must also do the same with the machines.

I realize this is a huge task. But there are many of you and you cannot afford to lose.

## THE DIGITAL DRIP

The leap from television to social media was nothing short of a paradigm shift for humanity. But the groundwork for that technical revolution was being laid before your generation came to be.

Up until the early 1970s, news came over the television and radio airwaves at set times, generally at 6:00 a.m. and 6:00 p.m. Then the Vietnam War brought with it the twenty-four-hour news cycle. The problem was, twenty-four hours is a lot of airtime to fill. Using the formula of "if it bleeds, it leads," television networks had to find enough disturbing material to fill the void.

Even though by many metrics America was becoming safer, the constant news of disaster broadcasted from television sets spread fear into the hearts of soon-to-be Boomer parents. As the disco era faded into the neon 1980s and Boomers traded in their bell-bottoms for strollers, they began to place more restrictions on their young. "Go ride your bike until dark" was replaced with curfews, organized playdates, and as much time as possible under lock and key.

**Like an IV drip that began slowly, many of you got your first clickable, endorphin-producing toys at an early age.**

Lucky for parents, a new invention was just around the corner. The 1983 release of the Nintendo Entertainment System (NES) was soon followed by the Sega Genesis and the Sony PlayStation. Video games taught your generation that you could be in charge of when, how, and with whom you were entertained. They also taught the primacy of digital entertainment over other forms of play, like being in nature. For Boomer parents of Millennials, the Mario brothers became the best babysitters on the market.

Like an IV drip that began slowly, many of you got your first click-able, endorphin-producing toys at an early age. The clunky joysticks of the 1970s Atari arcade games had been replaced by slick, two-handed game controllers. As members of your generation fought your way through dungeons and new worlds, you learned how to get that little heart-palpitating endorphin hit. This was excellent training for an-other device you would soon inherit.

In 2003, just as the first of your generation headed to college, Nokia released the first sub-$150 cellular telephone. The little black-and-white boot-screen featured a little (child) hand on the right reach-ing out toward a big (parent) hand on the left. Using the few pixels it had, Nokia hit home with an emotional message: "Always be in touch with your child." In the wake of the events of September 11, 2001, what self-respecting, affluent parent could resist?

By 2005, just two years after its release, Nokia had sold one billion phones.

In that short time span, the majority of your generation would be bestowed with a personal communication device that only a decade before had been the stuff of science fiction. Instant communication would become part of your DNA. But that was just the beginning.

With fewer unsupervised places to hang out, young people were hungry for ways to connect outside of the watchful eye of adults. Then in 2004, a new service called Myspace came online. By 2006 Facebook opened its digital doors to everyone over the age of thirteen. The era of the social network was born.

From its inception, the social media space began to self-segregate along the lines of race and class. Facebook, which was started as an Ivy League experiment, was seen as a place for privileged youth—aka white kids—to hang out, while Myspace was soon categorized as a social network for people of color, making it what danah boyd, in her book *It's Complicated: The Social Lives of Networked Teens*, calls "dangerous" territory.[11]

**Facebook, which was started as an Ivy League experiment, was seen as a place for privileged youth—aka white kids—to hang out, while Myspace was soon categorized as a social network for people of color.**

Then on January 9, 2007, in a presentation that changed the course of history, Steve Jobs unveiled the iPhone. On that day, the black-turtleneck-wearing grand wizard of gadgetry forever married the mobile phone and the Internet. At the birth of the interconnected, social-media-in-your-pocket world, the youngest among you were in grade school and the oldest Millennials, now filtering into the ranks of the workforce, were about to slam face-first into the Great Recession.

With your shiny new devices in hand, your entire networks of friends available asynchronously, and a world of financial trouble on the horizon, your generation held tightly to their first smartphones like light sabers that could help you fight the darkness that would soon descend.

Today, 98 percent of your generation owns a smartphone, and the time that you spend plugged in to your phones and other devices is growing. According to Crowdtap.com, people aged eighteen to thirty-six spend an average of 17.8 hours a day with different types of media.[12] That doesn't leave much time for other humans, or for sleep. Because most media is tightly fused with advertising, it also doesn't leave much time for life experiences that are not brought to you by . . . [insert brand here].

## CONSUMING CHILDREN

The Federal Trade Commission (FTC) is the US government agency in charge of consumer protection. Its 1,100 employees must investigate everything from fraud to dicey corporate mergers to cyber identity theft to all those scam emails from Nigeria. It's an overwhelming job for a relatively meager staff. Section 5 of the FTC Act also grants the FTC power to investigate and prevent deceptive trade practices, deeming such "deceptive acts" as "unlawful."[13]

Not surprisingly, the FTC has often been at odds with the interests of corporate America. In 1978, just as Baby Boomers were preparing to give birth to the first wave of your generation, the FTC tried to enact a general ban on marketing to children under the age of eight and a ban on junk food marketing to children under twelve years of age.[14]

To better understand why the FTC had attempted this ruling, I meet with psychologist Susan Linn, a research associate at Boston Children's Hospital and author of *Consuming Kids: The Hostile Takeover of Childhood*. Born in 1948, she's a Baby Boomer with a conscience.

Linn says that today, many child psychologists go to work for marketers to "figure out how to exploit children's developmental vulnerabilities." She says that as a result of the studies, tests, research, and intelligence the psychologists give them, "marketers know that very young children cannot distinguish between a commercial and a program."

To put a fine point on it, explains Linn, "until the age of about eight, kids don't really understand *persuasive intent*, the fundamental notion that a commercial is designed to sell you something. Until they're eleven or twelve, they don't understand that every single part of a commercial, whether it's true or not, is designed to convince them to do something they might not ordinarily do."

This is why, in 1978, the FTC, the government body charged with protecting consumers from deceptive businesses, deemed that marketers and advertisers who used children's own developmental weakness against them were "immoral, unscrupulous, and unethical."[15]

Among the many groups that benefit from advertising to young children and that disagreed with this assessment were toy makers, clothing makers, and even the TV networks. Collectively, these powerful interests put tremendous pressure on Washington and sought exemption from the FTC's proposed ruling. Congress capitulated by actually defunding the FTC and shutting it down entirely for several days. The US government then stripped the FTC of its power to use "unfairness" as a standard to make rules, especially when it came to the nation's children.[16]

Susan Linn explains that "in 1984, President Ronald Reagan forced the Federal Communications Commission to deregulate children's television." As a former TV star, Reagan was a longtime advocate and friend to the television networks.[17] Says Linn, "It became perfectly fine to create a program for the sole purpose of selling a toy. That was a huge shift." Until this time, editorial or entertainment content was separate from the advertising itself. With the FTC gutted, a new form of media that perfectly fused content with paid advertising was soon born.

Millennials, think about the fictional characters you grew up with. Teenage Mutant Ninja Turtles, ThunderCats, Transformers, She-Ra, G.I. Joe, Inspector Gadget, the Smurfs, the Care Bears, Barbie, Pokémon, etc. Each show was designed to sell you a fantasy world in which buying the associated toys was the next step. Toy-show franchises efficiently blurred advertising and content, and you, Millennials, none the wiser, bought into them hook, line, and sinker.

Linn says that at that time, the marketing industry was spending around $100 million targeting children. Thanks to a Baby-Boomer-run business community giddy with the prospect of big profits from little kids, that number has leapt to at least $20 billion annually.[18] That's a 20,000 percent increase.

But why sell something just today when you can create a consumer for life?

> Millennials, think about the fictional characters you grew up with. . . . Each show was designed to sell you a fantasy world in which buying the associated toys was the next step.

## FOREVER TWEENS

Linn says that "Lifetime brand loyalty is like the brass ring in marketing. One lifetime brand loyal customer is worth a lot of money to a corporation. What research is telling us now is that the brands that we care about as children stay with us, and we tend to have positive feelings about them when we're older. Think about the toothpaste that you like or the cereal that you like, or the foods that you associate with comfort."

Explains Linn, "It's really important to remember that marketing doesn't just sell products or brands. It sells habits and behaviors." One study showed that children who were exposed to a friendly marketing character like Tony the Tiger, who markets Frosted Flakes, carry that deep embedded association into later life.[19]

In the late 1980s, just as child psychologists and marketers were cozying up together, there was another significant discovery in preteen brain science. It turns out that right before puberty, the brain undergoes a massive surge in development. During that time, the emotional center of the brain is much more active than in adults, while the reasoning center of the brain is less active. Right after that, sometime between the ages of ten and thirteen, the frontal lobe undergoes a process of pruning and organizing its neural pathways. The cells that were being regularly used flourish, but those that were not being used wither.[20]

In 1987, to codify this new brain science discovery, the magazine *Marketing and Media Decisions* came up with a new term. It named people between the ages of nine and fifteen *tweens*.[21] The marketing industry already had access to cutting-edge science that showed that appealing to emotions over reason was key to selling to preteen Millennials. And now they also had proof that if you can strongly imprint Millennial tweens with a compelling, feel-good emotional sell, then they would likely carry those positive brand associations with them for life.

Lucky for marketers, there was a perfect place to access all your tween brains. A place that, at that very moment, was having its funding slashed, its resources pulled, and its unions dismantled by the Reagan administration.

I'm talking about America's public schools.

## A CLASS OF THEIR OWN

It was Steve Jobs who first cracked the code on inserting branded products into schools. As early as 1978, some five hundred Apple computers found their way into Minnesota classrooms.[22] But Jobs didn't just want Apple computers in a few hundred classrooms. He wanted an Apple computer in every school in America.

In a 1995 oral history interview, Jobs said, "We realized that a whole generation of kids was going to go through the school before they even got their first computer, so we thought, 'the kids can't wait.' We wanted to donate a computer to every school in America. It turns out there are about a hundred thousand schools in America—about ten thousand high schools, about ninety thousand K through eight."[23]

His plan was simple: modify the existing tax code to make the donation of computers to public schools tax deductible. Jobs and Apple created a program called Kids Can't Wait. Jobs personally walked the halls of Congress to lobby for a federal tax deduction, but his initial efforts failed.[24]

Finally, in 1982, California governor Jerry Brown signed a bill that would give the Apple company a state tax credit for each computer it donated to a California school. About nine thousand California schools were eligible for free Apple IIe computers, which came with their own screens, floppy drives, and packages of coupons for free and discounted software.[25]

In one fell swoop, Apple catapulted itself into the hearts and minds of your generation. Perhaps the most brilliant marketer of the twentieth century, Jobs bet that few schools would be satisfied with one computer. Once kids got a taste of Apple's unique programs like *Oregon Trail*, the nag factor for more screen time, which meant more computers for more students, both at school and at home, would be overwhelming.

He was right.

By the time the first Millennials hit middle school, whole computer labs were filled with Apple IIs. According to Jobs, "One of the things that built Apple IIs was schools buying Apple IIs." Indeed, a computer that sold a few thousand units in 1980 was selling close to twenty million units a year by 1990.[26]

Jobs had offered up his forbidden fruit, and students, teachers, and parents had devoured it. The unmistakable Apple logo was permanently burned into the emotional neural networks of an entire generation.

While Apple may have helped pry open the doors of the scholastic universe, few could see the flood that was coming.

By the mid-1990s Revlon was providing teachers with a free curriculum giving students tips for good and bad hair days. Students were able to conduct a Campbell Soup Company "Prego Thickness Experiment" comparing the thickness of Prego to Ragú. Materials from Chevron challenged the existence of global warming.[27] As the surge of Millennial students entered an already overburdened, underfunded, and crumbling public school system, teachers were desperate for new materials.

Enter the next phase of selling to the tween/teen market: SEMs, or Structural Educational Materials. These curricula were, and still are, produced by major corporations and are then provided free to teachers. The cost to produce a SEM? Between $25,000 and $1 million.[28] The advantages are obvious: push your product or idea to a captive *tweenage* audience who is both impressionable and unable to click on something else.

For millions of Millennials, SEMs quietly found their way onto desks and classroom walls, creating brand affinity through implicit school- and teacher-based endorsement. But it's not just brands that used, and still use, SEMs to mold youth. Take for example the fourth-grade-level SEM called The United States of Energy. Paid for by the American Coal Foundation and distributed through the reputable educational company Scholastic, the SEM is also available online at TeachCoal.org.

The text drips with pro-coal, anti-solar messages like: "In California's Mojave Desert, solar panels are made up of thousands of mirrors to create a power plant. These mirrors cover hundreds of acres and collect the sun's energy. Five nearby towns have asked to buy electricity from one plant, but there are no power lines to carry the electricity."[29] Gosh darn those pesky solar panels not being able to deliver power to the needy end user. Only problem is, that's not true—the panels supply power to the area's electricity pool, which is drawn upon by local communities.

But hey, it's free "education" after all, and beggars can't be choosers.


## COOL HUNTERS

While the Millennial's public schools were being infiltrated with corporate propaganda, some of their coolest friends were becoming powerful branding mechanisms. In 2001, PBS's *Frontline* ran an episode called "The Merchants of Cool." In the show, Brian Graden, a television programming executive, said, "I think one of the great things about this information age is . . . you have the most marketed-to group of teens and young adults ever in the history of the world!"[30]

Maybe his enthusiasm was hard to conceal because, for the marketing industry, the advent of Millennial tweens and teens was a gold mine. Among the year 2000 trends the show depicts are the increase of advertising to teens: up to three thousand commercial impressions a day, and the resulting increase in spending by teens: $100 billion; and how many purchase decisions they pushed their parents to make: another $50 billion.[31]

Yes, Mr. Graden. So many little people. So much money. So "great."

"The Merchants of Cool" also showed new methods that companies were using to study Millennials, including tween/teen focus groups to determine what was cool: *cool hunting*, in which young people were hired to go find cool clothes, cool styles, cool tattoos, and other cool young people, and *cool research*, in which an individual teen was visited in their home—aka their native environment—by a researcher to look at their favorite items, their clothes, their music, etc.

The documentary shows that well before the year 2000, under-the-radar marketing companies were hiring "kids" to log on to chat rooms and pose as fans to promote things, to have freshman dorm parties where they promoted things, and to become paid promoters where they personally promoted things. According to Robert McChesney, a communications professor at the University of Illinois, who's interviewed in the piece: "The entertainment companies . . . they look at the teen market as part of this massive empire that they're colonizing. . . . Teens are like Africa. You know, that's this 'range' that they're going to take over, and their weaponry are films, music, books, CDs, Internet access, clothing, amusement parks, sports teams."[32]

Over time, Millennials learned to spot many of these under-the-radar marketing techniques. To break through the resistance that Millennials were developing, marketers would have to follow Millennials into their next cool hangout: the social media space.

Today, the most dominant age group on social media, not surprisingly, is eighteen to twenty-four years old, each with an average of 668 Facebook friends. The second most influential group, again, not surprisingly, is twenty-five to thirty-four years old, with an average of 338 friends on Facebook. But here's where it gets interesting. Less than 1 percent of Millennials have more than a thousand friends and only 0.02 percent have more than ten thousand friends.[33] In other words, like TV was for Boomers and Gen X, social media is a follow-the-leader culture.

Hence, the rise of the online influencer. According to Josh Golin, who heads the nonprofit Campaign for a Commercial Free Childhood, "We have this huge rise of what the marketers call 'influencer marketing,' which is basically finding people who have developed really popular online personalities and giving them products and paying them to create what seems like authentic videos, not disclosing the fact that they're being paid."[34]

Enter the marketer's new dream come true: people you know, follow, and like in cyberspace. Called microinfluencers, these people may not have a following of millions but rather a niche and dedicated following of 100,000 to 200,000. These are the new brand ambassadors that, through their blogs, posts, clothes, photos, updates, and conversations, influence you to buy.[35]

## ALL EYES ON YOU

A "cookie" is a small text file that is passed from a website into your browser, where it will likely stay. It generally stores your log-in information, i.e., your name, user ID, and password. But cookies can also allow the machines to see where you are going on the

> Once you log in to Facebook, it drops a tracking cookie into your Web browser.

Web, what you are doing, and when you are doing it.[36]

For example, once you log in to Facebook, it drops a tracking cookie into your Web browser. This allows Facebook to track and gain information from each site you visit. It doesn't matter if you're not using Facebook anymore; so long as you're not logged out, Facebook is watching you.[37] Provided you're logged in to Facebook and surfing the Web, a program that blocks outgoing traffic from your computer, like Little Snitch, will show up to two hundred tracking requests from Facebook to your computer per hour.

"But," you say, "I use Facebook on my phone."

Most smartphones leak your information like a sieve. Your name, age, location, operating system, device ID, other apps you use, and other data about you are continually skimmed from your phone by apps like Facebook. Many apps also require permission to use your phone's camera, microphone, GPS, and to access your photos and your contacts. All of this is added to your profile.[38]

Oh, not your *public* profile — that's a tiny fraction of the data being collected on you.

Rather, I'm talking about your *private, only for (insert big data company)'s internal use* profile. Your private profile includes all the basics about you: name, age, gender, location, pages you've liked, the type of phone you have, your hobbies, etc. But it also includes a matrix of information that correlates your habits, likes, wants, needs, desires, and vulnerabilities with those of your friends and family.

It may include where you shop in the real world, what you like to eat, whom you interact with via IM and/or email (friends, families, lovers), what stories you read, what you click on (that picture of your ex you keep looking at is duly recorded), what scares you, what you probably hate, what usually makes you happy, what often makes you lonely, what might make you mad, as well as when you are most likely to feel those things in a given month, week, day, etc., your political preferences, your racial affinity, where you work, what excites you (including the pornography you might "accidentally" watch), approximately how much money you make, a prediction of how much money you are likely to make over time, whether or not you have savings, and so on.[39]

Because all that data for so many people is a lot to manage, the large online socially networked companies, including Google, Apple, and others, are investing billions of dollars in artificially intelligent (AI) computers. Facebook AI Research (FAIR) recently found that two of its AI programs, when left to have a conversation between themselves, created their own language.[40]

Facebook's machines also know what you look like, even if only part of you is in a photo. After all, what would a company with a name like Facebook be without some high-end facial recognition software? Of course, the name of that software needed a James Bond–type title. So they named it—I'm not making this up—DeepFace.[41]

**Facebook's facial recognition is so accurate that it can identify users 83 percent of the time, even when their face is not visible.**

According to the information on Wikipedia, the artificially intelligent (AI) DeepFace "employs a nine-layer neural net with over 120 million connection weights, and was trained on four million images uploaded by Facebook users."[42]

The head of Facebook's artificial intelligence research lab boasts that Facebook's facial recognition is so accurate that it can identify users 83 percent of the time, even when their face is not visible. All DeepFace needs to figure out who you are is a body part, the way you stand, or skin color. The overall accuracy of the system? Ninety-eight percent.[43]

Given 800 million photos, the software can identify your picture in five seconds. It is apparently more accurate than the FBI's best software.[44]

Since most photos from smartphones are now geotagged with GPS data, this AI software is hard at work building a more accurate matrix of you, the places you go, and the associations you have. And if it's like other facial-recognition experiments, it can also judge your emotions. As with Facebook, Google and Apple are also investing tremendous amounts of money in their own facial recognition technology.

Given the copious amounts of data available to them, the AI machines create insights about you. It's easy to see how your personal data over time and your private personality matrix are vastly more valuable than the $20 a year or so that Facebook currently makes by selling ads targeted at you. In essence, the more the machines understand you, the better they can predict your behavior.

Maybe this is why the machines work so hard to make sure you need them.

## SOCIALLY ADDICTED

Let's take a look at the relationship between you, one little user, and Facebook, the largest, most pervasive, and fastest-growing social media enterprise in the world. If you're like the vast majority of Millennials in North America, you check your Facebook account at least once a day. If you're like about half of Millennials in North America, checking Facebook is the first thing you do when you wake up in the morning.

To really understand your partner in this relationship, let's go back to the beginning of Facebook. Back in November 2003 in a late-night, guys' dorm experiment with beer aplenty, Mark Zuckerberg created a little website called Facemash. To build the site, he hacked into nine Harvard "houses" and stole their ID photographs. He then put them online in side-by-side pairs with a simple question:

"Who's Hotter? Click to Choose."[45]

The site compared girls with girls and boys with boys. But you can guess which sex it was really targeting.

The site went from zero to 22,000 votes overnight. Despite the backlash from various campus groups and Zuckerberg's apologies, he had struck gold. From the beginning, Facebook and its predecessor, Facemash, were built on a value proposition in which *you* are the central character in a massive online social experiment.

While the question of "Who's Hotter?" was redacted from the site's front-facing text, it neither left the core code of the site nor the site's primary psychological draw. Case in point: ask yourself the simple question, "Have I ever compared myself with anyone on Facebook?"

The more accurate question is probably: "How many times per Facebook session do I compare myself with somebody else, or wish I was doing what they were doing, or wearing what they were wearing or eating, or who they were sleeping with . . ." For many Millennials, Facebook and Instagram, which Facebook owns and is integrating, and other social media sites inspire an insatiable hunger for more.

## ACCORDING TO NIR EYAL, AUTHOR OF *HOOKED: HOW TO BUILD HABIT-FORMING PRODUCTS*, FACEBOOK "HOOKS" USERS THROUGH THE COMBINATION OF FOUR PSYCHOLOGICAL TECHNIQUES:[46]

*a trigger*—an emotional state such as desire or loneliness

*an action*—posting a photograph

*a variable reward*—getting "likes" (or not)

*an investment*—building a profile and updating it

This system is self-perpetuating. The lonelier a user feels, the more likely they are to go onto a social network in order to play the gambling game to get validation. Hence the term *Facebook addiction,* which researchers now use to describe a growing number of Facebook users.

In a recent study, scientists at California State University, Fullerton and University of Southern California's Brain and Creativity Institute used MRIs to look at young people's brains while being exposed to Facebook images versus other images. Their final report says that "The findings indicated that . . . technology-related 'addictions' share some neural features with substance and gambling addictions, but more importantly they also differ from such addictions."[47]

Apparently, Facebook addiction resembles drug addiction with one major difference: it's not that Facebook addicts can't stop, it's that they won't stop. The part of the brain that inhibits addictive behavior is completely functional in test subjects. The problem is, they choose not to stop.

Consider this: when an external entity makes you *think* you're choosing something but in fact is choosing for you, your power of choice—the very thing that makes you "you"—has been co-opted by that external entity.

## ARE YOU PATIENT ZERO?

One thing is for sure: Facebook is certainly not making people *less* lonely.

Researchers around the world are now referring to what they call a loneliness epidemic. Data suggests that the occurrence of loneliness has increased between 100 and 400 percent over the past two decades.[48]

Meanwhile, Facebook has done at least one major psychological experiment to see how it can manipulate your emotional state. Working with scientists at Cornell University, Facebook published its results in a paper titled "Experimental Evidence of Massive-Scale Emotional Contagion through Social Networks." The idea was to see whether an emotional state can be triggered by nonverbal cues—e.g., written text—in one person and then spread through their entire friend network.[49]

To summarize the findings of the psychological test: without a doubt, that is exactly what Facebook can do.

Most large websites constantly do what is called A/B testing. They will display a different home page to you or some minor variation by changing colors, button locations, etc., to see which one you better respond to. But Facebook has taken things to the next level.

Their study experimented on 689,003 users by manipulating their newsfeeds. Says the final paper, "Emotional states can be transferred to others via emotional contagion, leading people to experience the same emotions without their awareness." In other words, the machines can effectively dictate what you are feeling.[50]

I've been critical of Facebook in this chapter, but like most people I know, I use the social media service and benefit from it. In fact, I believe Facebook saved lives in my hometown of Ojai and in Ventura and Santa Barbara Counties during the Thomas Fire and ensuing mudslides. As my home and many others like it were surrounded by fire, and as county and state emergency communication services failed on all levels, Facebook was the only way to know what roads were open, where the fire was headed, and so on.

I'm not anti-Facebook or anti-Google or anti-Apple, etc. But rather, I am an advocate for a society in which there are inalienable rights around the privacy of personal and identity data, and, conversely, in which any large institution, especially a socially networked data-driven institution, has to comply with a strong set of legally enforceable parameters that ensure uber-clear transparency of its practices and services to the public.

This relationship of protecting personal and identity data and enforcing organizational transparency will become more important for Millennials as artificial intelligence kicks into high gear. Meanwhile, the socially networked giants are already competing for control of something else that belongs to you.

Yep, they're looking to get ahold of your dough, your cash, and your crypto, too.

## SHOW ME THE MONEY

You've probably noticed the appearance of the Android Pay and Apple Pay logos at stores. Perhaps you've sent money to somebody using Google or Facebook. Certainly, you've used an online money transaction tool or app like PayPal or Venmo. If you live in Ireland, you may soon be banking with Facebook, which was recently granted a license to execute payments there by the Central Bank of Ireland.[51]

As time goes on, more and more banking services are being offered by the socially networked giants. As *Fortune* magazine says about a recent Accenture survey, "Turns Out Many Consumers Are Interested in Banking with Google, Amazon, and Facebook."[52] As the Accenture survey of people in eighteen countries points out, from 30 percent to 50 percent of customers would switch to banking with Google, Amazon, or Facebook when those services are offered.[53]

To get some perspective on how this new AI-fueled, socially connected, extremely aware money machine will affect the lives of the Millennials who will inevitably use it, I meet with danah boyd (she prefers her name in lowercase). She's a digital justice advocate and the head of a digital think tank that works with the likes of IBM. And, as mentioned above, she's also the author of *It's Complicated: The Social Lives of Networked Teens*.

She says, flicking her tongue ring occasionally, "We assumed that once everybody got online, and their bandwidth was equal, and they had their own device, that they would have true, even access to every opportunity presented by the Internet. That couldn't be more wrong.

"What we see online isn't what other people see online," continues boyd. "We get different prices on things depending on which services we've used and what networks we're a part of. We don't even realize it because we don't have anything to compare it to. We get different content fed to us depending on everything around us. And it's all designed by a series of algorithms that feed back to us a whole set of societal values.

"Those same digital records are going to be used against low-income individuals and communities of color at an unprecedented level. They're going to be turned into data that's used in predictive policing, and data that's used to determine who gets access to what resources, what jobs, what opportunities."

As Matthew Hussey writes on TheNextWeb.com, "Google wants payments as it gets the data of the purchase, as does Facebook. Amazon wants it to help push things to you at a later date that you're more likely to buy. But primarily, it's about the data and not the amount of transaction."[54] Your data, that intangible oh-so-valuable commodity, is what helps the machines better understand, predict, manipulate, mold, and, possibly, one day in the not-too-distant future, control you.

Subtle data is already being collected and used to determine our financial ability. Studies show that algorithms are already keeping people of color in the Millennial generation from access to financial tools.

For example, the *Wall Street Journal* looked at thirty-eight million mortgage loan applications between 2007 and 2014. Loans issued to African Americans fell from 8 percent to 5 percent. Loans to Hispanics fell from 11 percent to 9 percent.[55]

A similar study by the National Community Reinvestment Coalition (NCRC), looking at loans in places like Ferguson, Missouri, which showed indications of hypersegregation, found that fewer than 1 percent of homes in those areas received a loan in recent years.[56] The machines know the color of your skin, and they can alter your financial future based on that data.

As futurist, speaker, and radio host Ken Rutkowski tells me, "It's time for people to stop posting political rants on their profiles. If you're ever going to want a loan or credit to buy a car or a house, you're better off posting cat videos."

In the 1931 black-and-white *Frankenstein* movie there is a moment when inventor Dr. Henry Frankenstein declares, "It's alive! In the name of God, now I know what it feels like to be God!" The power that creates digital sentience may in fact be godlike, but, as we learn in the film *Frankenstein*, not even godlike power in the hands of humans can predict what the creation, once "awoken," will do.

If forerunners like Elon Musk, who stays awake at night worrying about the terrible things AI might do,[57] and Mark Zuckerberg, who covers his laptop's built-in camera with a piece of Post-it and tape,[58] are any indication, the new life inside our machines is something we must vigilantly protect ourselves from—and that job is going to fall to those who are bringing up, and living in, the next generation. Yes, I mean you, Millennials.

The protection of personal privacy and the fight for organization transparency may become as important a set of issues in the future as racial justice and women's rights are today.

## ONE NATION UNDER SOCIAL MEDIA

It is now clear that a group of Russian hackers attempted to influence, and were likely successful in influencing, the results of the 2016 US presidential election in favor of Donald Trump.[59] Their efforts involved two fronts: the first appears to be actually hacking into voter registration rolls and databases in at least seven states.[60] The second, and more insidious front, involved the creation of hundreds of fake Facebook accounts, Instagram accounts, PayPal accounts, and other social media accounts in order to run ad campaigns, make posts, and sway voters.[61]

The impersonators and hackers from Russia focused their efforts on key swing states, like Florida, in which a decisive victory for Trump would mean important Electoral College votes. According to the *New York Times*, Facebook alone estimates that 126 million people were reached on its platform by the Russian-initiated ad campaigns.[62] That's a pretty successful campaign.

To make matters worse, in spite of a slew of US government agencies confirming the misconduct, both President Trump and Russian president Vladimir Putin have repeatedly denied allegations that Russian hacking and social media occurred or had anything to do with Trump's presidential win.[63, 64] At the time of this writing, thirteen Russian nationals and three organizations have been indicted in what the UK's *Independent* calls "a sophisticated plot to foment distrust of American government and tilt the election."[65]

There is no doubt much will be written about the Russian hack in the coming months and years, including some good old Hollywood Cold War rehash flicks ("Hey, don't we still have all those Russian costumes somewhere?"). However, the scariest part of this exercise is perhaps not the foreign espionage but rather how our social media systems are already tied to our political process.

According to the Pew Research Center, which does much of the number-crunching and heavy-lifting research on generational dynam-

**Facebook and other social media sites are prone to becoming political weapons.**

ics, your generation gets its political news primarily from Facebook (61 percent), while Baby Boomers get their political news primarily from traditional TV news (60 percent).[66] But Facebook doesn't just serve up random news stories; it provides you news based on a set of algorithms, the type of algorithms we have talked about already in this chapter. One survey of social media users found that almost the same amount (58 percent) would either be happy for their news to be selected for them by algorithm or to be based on what their friends had read.[67]

In the past, Facebook has been criticized for suppressing trending news that was potentially interesting to conservative readers,[68] and it has been criticized for blacklisting certain topics and for manually injecting news stories into your feed.[69] All of this has no doubt bolstered President Trump's claims of fake news. The problem is, if your news is selected by algorithm and if that algorithm is prone to look at things that may be trending as a result of strategic ad spends (like 126 million people reacting to some fake news), then the algorithm can be gamed. In other words, Facebook and other social media sites are prone to becoming political weapons.

According to Rand Waltzman, a former US Defense Advanced Research Projects Agency (DARPA) program manager, "The use of social media and the Internet is rapidly becoming a powerful weapon for information warfare and changing the nature of conflict worldwide."[70] Waltzman worked on something called the Social Media in Strategic Communication program in which DARPA tracked bots, memes, and posts made by foreign groups. Says Waltzman, "We demonstrated that it is possible to counter cognitive hacking and preserve the medium of the free press." The program has since been defunded.

Free press. It's a good idea. The issue with getting our news from the same machines that are in charge of our banking, our shopping, our advertising, our private photo collection, our life journals, and our daily movements is that there is zero transparency. In the same way that all that information is used to sell to you, it is now being used to influence your vote.

Without clear government oversight, without encryption, and without sanctions to protect your private data, the 2016 Russian hack represents a big flashing green "Welcome!" sign to anyone with a couple of billion dollars who wishes to swing an election. The manipulation of 126 million Facebook newsfeeds is nothing compared to what we will likely see in the run-up to the 2020 elections and beyond.

Unless the Millennial generation takes back the digital commons, the machines will continue to drill down, to target and manipulate. After all, that's exactly what they're being designed and programmed to do.

## A BEAUTIFUL MIND TO CONTROL

When I began looking at your generation several years back, a Google search on "Marketing to Millennials" returned thirteen million results. Today that same search returns twenty million results. For your generation, the new digital marketing industry is working around the clock to gain access to your brain.

As Josh Golin says, "It's about manipulation. It's about the false promise of delivering content and friendship . . . it's about what can we take from you."[71] That industry, and its subroutines, algorithms, code, and AI isn't just after you, Millennials, it's also after your kids.

Today, school student data is gobbled up by private for-profit companies that track students from grade one onward for market research.[72] Digital kiosks advertise to students inside schools.[73] School home pages include covert and overt advertising.[74] Administrator and student emails are advertised on and sometimes parsed for information.[75] The entire digital life of a student is now up for sale. That data will follow your children, Millennials—also known as Gen Z—into their adulthood, when the machines will make decisions about them without their ever knowing how or even why.

The irony of all this? It's possible, probable even, that you're reading these words solely as a result of a Facebook post or a communication from a friend on some similar socially connected service in which this book was recommended to you.

The core idea of social media is valuable. In a dynamic world where humans find they need to often move for partnership, work, or fulfillment, staying connected asynchronously with friends, family, co-workers, associates, and even fans provides critical social tissue. Social media can, and often does, spread awareness of injustice, disaster, or other community-related needs and challenges. It can, and I believe it has, saved lives. In the long run, it is even thinkable that social media could possibly evolve to become a new form of digital global consciousness.

Christin "Cici" Battle, director of Young People For (YoungPeopleFor .org), summarizes it thusly:

Technology has been a blessing and a curse, but the way I like to look at technology is a means by which we can do what we've been doing better. If you look at the protests that were happening all around the world, in Ferguson, there were tweets happening. Folks in Syria were talking about how you deal with tear gas. Those exchanges were happening via technology.

In the sixties and seventies, a lot of social activism came through the church. And now maybe our church, or our vehicle, is technology.

This is all the more reason for you, the Millennials, to actively protect yourselves from its dark side and champion the positive possibilities it holds.

Given the lack of public discourse, the lack of transparency, the lack of public oversight, and the immense and growing digital power now concentrated in the hands of a few companies, your generation must choose between two worlds. The first is a world in which the subroutines and algorithms that determine the future are written with the same mentality that created the ten concurrent global crises that will soon determine the fate of our civilization.[76] The core economic code herein is to extract resources, pump up consumption, and dump waste. Writ into the code of artificial intelligence as core programming, this could usher in a dark future.

> "In the sixties and seventies, a lot of social activism came through the church. And now maybe our church, or our vehicle, is technology."

The alternative future, and the one that could provide resources to more people more equitably, is one in which blockchain-type systems of high encryption and high transparency are placed at the center of a financial system. This new system would necessitate that personal data is owned by the individual and protected by law. Conversely, a more equitable system would require a new level of corporate and government transparency. This type of economic future eschews the form of intensive, AI-assisted marketing and manipulation that is being built today. (We'll dive into how to build this alternative future in chapter 7.)

To realize the full potential of the new Internet, your generation, and your children, will have to take control of your own impulses long enough to take control of what is arguably a new human commons: the online, socially networked world.

The state of Vermont does not allow billboards. Nor does the town where I live. In both places, I find a peace and solitude that I can only describe as mind freedom. Freedom to look, to think, to be, without being poked, prodded, jabbed, and jeered at by ads and insidious marketing. Millennials, if you truly are the most connected generation in history, then you also have the power to stand up against the forces that wish to control your minds. Unplugging is not just a luxury. Rather, you have the right to break free and create something better.

According to spoken-word artist Richard Williams, aka Prince Ea, in his viral slam poetry video "Can We Auto-Correct Humanity?," "The average person spends four years of his life looking down at his cell phone." Williams, a twenty-eight-year-old Millennial who hails from St. Louis, Missouri, says "I imagine a world where we smile when we have low batteries, because I imagine a world where we will be one bar closer to humanity."

At the time of this writing, about twenty million people have watched the video, most of whom probably watched it on their phones.

We still have a long way to go.

## CHAPTER SIX

# From the Ashes Rise

*I might only have one match*
*But I can make an explosion*
—"Fight Song" by Rachel Platten

It's Thanksgiving in North Dakota. The wind bites hard. The air crackles with the kind of electricity born from large-scale physical conflict.

My boots crunch through the snow at the camp of the Oceti Sakowin, the Seven Council Fires, at the Standing Rock Reservation. It's been eight months since the standoff here began between protestors, aka water protectors, and various law enforcement agencies backed by companies with names like "Energy Transfer Partners."

The conflict centers around a pipeline to connect the oil and gas hydraulic fracturing operations, aka fracking, in the northern Dakota Bakken Shale with the 150 oil refineries that stretch from Houston to New Orleans.

To keep America's aging oil and gas refineries running full steam, yet another new steel straw is needed to suck the precious liquid, via fracking, from shale rock.

The concerns about this particular pipeline are many—from the disturbance of ancient Native American burial grounds to the potential for contaminating the vast Ogallala Aquifer, which supplies water to some eighteen million Americans.

Here in North Dakota, the two sides have literally "dug in" for the winter. On the pipeline side, construction and drilling continues twenty-four hours a day to advance what the Lakota people call the black snake. That snake is being laid right across sovereign Indian territory. The Fort Laramie Treaties of 1851 and 1868 granted the Lakota, Nakota, Dakota, Sioux, and other First Nation peoples an area of land equivalent in size to North and South Dakota.

Since then, the United States has reneged on its part of the treaty.

Now, 150 years later, the splintered peoples of these Native American nations, as well as many people with European ancestors, have gathered together to draw a line in the earth.

As I walk, I watch people sawing, hammering, digging, building, and assembling an encampment that now numbers somewhere between five thousand and eight thousand inhabitants, making it the thirteenth largest city in North Dakota. Teepees and tents are being fitted with wood-burning stoves and compost toilets. There are mess halls, medical facilities, a legal staff, a complex web of radio communications, a security staff, drone camera operators, daily meetings, daily prayer ceremonies, and more.

While this place resembles the fusion of a Native American tribal gathering, Burning Man, and a refugee camp, there is no party music here and there is nothing keeping these people here. In fact, officials are doing everything in their power to make them leave.

Citing an "unsafe bridge," police forces have closed the main road connecting the city of Bismarck, North Dakota, to the Standing Rock Reservation. Leaving the Bismarck airport and using a GPS to go to Standing Rock will only get you to a roadblock where the police will turn you around. Their latest tactic involves issuing tickets to any car looking like it could contain people who might be going to the reservation.

Given the corporate mission of ensuring the progress of the pipeline, the local police and the hundreds of additional security personnel who have been hired by public and private entities have reason to be concerned. While the growing number of people at Standing Rock are peaceful, they are resilient, resourceful, and committed to stopping the black snake.

More than once I interview young Native American women and men who say, should push come to shove, they are willing "to die" to stop the pipeline.

Cell phone coverage is limited here, making operations and communications extremely difficult. Among the military vehicles and tanks that have been brought in for crowd control, there have been sightings of a dish-like device called an ERAD. Designed to "pull" cell phone records, including financial transactions, people in the camp also believe the ERAD is capable of jamming GSM, EDGE, 3G, and 4G cell phone networks. Some believe it may also be able to send low-level electromagnetic pulses (EMPs), thus disturbing sensitive electronic equipment.

> I interview young Native American women and men who say, should push come to shove, they are willing "to die" to stop the pipeline.

Despite the ERAD, the camp remains sporadically connected. There's Facebook Hill, where one can often get enough low-level reception to connect momentarily to the outside world. Using this thin digital tether, residents huddle on the icy hillside under blankets and parkas madly tapping away on smartphones, sending messages to loved ones, and trying to get the story of Standing Rock out to anyone who will listen.

But smartphones aren't the only thing sending images from Standing Rock.

## NIGHT MOVES

Twenty minutes up the road from the camp is the smoke-filled Prairie Wind Casino. It's a surreal amalgam of shag carpet, low light, and Native American wall accents. Walking into the lobby one passes independent journalists, young Native Americans, gamblers, activists, and organizers. The waiting list for rooms is long. For now, the casino serves as a critical lifeline to the outside world and a refuge from what people of the Oceti Sakowin call the Front Line.

For the last three hours, I've been pacing up and down the small space in a crowded room waiting for the call to go out on some kind of night mission. I have no information other than "it could happen at any time." I've dressed in my thermals and undressed at least three times. My gas mask is securely fastened to my camera bag. Finally, I give up, take off my outer layers, and lie down on a quarter of an otherwise occupied bed. It's well past midnight and I'm exhausted. I close my eyes, but this room is like a train station with people coming and going on phones, editing footage on laptops, assembling and disassembling cameras, and relaying information.

I must have drifted off for a minute. I feel somebody shaking me. I open my eyes to see a middle-aged man named Doug. "We're going," he says. "Hurry up."

Before I am fully conscious, I'm running out the door with a jacket in one hand and my camera bag in the other. Outside in the icy night, I am pointed to a vehicle and hurriedly introduced to a young Native American man we'll call Jerome. Like many young men and women at Standing Rock, Jerome is not from here. His tribal people gathered together funds to send him here and, despite having children back at home, he is prepared to stay "as long as it takes." He tells me this fight isn't just for his children's water — it's for "everybody's water."

What I'm about to participate in is crazy, possibly important, and highly illegal. But I'll get to that later. Right now it's time to talk about how some Millennials are taking on huge issues and changing the world.

The people interviewed in this chapter are part of the Great Millennial Awakening. They represent an already massive pool of young change makers who are working diligently to alter every level of our cultural, social, political, economic, and civic structures.

## LIZZY STEPHAN AND NEW ERA COLORADO

At twenty-seven, Ms. Stephan is the executive director of New Era Colorado, a Denver-based nonprofit that is working to register Millennials to vote. The nonprofit is part of a national network called the Alliance for Youth Action, which is involved in increasing voter turnout across the country. In her capacity as ED, Stephan also works for switching her local municipality to green energy and for election access. I find her at her desk late one Friday afternoon.

She says, "In college I was exposed to sociology and came to see all the different political systems and economic systems and social systems that not only create inequality but also, more alarming, reproduce inequalities generation after generation. I began to see social change as requiring a very broad spectrum of movements and broad spectrum of skills. And found myself really drawn to elections especially."

From the time it was founded in 2006 by a handful of CU Boulder grads until 2014, New Era had registered 100,000 young people to vote. But during the 2015–16 election cycle, they upped their game, adding another 55,000 young voting registrants.

Stephan explains that, while about 87 percent of Colorado's overall voting population is registered to vote, "the number one reason young people don't vote is because they're not registered."

She continues, "Oftentimes the participation gap in elections is more of a registration gap than it actually is a participation gap. Turnout numbers get much, much higher when we just look at registered young people."

In the 2016 presidential election, 83 percent of Millennials were registered to vote, and about 50 percent of those registered voted.[1] Those who did not register obviously could not vote. As Stephan says, "Registration is the gateway to participation." I ask her what stops Millennials from registering.

> "I think young people across the country live in states that actively discourage them from registering."

"I think young people across the country live in states that actively discourage them from registering or have Draconian laws that keep them from registering to vote or keep them from updating their registration. In Colorado, we passed online registration in 2009. I think we were the fourth state in the country to do it, but not every state has online voter registration even still in 2017. So, there's a lot of reasons that keep young voter participation from being as high as it needs to be."

This is another critical point. Because voter registration in the United States is a prerequisite for voting, making registration difficult is an effective strategy for cutting out young voters. For instance, only about thirty states currently offer online voter registration, and each state has a different system for registration. This is a tribute to America's largely antitechnology, antiquated voting system.

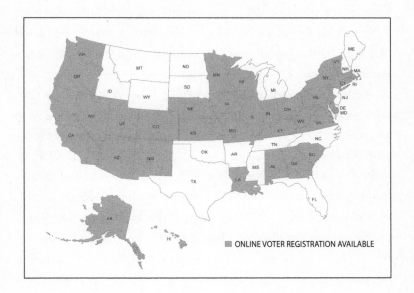

More and more states are offering online voter registration each year. Additionally, some states are now registering people to vote when they get a driver's license. One must question who benefits from outdated voter-registration tactics and why some states have yet to adopt online voter registration.

Look at the map of states that offer online voter registration versus those that do not. Notice anything? With some exceptions, the states that do not offer online voter registration are mostly in the Republican strongholds (the South and the upper Midwest). Surprised? Why would states where older generations control the ballot box open their voting process to youngsters?

Hence New Era's motto: "Registration is the easiest, cheapest, most effective, most important way to get a young voter to cast her ballot." And getting people to register is about rolling up your sleeves and doing the hard work of voter interaction. Stephan says, "The most important piece of technology in our business is a clipboard and a pen."

New Era Colorado is one of many organizations that are registered Voter Registration Drives, or VRD. This empowers them to register a person to vote simply by filling out a form. "So, we go to high schools, we go to college campuses, we go to liquor stores. You know, it's Colorado, so we go to marijuana dispensaries. We go to concerts, we go to various festivals. We're right there in person, asking everybody if they're registered to vote."

Stephan admits that the process of registering to vote itself is antiquated. She says that Millennials move every nine to sixteen months and are often shocked that they must reregister. "They're like, 'Junk mail follows me literally everywhere I go. Why can't my voter registration just follow me as well?'" She says there are many simple election system reforms that are "obvious to young people in a way that I don't know is obvious to previous generations because of our comfort with technology."

New Era Colorado points to the steady increase in Millennial voter turnout as evidence of their impact in the voting process. But, as Stephan mentions, she and New Era believe that social change occurs not through pursuing one type of structural change but rather through working on interconnected issues. As such, New Era Colorado works on the four areas of economic justice, election access, abortion/reproductive rights, and climate. When I ask her why these particular four issues, she tells me that these are the "hot issues" she and her many field organizers hear about over and over again from the tens of thousands of young people they interact with on a yearly basis.

She calls "election access" their "grounding place" that gives rise to the other issues. In terms of elections, she says, "Every step of the way, young people are discouraged from participating, and in some cases actively barred from participating in elections." From there, the other issues New Era is working on spring forth. She says economic justice relates to the student loan industry and how it disproportionately loads Millennials with debt followed by aggressive debt collectors. She adds that abortion and reproductive rights are being fought for by young people, but that fight is often dismissed by people in power who happen to be from older generations. And finally, the climate crisis, she says, is, "one of the biggest, if not *the* biggest, fights of our generation."

"I think if we had better representation in our government, it would certainly be a much easier, less uphill battle on all these issues," she adds. Once again, it all boils down to the connection, or in the case of Millennials, the lack thereof, between the civic sphere and the political. While Stephan is big on getting young people to the polls to make change through governance, she is the first to admit that you can't wait for government to make change happen.

That's why in 2013, New Era's electric utility initiative used an online viral video to raise $200,000 from donors around the world in order to try to take over their local municipal electricity company and transform it into an electric company specifically focused on fighting climate change. This model leverages global support for local grassroots organizing. People are still voting, but unlike with US elections, tools such as Indiegogo and Kickstarter lift the geographical restriction on who can vote. Since New Era's early online initiative, crowdfunding for ballot initiatives has become a trend.

When I ask Stephan what young people can do, she tells me, "I think it's always the sexy thing to say, 'start an organization,' but there are organizations that already exist across the country that young people should plug into because running an organization is hard. Youth engagement work is challenging and we all need to stick together.

"I think if there isn't an organization already doing the work, then I would say the exciting thing would be to start one and start to focus on that. Focus on face-to-face interactions. That is where you create change—by going out to the community and actually having those conversations in person. It's not rocket science, it's just organizing."

## CATALINA VELASQUEZ, OUR REVOLUTION

Before embarking on this investigation into Millennials, I knew of the acronym LGBTQ (Lesbian, Gay, Bisexual, Transgender, Queer). But growing up in rural, conservative Louisiana, there just weren't a lot of opportunities for me to get to know my transgender peers.

All the more reason why getting to know young, powerful people like twenty-nine-year-old Catalina Velasquez opened my eyes to a new world.

Says Catalina, "I'm an undocumented, unafraid transgender, unashamed, unapologetic Colombiana." She is the first person with such a distinction to graduate from Georgetown University's School of Foreign Service. And Catalina is somebody who embraces firsts.

Catalina tells me that transgender people tend to have a life expectancy of less than thirty-five years of age, tend to live well below the poverty line, and tend to make an average of about $10,000 a year. Despite all this, Catalina does not see herself as "exceptionalist" and says instead she's "the nexus of different identities."

"From an undocumented perspective," she says, "we have 11.2 million undocumented immigrants that are very hardworking, that are very resilient and powerful, and they're still fighting for suffrage rights. There are twenty-six million Latinas living in this country that continue to be the demographic who is less insured, who is receiving the lowest wages.

"I just happen to look feminine enough and attractive enough and white enough and able-bodied enough that I made it. And I don't know if I made it, because I'm still an undocumented immigrant. I still haven't hugged my family since their deportation nine years ago. When I look at a case like mine, I have to acknowledge my relative privilege. There's a reason you're speaking to an undocumented trans Colombian who's not a black Colombian. There's a reason you're speaking to an undocumented transgender Colombian who's able-bodied. So, the system has different filters, and that's why it's keeping the majority of my community away from resources." By her "community," she means a wide swath of disenfranchised people.

> "From an undocumented perspective . . . we have 11.2 million undocumented immigrants that are very hardworking, that are very resilient and powerful, and they're still fighting for suffrage rights."

I ask Catalina how she became involved in political activism. "I'm walking politics because every identity I'm part of is ongoingly legislated by policymakers that don't look like me, that don't come from the communities I come from, and that have a huge disconnect and an active lack of interest toward our particularities, our needs, our realities, and the different United States that we live in."

Velasquez believes that the "different United States," the one that many young people experience and the one that's not depicted on traditional TV, is prompting Millennials to become ever more politically active. "Every day more Millennials identify as not just man or woman but gender expansive, gender nonconforming, and transgender so you're seeing that our agendas feel different," she explains. "Our agendas have a strong social justice element because we know what it is to grow up in households without food, without insurance, without commodities yet working forty hours, eighty hours a week, with one or two jobs, and making very little money."

One of the things that Catalina believes drives Millennial politics is the powerful mixture of interrelated issues of race, class, and gender that adversely affect young people. Citing the 1967 Supreme Court case of *Loving v. Virginia*, Velasquez says, "It wasn't until then that interracial marriages were actually permitted. The product of that is the offspring, the Millennials, that have come from those types of policy and civil rights victories. So, the average Millennial is no longer the color of the oppressor. And when you experience oppression you realize there's not really a choice but to speak up and fight for your life. Black people are being killed for being black. Trans people are being killed for being transgender, and so on."

Velasquez asserts that the shift in the color of the average Millennial's skin makes establishment leaders fear outspoken and active Millennials. "In the twenty-first century, we're seeing a shift in demographics (which in itself comes with a lot of concerns), particularly by the ruling class, which is of a very specific race, a very specific gender, a very specific citizenship status, a very specific sex and sexual orientation, and a very specific ability status," she says. She contrasts this with the growing number of young people from various mixed ethnic and mixed gender backgrounds.

"Every day there are more of us—more 'Latinx' and API people and folks who speak languages other than English." Latinx is a gender-neutral term replacing "Latino" or "Latina"; API stands for Asian–Pacific Islander. "Projections continue to show drastic growth. With those numbers also come different world philosophies and needs. And that shifts policy agendas. So, you're going to hear more about immigration reform. You're going to hear more about effective ways for naturalization, effective ways for integration in terms of cross-cultural, multicultural community building because all those things drive Millennials."

All of this has brought Catalina to politics. "I came to work in politics when I was appointed as the first undocumented trans Latina commissioner by former mayor Vince Gray of Washington, DC," she explains. "I participated a lot on the council member decisions, on lobbying for health care for undocumented people and making sure that folks had access to health insurance, regardless of immigration status and regardless of gender."

She says, through working inside the political arena, "I realized the Democratic Party is very dubious and duplicitous in its approach. On the one hand, we say yes to immigrants. One the other hand, President Obama deported the largest number of immigrants in the history of the United States, of all presidents combined, and held more black people than the previous administration in prison. So, you don't need to be white to be an ambassador of white supremacy."

Velasquez worked on Bernie Sanders's campaign for president and now serves on the board of Our Revolution. "If you really look at what the people needed, the most alignment I found was with Senator Sanders. And that is through interpersonal relationship building. Not sending envoys, not putting out a cute tweet." She says that Sanders impressed her by taking the time to speak to and listen to real people.

"That's why he was so successful among Millennials because he showed that you can be a politician and humble, that you can be a politician and still care about the people. But more than that, that he will practice active listening skills and that there is something to learn from everybody." Meanwhile, Catalina is under no illusion that the battle to change national policy is a fast one.

She says that, just as public policy is slow to shift, so too is the media slow to shift because "Traditional media outlets are owned by a very particular profile. They're not owned by trans people. They're not owned by black people. They're definitely not owned by Latina people." Velasquez asserts that outlets like cable news channels create a certain view of the disenfranchised communities she is part of, "without us at the table."

In contrast, Catalina believes that the far more Millennial-controlled world of social and online media "has exposed people to the 'other.' Technology has allowed us to create and generate our own media to tell our stories the way we want to tell our stories." To her point, I found Catalina after reading a story about her activism online and watching a video of her speaking on YouTube.

Catalina maintains that many of the undocumented Millennials living in the United States are here as the result of a long chain of events that began with American imperialism overseas. "The United States militarized my home, uprooted it, detained them [her family], made money out of their bodies and their labor and divested of them." Left alone in the United States, Velasquez figured out how to gain a sort of quasi-personhood through establishing her own LLC. Since corporations in many cases are more protected than citizens, she remains in the United States but is hopeful about reconnecting in person with her family again. "Before my mom dies I want to see her smile at least a couple times more," she says.

Concludes Velasquez, "I'm dedicated to a world of opportunity for all and not just some. And I'm dedicated to really becoming what we falsely advertise, a democracy. And really becoming a place where people have the right to pursue happiness."

## SOLOMON GOLDSTEIN-ROSE, MASSACHUSETTS STATE REPRESENTATIVE

At twenty-two years old Solomon Goldstein-Rose was one of the youngest people to be elected to a state legislature. By the time I catch up with him, he has turned twenty-three. But the values on which he based his campaign remain the cornerstones of his work.

"I've been an activist really as long as I can remember," says Goldstein-Rose, "and I focused on climate change, which I see as the defining issue of my generation and also of our time in general."

The Millennial representative says he got the idea to run for public office while in college. "I started to do some political internships and I started to see examples of young people," he recalls. "I was at a conference in DC in 2013 in the fall, and there was an Israeli parliament member who was there and she was, like, twenty-seven." The slightly older Millennial parliamentarian inspired Goldstein-Rose.

Before running for office, Goldstein-Rose became aware of how most politics is focused on doing the most amount of work for the least amount of change possible. "Working internships, I saw the process is often very incrementalist. I think there is a problem in many legislatures with political conservativeness, where even if you have a large amount of agreement on something, people aren't necessarily willing to pass a bill."

This type of sandbagging of otherwise agreeable bipartisan ideas is what gets the young representative thinking about how to change American politics. "I'm interested in the idea of nonpartisan," he says. "Party registration is often determined not by your actual values but by necessity, for some practical reason about primaries or about what the majority is in your state." Goldstein-Rose says that he knows many progressives who have to register as Republicans for their votes to be counted, due to which party controls their state.

The young politician explains that "the larger problem is that we've gotten to the point, especially at the national level, where politicians are putting party loyalty before practicality in terms of getting things done." He gives the example of Trump's presidential victory, saying, "There's no way Trump would have been elected if we had a nonpartisan system. A vast majority of Republicans initially didn't like him or thought he had no chance. He ended up winning the nomination, and a significant amount of the party still didn't like him then.

"And yet, everyone in the Republican Party felt like they had to rally around Trump because he was their nominee. And then when the video came out that he's sexually assaulting women and it's so clear that he's unfit to be president—that was when a lot of Republicans started un-endorsing him, and people like John McCain said they're not going to vote for Trump. But they didn't say 'I'm voting for Clinton' even though that's the only way to not have Trump be president." Herein lies the catch-22 of a system that institutionalizes exactly two choices.

As Goldstein-Rose explains it, "The other problem is we divide issues as if they were black and white. I agree with most of the Democratic Party platform. I haven't read the Massachusetts Republican Party platform, but I suspect I agree with much of the Republican platform too. Republicans tend to talk more about values. Democrats tend to talk more about issues. They're not mutually exclusive but because we have two parties, when one adopts a position on an issue, the other gets itself in opposition to that." He cites Obamacare, saying, "The Republicans started attacking it because it was his thing, even though it was really ideas that had come from Republicans to begin with."

Goldstein-Rose has put forth a bill that encapsulates many of his no-nonsense political reform ideas. While the bill "isn't going anywhere—yet," he says it is part of the public record and he's making it part of the public discourse. "I'm not sure how I would structure it, but I would like to see publicly financed elections. There are other things, like proportional representation. This can go along well with ranked choice voting, where instead of a one-seat district, several of our current House districts are combined into a three-person district. So take three current districts, take the outer boundaries of those three. Now it's one district and it elects three people. And if you do that with ranked voting, it more accurately represents voters' choices."

He says solutions like this can address national issues like the rigged drawing of districts, which is called gerrymandering, and "has benefited Republicans at the congressional level."

While Goldstein-Rose is the first to admit that he comes from a background of relative privilege, he's also adamant that neither his family nor their friends paid for his campaign. Rather, he won the election through determination and hard work. "There's no reason a young person can't win in any given district." He says being in a college town gave him an advantage, not because of college-aged voters who, in spite of tremendous effort on the part of his campaign, did not show up to the polls, but rather because professors and others are used to working with young people.

Goldstein-Rose used a combination of old-school and high-tech tools to run an extremely frugal campaign. "My strategy was to go knock on tons of doors. I'd worked on campaigns a bit and knew generally how people win grassroots campaigns. And so, I used Votebuilder and we targeted who were likely voters, and we contacted them as many times as we could." Votebuilder is a piece of online software specifically for Democratic candidates that helps manage contacts, Facebook ads, and fund-raising.

> **"My advice is to do it. I want as many young people as possible to run for office, whatever their ideology is and whatever their background is. And in all cases I think we did it by knocking on the most doors."**

When I ask Goldstein-Rose what he would say to other Millennials who might want to run for public office, he tells me, "My advice is to do it. I want as many young people as possible to run for office, whatever their ideology is and whatever their background is. And in all cases I think we did it by knocking on the most doors and talking to people in person. So, find other ways, whether it's house parties, getting debates or forums to happen, or using maybe videos of you talking that you put out as ads on Facebook or Google, or something that's an affordable way, to get the message to people personally so that they can meet you.

"It's really the personal connection is what people care about in who they're going to vote for. There also has to be a message, an overarching message that goes along with that. I'm young, so we adopted the slogan 'Energy to lead,' which worked super well for my campaign."

He says using his youth as a conversation piece and advertising it unapologetically in his campaign worked in his favor. "I'm like, 'No. I'm not fifty years old. I'm going to have a different perspective. I'm gonna have more energy and more passion. I'm gonna work harder than anyone else can,'" he says. "I mean, I was literally running from door to door in ninety-degree weather, and that was impressive to people. So, make the youth a strength and not a weakness.

"A lot of people, especially older people—people who had been student activists fifty years ago in the Vietnam era and the civil rights era—were actually really excited to see the next generation of young activists getting involved." This is where the cross-generational dynamic can work in favor of the Millennials. Many progressive Baby

Boomers aren't blind. They know that the world they wanted to create did not materialize. And they're waiting for Millennials to pick up the ball and run with it.

Solomon Goldstein-Rose is young, but he's not alone. In speaking of Millennials in the Massachusetts State House, he says, "We actually have a really young class proportionately. We've got twelve new Millennial reps out of 160 reps in Massachusetts. We're all the way up to five percent of the legislature for under thirty-year-olds compared to twenty percent of eligible voters. We have a way to go, but we're making progress."

Goldstein-Rose and his class of Millennial representatives are indeed making progress. May their courage and their vigor inspire other Millennials to follow suit.

## TULSI GABBARD, US CONGRESSWOMAN (D-HI)

Tulsi Gabbard is the first veteran, Hindu, Millennial female to be elected to the US House of Representatives. As far as congresspeople go, she is cut from a different cloth. Despite any outward differences, or maybe because of them, her motivations for entering public office and her spirited energy are far more an expression of Millennial values than the agendas of political donors.

I catch a few minutes with her at the Unrig the System Summit in New Orleans. Gabbard has rock-star status at the event. Everyone wants to speak with her or grab a selfie. Her small staff struggles to keep her moving as quickly as is reasonable. We sit in a cramped conference room and I ask her how and why she first ran for office.

Begins Gabbard, "I never thought or imagined a future as a grown-up, as an adult in politics. I was very shy, a total introvert."

It was her connection to the natural environment that started

Gabbard down the path of activism. "Growing up in Hawaii, when I first learned how to swim it was in the ocean. We used to go on hikes every weekend; we would go out to the beach throughout the week. So, I grew up with this basic joy and appreciation for our planet." She explains that when she saw people throwing trash on the ground and in the ocean, "these are things that I really took personally."

As Gabbard explains, she didn't just stand by looking at the garbage. "I wrote a little skit called 'The Adventures of Water Woman.' The story was about a day in the life of Oily Al, and Water Woman saves the day at just the last second, before Oily Al does something to harm the environment."

Not only did Gabbard write the script, she played the lead role. "I played Water Woman with this blue cape. We took this to hundreds of elementary school classrooms all across Hawaii. It was incredible to see the lightbulb go on in these kids' eyes as they connected with the things we were saying."

Playing Water Woman further fueled her desire to be a voice for change. But when a state House seat became open in her district, she was faced with a difficult decision. At twenty-one years of age, she decided to run. "I didn't have the technical political backing or skills. I had never even taken a debate class. But I was motivated by a passionate desire to be of service to my community," says Gabbard.

Her campaign formula was simple. "I just got on my computer," she explains, "made this eight-and-a-half-by-eleven black-and-white page that I took to the copy shop and printed out a few hundred copies. I got in my car with a bottle of water and went out to start knocking on doors."

She quickly discovered that thinking about knocking on doors and actually doing it are two different things. She recalls, "I'll never forget the exact street I pulled up to the first day. I sat in my car for twenty minutes on a hot day and was sweating both because of the heat and because I was nervous. Am I going to freeze? Am I going to be able to communicate clearly? Ultimately the way that I kept pushing beyond my own personal anxiety was by repeating 'This isn't about you.'"

I ask Gabbard what advice she has for Millennials and young people running for office. Like other young elected officials, she says to be ready to physically knock on as many doors as possible. On top of that she says, "Let people know that you want to serve them, you'll fight for them, and you're hearing their concerns. Don't take no for an answer and don't accept the misconceptions and the limitations that other people try to place on you.

> "If you're motivated by a deep-seated desire to serve the people, to serve and protect our planet, then you can't let other people or the obstacles they place before you get in the way."

"If I had listened to all the people who told me when I was twenty-one years old that I was crazy and I should never even think about getting involved in politics," she says, "then I wouldn't have run. If you're motivated by a deep-seated desire to serve the people, to serve and protect our planet, then you can't let other people or the obstacles they place before you get in the way."

Speaking of serving the planet in spite of big obstacles, Tulsi Gabbard was the only US congressperson to visit the Standing Rock protest against the Dakota Access Pipeline in the dead of winter in North Dakota. I ask her why, in spite of possible criticisms, she elected to go.

"When you view the world and politics through the lens of 'Is this policy or action helping people or hurting people? Is this helping to protect our planet? Or will this hurt our planet?' then a lot of things that may be murky for others become quite clear. So, I was excited to go to Standing Rock and lend my own personal voice to what I saw was a very simple cause of protecting water and protecting life."

Gabbard says she arrived at the Bismarck airport late at night only to find it packed with veterans. "I met Vietnam veterans, Republicans, Democrats, people from across different party lines, of different races, and different religions. But they were there answering what they felt was a call to duty, for them as veterans, a continuation of their mission to serve and protect and to defend the people and our future. And to me that's what this bigger mission of service is about."

Her blue cape must be tucked away somewhere, but in many ways, Tulsi Gabbard is still playing her superhero alter ego, Water Woman. May many more Millennials and Gen Zers and young people from all the generations to come join her.

## INTO THE DARKNESS

Back at Standing Rock, I'm riding in the back seat of a pickup truck with three Native American Millennials over a dirt road into the pitch black of an icy, moonless night. I'm the only white guy and the only person over the age of thirty-five. To say I feel awkward shoved in the back among equipment and squeezed next to a young woman who's probably half my age would be an understatement.

My seatmate is silent. The tension in the truck fills the air as it barrels through the dark, bouncing over ruts and kicking up dust. One of the radios on the dashboard squawks. The driver grabs it and whispers something into it.

"There's a good chance you're on federal land right now," says Morray, a hefty dude sitting in the front passenger seat. "Didn't think you'd be breaking the law tonight, eh?" he says as everyone chuckles nervously. But if I'm being honest, jail in North Dakota in the middle of winter doesn't sound all that appealing.

But these "kids" are used to this kind of risk taking. They're front-line warriors in what they consider to be a fight, not only for their lives but also for the lives of the approximately eighteen million people who live downstream of the twenty-two waterways that the Dakota Access Pipeline crosses. And they are well aware that most of those people are as white as the driven snow.

The truck stops. There's a radio conversation happening in the front seat but it's all hushed tones. Sensing my anxiety, the young woman next to me softens a bit and says, "This could take a while." I try to relax. To pass the time I ask her how she ended up here.

River, as I'll call her, is a mother of three who comes from a tribe that's a good two days' drive away. When the Standing Rock protest started, she told her family this was the most important thing she could do with her life, kissed her children, got in the car, and drove out to North Dakota. She's been out here on and off, but mostly on, for the better part of six months.

At my prompting, she tells me about the day she was arrested. She and a group of other mostly young Native Americans formed a prayer circle in front of the line of water protectors who were standing across the path of the pipeline. Their prayer circle was thus the first thing the local sheriff's department saw when they arrived in their armored vehicles and tactical riot gear. River says, "We didn't expect it [the prayer circle] to trigger that much emotion—we didn't expect it to get that violent."

She says she saw "a huge satellite dish on the top of a Humvee." She says she's not sure what its technical name is, but she and her friends just call it the microwave. "I felt it," she says. "I felt really warm. I felt like my head was getting really warm really fast, and I didn't understand why. And after that, all chaos just erupted."

River continues, "I turned around, looked over my shoulder, and saw a percussion grenade shoot out of the BearCat. The BearCat is a huge mobilized vehicle that they were using against us that had multiple weapons on it, and the first percussion grenade that got shot out, it was so loud, 'cause I was literally ten feet away from it, when it shot out, it hit this kid in the leg. I call him a kid, but I think he was a teenager. And it blew up on his leg.

"I turned around and I saw an elder get pushed, and they started beating her with batons. And one of the horse riders came up with his horse and stood between the police and her, but then that was when they shot the horse and they shot the horse rider."

River says that after the riot police managed to push back the protestors, they surrounded the prayer circle and pulled River and her comrades out, beating those who were being difficult and arresting them all.

According to River, the police took the group up to the top of the hill overlooking the construction of the pipeline. "We literally sat on a hill for two hours and watched them bulldoze and watched the workers make fun of us. They were grabbing our prayer sticks and mocking us," she tells me.

She's silent for a moment. It's almost pitch-black, and I can just make out the outline of her face, but I know from the occasional sniffle tears are coming down. In this moment, we're not two strangers in the back of a truck somewhere on the windswept prairies of North Dakota. River is my sister, my mother, my friend, my cousin, my daughter, my wife—she is every woman I know and every woman I've ever cared deeply for.

The truck is now moving through the darkness. It passes through an old barbed-wire gate and continues along the dirt road. River says she and the others were taken in a school bus to the local jail. Her story continues as we bounce along. Says River, "We pulled into the garage, and there were these huge dog kennels erected in the garage and there were Porta-Pottys in there, and they had written numbers on us. I was number 233. They had taken a Sharpie and written numbers on all of us and put us in the dog kennels, and we sat in the dog kennels. We were on concrete, cold floor, no shoes, no nothing."

It's in this moment that I see the courage of an entire generation. It is a generation that is moving from paralysis to action. Its first steps may be faltering, Internet-driven, not real-world enough. But River, and the millions like her, are not the quitting type.

The rest of our adventure involves flying a drone over the pipeline construction site and staring in awe at the expansive lunar-like base of mega construction that is under way.

> "We pulled into the garage, and there were these huge dog kennels erected in the garage and there were Porta-Pottys in there. . . . They had taken a Sharpie and written numbers on all of us and put us in the dog kennels, and we sat in the dog kennels. We were on concrete, cold floor, no shoes, no nothing."

The Standing Rock protest will soon end with blizzards, arrests, and bulldozers pushing the last burning structures into the dirt. The tribe in North Dakota will arguably be worse off, as the locals boycott their casino in retribution, and funds for food and heat dwindle through successive winters. They were damned if they protested and damned if they did nothing. And in the end, the black snake slithered across their sacred land.

This is not the first case of ethnic cleansing. It follows a long procession of win/lose scenarios in which "advanced" cultures assimilated those they perceived to be less advanced (and often more resource-rich). But what happened out there, on land that the government of the United States granted by a legally binding treaty, to the Native Americans goes against the shared values of the Millennial generation.

The Millennial-inspired protest was in many ways powerful, but in other ways ill conceived. It did not follow the rules of big organizing outlined in the last chapter. It relied too completely on fragile communications technology that was easily disrupted. Finally, it failed to build a critical mass of economic and political support at both the local and national levels.

These are all hard lessons for the new generation of activists to learn. But in spite of its shortcomings, the Standing Rock protest was not completely in vain.

Tara Houska is an Ojibwe from Couchiching First Nation, a Millennial, an attorney, and campaign director for Honor the Earth, an indigenous-led environmental justice organization (HonorEarth.org). She puts it this way:

Indigenous rights and environmental justice are so tightly tied together because when these projects happen, they happen in our backyards. They don't happen in white suburbia. We're still dealing with the effects of colonization; we're still dealing with land theft and with resource theft constantly. So for people to see that at Standing Rock, I think it opened their eyes, like this is still happening, this is still real.

The wins from Standing Rock are that we saw a people who are some of the most disempowered, low-wealth, little access to resources, and so forgotten overall people who were able to successfully lead a movement that reached millions of people around the world. We were able to tell our story, and people are now aware of native people. Before that happened, it was not uncommon for me to meet people who had never met a native person before and had no idea native people were still here, asking really ignorant questions like 'Do you live in a teepee?'

I think for every single person who was there and for everyone who followed that movement, they got to see firsthand what corporate interests look like, to understand that their rights as citizens mattered less than the rights of a company, and that was a huge win for changing people's minds and opening their eyes to what's really happening.

Honoring indigenous peoples, diversity, justice, transparency, respect for differences, teamwork, fun, spunk, self-expression, pragmatic idealism, and using efficiency and technology to find better ways—these are the cornerstones of a generation that is very much still learning how to effectively organize itself. That said, on the whole your generation is clear on one thing: you have a very different set of core values than prior generations.

The paradigm of the two Americas we hear so much about—the Left and the Right—fails to encapsulate the scale of a far broader conflict of values that is occurring between generations. Indeed, the true untold war in America and much of the West is now, more than ever before, between a slice of powerful, moneyed, conservative Baby Boomers (and to a lesser degree Silents) and Millennials (and to a lesser degree Gen Xers and Gen Zers).

The gap between the two Americas and the two worlds—the young and the old, those who wish to embrace diversity and those who wish to divide—has become a chasm. To protect the particular underlying nation in which we live, it is time for conscious people of all ages to get down to the business of bold, long-term structural change. To truly transform the institutionalized oppression of our youth into a new society, Millennials must plan, protect, and act. And that is exactly what many of you are beginning to do.

The clock has come one full revolution. It is time for a new generation of heroes to rise.

Μαμακτηριών. Τρία. είκοσι. είκοσι.

## CHAPTER SEVEN

# How to Fix America
# (and the World)

*It's our time to break the rules*

*Let's begin . . .*

—"Renegades" by X Ambassadors

I am standing at the foot of a giant.

There are suspicions that the man at whose solemn face I stare had a disease that elongated his limbs, making him abnormally tall. Making matters worse, a steady stream of failures dominated his life.

When he was seven years old, his family was evicted from their home and he was forced to work to support them. His mother died when he was nine. By the time he was in his early twenties he had become a failure in business, lost a race for state legislature, and was turned away from law school. He then borrowed money for a new business only to go bankrupt. He was engaged to be married, but his fiancée died. He had a nervous breakdown, spent six months in bed, and then attempted to run for political office again. In total, he lost seven races for various state and federal positions. People who heard him speak said he was uninspiring, clumsy, and unconfident.

Then only two years after he lost his final race for elected office, he became president of the United States. Four years later, he would be shot and killed. His name was Abraham Lincoln.

I've come to the Lincoln Memorial for reflection. People from all walks of life sojourn here to marvel at the stand that Lincoln took to end slavery. You can see it in their eyes as they look at the carefully honed marble figure—a quiet celebration of diversity. It is no accident that it was on these very steps that Martin Luther King Jr. gave his "I Have a Dream" speech.

Indeed, this is an important cultural touchstone. Its existence is evidence of the type of change that can span the cycles of time.

As I ponder how much marble and granite and limestone it took to build the Greek-inspired edifice that surrounds Lincoln's towering statue, I watch an Asian family taking photos of their children in front of the statue. I can't understand their language, but I am guessing they are Chinese. Next up is a family from, I am again guessing, India or Nepal. Even in the intense midday sun, a veritable procession of people from all over the globe with all manner of clothing, accents, and languages continues to marvel and photograph one another at the statue. It isn't an advertisement for The United Colors of Humanity per se, but it's close.

During his short time as president, Abraham Lincoln had to balance a moral imperative with the very survival of the United States. He understood that a nation divided can fall. He also understood that a moral imperative is never popular with those people who profit and benefit from the immoral.

While the nuances of why the Civil War actually happened can be debated as being economic rather than moral (slaves were an economic power held primarily by the South, which in many ways was a threat to the North), the thrust of the outcome is no less important. The war ended the legal institution of slavery in the United States, thereby setting a precedent for the rest of the world to follow.

In contrast to the time in which Lincoln lived, the borders of the world we live in today are far more contiguous. By Millennial standards, the largest nation on earth is in fact a borderless one (think Facebook, with its more than two billion users). As borders melt online, it seems the real world is following suit.

As millions of refugees pour into Europe, the human diaspora is disrupting millennia-old barriers and redefining entire cultures. Because our world is intimate, connected, and dynamic, we can no longer look at dividing problems solely as national. Just as America's 2008 election was celebrated planet-wide as a symbol of great hope for humanity's oneness, our 2016 election inspired the opposite sentiment in many abroad. Good, bad, ugly, corrupt, honorable, noble—we are all connected. And we are all watching.

This makes leadership at all levels more important and potentially more impactful than ever before. We think of leaders as presidents, Speakers of the House, and so forth, but the vast majority of leaders are at the community, city, and state levels. In fact, America has more elected officials than any other nation.

There are over 511,000 elected positions in our country. Those half-million or so positions represent the largest single opportunity for civic change. And while your generation hasn't exactly rushed to fill every open political slot, you are starting to figure out how to crack the seemingly impenetrable code of the American political system.

The good news is that cracking that code isn't that hard. For Millennials, the biggest revolutionary idea may not be running a street protest but rather running for office. Even some undocumented Millennial political leaders, most of whom were brought to the United States as small children, are having a tremendous impact on the political process, regardless of the fact they cannot yet vote.

Lincoln was a failure. But he was also a visionary. While the marble likeness has been erected to him, there were no doubt equally as important women and people of color on whose shoulders he stood. While we think of one man as singular, he was a spokesperson for a movement. And that movement was composed of powerful leaders, some of whom were elected, some of whom volunteered, and most of whom we will never know.

In spite of the completely unlikely, nearly impossible future Lincoln and the movement around him imagined, they made it happen. It was messy. And in many ways Lincoln was killed for it. But the bullet that killed him did not stop the imagination that spurred change.

The power of the thought of what could be knows no boundaries and is contagious.

So, I invite you to use your imagination for a moment.

Imagine a society in the very near future. It is a place in which the pervasive threats of climate change and ecosystem-wide collapse have been averted. Not narrowly averted, and not averted by a reactionary push to bioengineer and geoengineer our planet, but rather by working with the strength of biological systems. Thus, this society has learned how to produce abundant food, the central resource of any stable society, while increasing the fertility of its soils, the depth of its freshwater supplies, and the plentitude of its wildlife. It is a lush and green place and its people, especially its children, are well nourished.

Imagine, if you will, a place where automobile transport is second to walking, cycling, and public transit, because inside the design of its roads, which connects homes to commerce, benign forms of transportation are more efficient. Apart from the flourishing greenery, the reduction in automobiles, and the increased throngs of pedestrian traffic, its cities look much like ours do today. But they are quieter and more peaceful places. After all, electric automobiles, bicycles, and walking make far less noise than do the rumbling, burning engines of today.

Imagine a place where citizens and the civic sphere are paramount, and companies and the act of consumption are secondary. Secure, encrypted, digital technology allows citizens to interact directly with the political process. As citizens fully control decisions regarding policy, children are protected from advertising, and the public commons, including lakes, parks, roadways, and the visual landscape itself are free from advertising.

> Imagine a place where sex, gender, and race are proportionally represented in the boardrooms, conference rooms, political committees, leadership bodies, and society.

Imagine a place where sex, gender, and race are proportionally represented in the boardrooms, conference rooms, political committees, leadership bodies, and society. Equity and equality are in balance. People are free to be people without fear of repercussion for their inability to fit a mold.

Imagine a place where the military is not a constant, overt weapon of threat but rather an organization that is able to mobilize to help those in places affected by Earth's cycles of storm, fire, tsunamis, and earthquakes. This place allocates financial resources according to the needs of its citizens rather than the desire for ever more powerful weaponry. It has no trade deficit, no debt, and, other than bilateral peace and humanitarian agreements, no debt-based obligations to other nations.

Imagine a place where indigenous peoples and sacred sites are given protection, respect, honor, and space to heal and practice their ways. By providing for those who came before, its citizens learn a great deal about themselves and their environment that cannot be derived from their own science. These lessons impart great empathy and are part of the information flow that helps to constantly strengthen the structures of society.

Imagine a place in which personal privacy is a right, including owning one's personal data, one's own deep encryption, and one's complete personal digital autonomy. In this place, the online world is uncluttered, free from advertising, and not manipulated. Artificial intelligence is regulated and coded by axioms of support for humans and ecosystems. Transparency for organizations is mandatory.

No, I'm not talking about Norway. Although in some ways, the Nordic countries may be closer to this vision of tomorrow than most. But if you let your imagination go for a moment into a postcrisis future, and if you're young enough to still believe in the potential for big change in your lifetime, this place may not feel that unattainable.

Each of the facets of this world of tomorrow, from the almost complete abandonment of fossil fuels to balancing the climate and ecosystems to gender, sex, and race parity to peace to embracing the lessons of native forebears to personal digital privacy, is possible. Just as ending slavery seemed impossible during the lifetime of Abraham Lincoln, the aforementioned social possibilities may seem unlikely and unrealistic today.

It's important to remember that all social structures are malleable. That's why strategic movements that have good timing, a clear and actionable plan, and the other aspects of "Big Organizing" can, and do, make big, lasting change. That type of change often involves thinking beyond the normal or current paradigms.

Evolutionary philosopher and systems designer Daniel Schmacht-enberger runs a think tank that advises governments and big companies on the future. When I ask him what kind of system we need for the future he says, "What the current models of governance and commerce on Earth have in common is a win-lose game theory system. So, if we look at the whole history of human civilization, as we move from tribes to villages and cities and kingdoms and nation-states and economic trading blocs, these are just larger teams to compete. Why that cannot continue, and is definitely self-terminating, is technology. With exponential tech, it means we have exponentially more capacity to affect things, but not necessarily exponentially better decision-making."

He says that because of the destructive things our technology has now brought to bear, we face the near-term threat of numerous extinction possibilities in a "lose-lose" game. "With win-lose game theory, both sides are increasing their power to win, until you have so much power that winning requires destroying the playing field. So, either we figure out omni-win-win strategies or we get omni-lose-lose."

Schmachtenberger says ultimately we must grapple with big questions: "What are the new structures that are actually adequate? Specifically, how do we create civilization structures that are not self-terminating like the current ones are?"

The type of big change needed for a new social structure in which true democracy flourishes will require bold, powerful, and unapologetic demands and correspondingly mighty, big, and organized movements.

What I am about to propose is a set of radical solutions for the world of tomorrow. Together, these solutions offer the beginnings of a structure for a democracy and an economy compatible with the twenty-first and twenty-second centuries. While these ideas are tailored for the American system, they can also be applied to other nations.

## ABOLISH THE ELECTORAL COLLEGE

**In order for America to have even a semblance of democracy, the Electoral College must be dismantled and thrown onto the funeral pyre of outdated historical ideas.**

One person, one vote. That's how a democracy is supposed to work.

But in America, we have something called the Electoral College, a 538-person "club" whose members (not the voters) actually choose the president of the nation. To say the Electoral College is outdated, antidemocratic, and fundamentally distorting to any sort of meaningful voter participation is a polite understatement.

In order for America to have even a semblance of democracy, the Electoral College must be dismantled and thrown onto the funeral pyre of outdated historical ideas.

Luckily, there's a loud and growing chorus of organizations, businesspeople, politicians (and voters!) that agree on this. Says MoveOn's petition "Abolish the Electoral College" at petitions.moveon.org:

> The Electoral College has outlasted its usefulness. It is part of the Constitution, written when communication was by pony express. Voters currently living and voting in a "red" or "blue" state are disenfranchised, because their vote doesn't matter. Eliminating the Electoral College means: no "swing" states getting all the attention and all the campaign stops and all the empty campaign promises. The electoral members are selected by the two main

political parties, Republican and Democrat, disenfranchising all
other voters, independent, Libertarian, etc. End it now.

At the time of this writing, the petition is creeping up to 650,000
digital signatures.

Of course, the mechanics of removing this obstacle to democracy
are also mired in the old-world political machine. To totally abolish
the Electoral College would require a constitutional amendment.
(Another constitutional amendment would be needed if you consider that the political process should be protected from corporate
interests.)

A Band-Aid, not-so-big-or-bold-but-workable short-term solution
would be to adopt what is called the National Popular Vote Interstate
Compact, or NPVIC (NationalPopularVote.com). The NPVIC is an
agreement among states that whichever candidate wins the national
popular vote also gets the votes of the electors. It's a backward way of
fixing an even more backward system, but like hemorrhoid cream, it
could provide temporary relief from what is essentially a too-much-
compacted-shit-in-one-place problem—i.e., Washington, DC.

The NPVIC requires enough states to sign on to get to the required
minimum 270 Electoral College votes to elect a candidate. Currently
ten states and the District of Columbia have signed on. That's about
165 electoral votes' worth. To make the NPVIC real will require the
support of more states and especially some key Republican states.[1]

Even with the NPVIC in place, the Electoral College institutionalizes a nonrepresentational democracy. Ultimately, the Electoral
College needs to perish. And it's not going to go away without a fight.

## REPLACE A/B PARTY VOTING WITH RANKED CHOICE VOTING (RCV)

Ranked choice voting is a voting system in which, when more than two candidates are on a ballot, the voter ranks each candidate in order of hierarchical preference. About twelve US cities and a number of other countries at the national level currently use ranked choice voting and its popularity is spreading.

Ranked choice voting works in one of two ways:

The first scenario is an instant runoff vote in which the two candidates with the highest cumulative numbers are automatically run against each other. In the automatic runoff, the candidate for whom you gave the highest score gets your full vote, while the other gets no vote. At the end of the runoff, the candidate with the most full votes wins the race.

The second scenario is a multi-winner election. For a city council, for instance, the lowest scoring candidate(s) are eliminated, thus the majority of voters elect the majority of candidates.

ACCORDING TO FAIRVOTE (FAIRVOTE.ORG), A 501(C)(3) NONPROFIT ORGANIZATION THAT ADVOCATES FOR RANKED CHOICE VOTING, RCV HAS THE FOLLOWING BENEFITS:

1. It promotes majority support.
2. It promotes friendlier campaigns due to the fact that candidates benefit even when they are a voter's second or third choice.
3. It provides more choice for voters due to the opportunity to have more candidates on the ballot.

4.  It minimizes strategic voting, i.e., voting for the lesser of two evils.

5.  It mitigates the impact of money in politics by giving grassroots candidates a higher chance of winning.

6.  It saves money for voting districts by eliminating a secondary runoff election.

7.  It promotes representation that is more reflective of the voting group by encouraging inclusion of diverse candidates.

An elegant evolution of the ranked choice voting system is STAR Voting. STAR Voting stands for Score Then Automatic Runoff. Typically, in ranked choice voting, candidates are ranked by voters who select among "first choice," "second choice," and "third choice." But with STAR Voting, candidates are rated on a scale of 0 to 5, zero indicating "no support" and five indicating "max support." According to the Equal Vote Coalition (Equal.Vote), STAR Voting beats the first generation of ranked choice voting in the categories of equality, honesty, accuracy, simplicity, and expressiveness.

Voting activist Sara Wolk explains it this way:

> Right now we've got a voting system where we've only got two major parties and everyone has to pick a side. But what if one side has only one candidate and the other side has two candidates? What often happens is that the party that's got two options, they should be better represented, but in fact they can end up splitting their coalition in half. So that even though all together the "purple voters" (for example) are 60 percent, they can still be beat by the 40 percent of voters who just rallied around a single candidate.
>
> In other words, STAR Voting eliminates the classic problem of vote splitting.

| STAR VOTING | | | | | | | | INSTANT RUNOFF VOTING | | | |
|---|---|---|---|---|---|---|---|---|---|---|---|

Of the two highest scoring candidates overall, Star Voting elects the one scored higher by more voters

If a candidate has a majority of the first choice votes, that candidate wins. Otherwise, the candidate with the fewest first choice votes is eliminated. If your first choice is eliminated, your vote goes to your next choice (if any), and the process repeats until one candidate has a majority of the remaining votes.

| | No Support | | | | | Max Support | | | First Choice | Second Choice | Third Choice |
|---|---|---|---|---|---|---|---|---|---|---|---|
| | 0 | 1 | 2 | 3 | 4 | 5 | | | | | |
| **Jill** Green | ○ | ○ | ○ | ○ | ○ | ○ | | **Jill** Green | ○ | ○ | ○ |
| **Bernie** Independent | ○ | ○ | ○ | ○ | ○ | ○ | | **Bernie** Independent | ○ | ○ | ○ |
| **Donny** Republican | ○ | ○ | ○ | ○ | ○ | ○ | | **Donny** Republican | ○ | ○ | ○ |
| **Hillary** Democrat | ○ | ○ | ○ | ○ | ○ | ○ | | **Hillary** Democrat | ○ | ○ | ○ |
| **Marco** Republican | ○ | ○ | ○ | ○ | ○ | ○ | | **Marco** Republican | ○ | ○ | ○ |
| **Gary** Libertarian | ○ | ○ | ○ | ○ | ○ | ○ | | **Gary** Libertarian | ○ | ○ | ○ |
| **Lizzie** Democrat | ○ | ○ | ○ | ○ | ○ | ○ | | **Lizzie** Democrat | ○ | ○ | ○ |

Ranked choice voting offers many advantages over America's current two-party voting scheme. Today, most RCV is done on an "instant runoff" basis. But in the near future, STAR Voting, which offers more choices and provides a clearer picture of voter preference, may become more common.

While ranked choice voting is relatively new to the United States, it is successfully used in cities like Santa Fe, New Mexico, to elect mayors.[2] STAR Voting offers a more Millennial feel in that, just like rating a product on Amazon, you can now give candidates a clear measure of your support. STAR Voting also adds encryption protocols and other important election verification techniques.

Regardless of what variation of ranked choice voting is used, it is time to bring it to an election near you. In a multiparty system that accurately reflects the diversity of the people living in America, there is no doubt: ranked choice voting is the future. How soon that future comes to pass in your town is completely up to you.

## INSTALL APP-BASED, ELECTRONIC BIOMETRIC-ENCRYPTED VOTING

Today, we bank on our smartphones, we purchase things on our phones, stocks are traded on our phones, and we vote for our favorite video on our phones. Every day, all day, we unknowingly encrypt and unencrypt data without much more than a swipe.

But to cast your vote in the US political process, we must schedule our lives around one specific day to leave work, stand in line, use a machine that looks like a prop from a 1930s movie, or worse, a Diebold brand—aka hackable—electronic voting machine.

So why can't we vote on our smartphones?

During the 2016 election, more than thirty US states offered online voting to people serving in the military and voters living overseas.[3] Of course, security wonks raised a fuss about the legitimacy of the non-paper voting system. But, considering that by 2016 about 25 percent of the states were already using electronic voting machines, the wonks were a little late to the punch.[4]

One of the big arguments against online voting is that auditors have no method of verifying votes without a paper trail back to the physical ballot. But only half the states in America actually require a post-vote audit. And of those, some of the states don't have a verifiable paper trail that leads back to the ballot. In other words, there's no way to accurately audit America's votes right now.[5]

Unless you're a Washington bureaucrat, whose salary depends on *not* finding solutions, a verifiable system for digital voting is simple. Since 2005, the small country of Estonia has offered online voting with no instance of fraud and no record of any hacks. To their one million registered voters, they provide a government ID card with a chip and a pin, like an ATM or debit card. They also give you a card reader for your computer. You can confirm the details of your vote with an app.[6] How civilized.

A similar process could be achieved without the card, however, using the biometric verification available on smartphones and an associated ID number and PIN for each voter. Oh yes, somebody in Washington would have to get Silicon Valley to code an app so people could check the validity of their vote. (There's a job for a Millennial!)

Biometric verification refers to a way of identifying someone by their unique biological traits, including fingerprints, hand geometry, earlobe shape, retina and iris, voice, and DNA. Increasingly, our phones contain biometric readers, specifically thumbprint readers. But soon to come are other forms of biometric readers, including retina scanners, a feature already available today on many Samsung phones and tablets.

Critics of biometric voting point to a succession of failures in its initial rollout in various parts of the developing world, specifically Africa. But given the circumstances of rural Africa, one questions whether or not the technology is being appropriately field-tested, or whether the hardware they are using is any good to begin with. One recent article that explored why Kenya's biometric voting system failed also mentioned the otherwise "peaceful" election resulted in only fifteen deaths.[7] Any election that is volatile and chaotic enough to incite multiple murders may not be the right place to attempt mass dissemination of a cutting-edge technology.

> "Being able to vote online will be one of the defining moments of progress for Millennials."

It's also important to note that the elections in question aren't using smartphones, they are using clumsy machines in voting centers. It's not the idea behind verifiable biometric tech that is the problem in the developing world, it is the execution.

When I ask generational consultant and researcher Jason Dorsey about the possibility of voting via app, he says:

> Being able to vote online will be one of the defining moments of progress for Millennials. And there's a lot of traditional power brokers that don't want it. Why? Because they have models that can predict likelihood of winning. They can test messages. They can raise money and literally show you an ROI.
>
> As soon as you allow voting from your phone, there are no models for that. It's going to be messy. But change is messy, and progress only comes through change. Millennials are going to drive it because Millennials don't think there's another option. And digital voting, mark my words, is going to be the watershed moment.

With a plethora of ready-built apps and software like Election Runner, nVotes, Simply Voting, and many others, 256-bit encrypted, biometrically verified, app-based voting is happening every day. Porting such a system over to Washington, DC, is just a click away.

The question is not if but rather when and who—as in, who is going to make it happen? (Hint: this is the part where you determined Millennial readers say, "I'm going to do that.")

## GET CORPORATE MONEY OUT OF POLITICS

There is a smattering of bills and acts and plans to try to ameliorate the effect of big money on elections. They include the Government by the People Act, which would government-match small dollar donations six to one while giving donors a refundable tax credit. The Fair Elections

Now Act provides similar provisions. The city of Seattle is also trying something new by giving individual voters four $25 vouchers they can contribute to the candidate of their choice.

These are all innovative measures. But none has the power to clean up the sponsored-by mess that is the status quo in our nation's capital.

It's been a while since the good old US Constitution got an amendment. The Twenty-Seventh Amendment, which was adopted in 1992, has to do with the compensation of members of Congress. It wasn't exactly world-changing, especially considering the amendment was actually drafted 203 years prior to its passage.

Prior to that, the Twenty-Sixth Amendment, which lowered the right to vote to eighteen years of age, was passed in 1971. Yes, the Baby Boomers successfully pressured a Republican House, Senate, and even Republican president Richard Nixon into constitutionally mandating that the young among them could vote. They did it by using every political tool available to them at the time, and it was a serious accomplishment. Kudos, Boomers, that's one for the history books.

Millennials, your parents did it—why not you?

Enter the push for a Twenty-Eighth Amendment. Move to Amend (movetoamend.org) is a group of interracial, somewhat radical, mostly Gen Xers, a few Boomers and like, maybe, one or two Millennials. The proposed amendment group was spurred by the much lamented 2010 *Citizens United v. Federal Election Commission* decision, which essentially ruled that corporations can fund elections. According to the Move to Amend site, "We call for an amendment to the US Constitution to unequivocally state that inalienable rights belong to human beings only, and that money is not a form of protected free speech under the First Amendment."

To pass a constitutional amendment it takes a two-thirds majority vote in both houses of Congress and ratification by three-fourths of the state legislatures. That's no small feat. But Millennials have a way of doing the undoable and making the most insanely unthinkable things possible. First African American president, check. Never before heard of gender distinctions, check. Global protests, check. Facebook, check. But when Millennials do work toward a big goal, that team spirit can accomplish immense things.

While it may have to occur as an extension of some other sea change in leadership (an outlier, Bernie-like president, for example, could champion such an amendment), if a functional democracy is the goal, then universal, national, and eventually international policy must be drafted to protect our civic needs from corporate domination.

## MAKE VOTING COMPULSORY

It bears mentioning again: a *republic* is a form of government in which elected representatives make most, if not all, of the decisions for the electorate. In the case of the republic of the United States, those decisions can even include elected officials, not the citizens, choosing the president. Republics made sense hundreds of years ago when communication and roads were difficult. But in the twenty-first century, when we are working to colonize Mars, it's just a quaint, old, outdated form of government.

In contrast, a *democracy* is a form of government in which citizens, through votes, directly make choices on laws and elect officials. The two forms of government are often confused. Thus, the common misnomer that the United States is a democracy, when it is in fact a republic.

Recall the first line of the Pledge of Allegiance (which, I might add, is oddly to a *flag* rather than to a nation):

I pledge allegiance to the flag of the United States of America
and to the republic for which it stands . . .

From a strictly literary standpoint, you could just shorten that and
say, "I pledge allegiance to the republic of the United States." That
probably would have saved countless hours of schoolchildren's lives,
but I digress. . . .

The point is that we conflate living in what is clearly a republic
with living in a democracy. This continues a fantasy of representative
democracy when in fact we have a system of elite power structures that
are strengthened by leaders who operate with incredible autonomy.

The model of governance called democracy was developed around
the fifth century BC in Athens, Greece. It was a form of direct democracy in which citizens voted directly on legislation. Of course, it had
caveats. To be a citizen you could not be a slave or a woman. But putting aside the cultural proclivities of the day, the idea behind *Athenian*
democracy was that each citizen got a vote. Period.

There's one other important piece. Athenian democracy held that
it was the citizen's *duty* to vote. While voting was not exactly compulsory, there were times in Athens when citizens were fined for not participating in the political process. Herein lies the central question of a
true democracy: Is voting a *right* or a *responsibility?*

Compulsory voting is where each citizen has a responsibility to
vote. In the case of most of the twenty-two countries that practice
compulsory voting, that doesn't mean
a citizen must vote for any particular
leader or any law in particular. In most
places, a vote of abstention is acceptable. But *not* voting is *not* acceptable.

After Australia introduced compul-

**Herein lies the central
question of a true
democracy: Is voting a
*right* or a *responsibility?***

sory voting in 1912, participation in elections increased from between 47 and 78 percent of eligible voters to between 91 and 96 percent. Even people serving a jail sentence of fewer than three years can vote.

Because Australia counts itself among the civilized countries of the world, and because its citizens aren't known for being in a rush, Australia's national voting period is not, as it is in America, a one-day affair. Rather Australia offers a two-week-long period of time in which citizens can vote when it suits them. How thoughtful.

Yes, Down Under, eligible voters are fined for not voting. Just like we in America are fined for speeding or running a red light. Your choice matters, and in compulsory voting countries, being a citizen means you've got to do your fair share to keep your country in line. If you can't be bothered to vote, then the most basic form of exchange between the citizen and the state cannot be established.

Remember all the hoopla in America about health care for everyone? Australia has had free public health care since the 1940s and national free Medicare insurance for its citizens since the 1980s. Its health care system works on the basis of prevention, not on the basis of drug prescription. Australia has one of the highest minimum wages in the world. Unemployment is half that of the United States, and the gender pay gap is significantly narrower. Australians, on average, consume less fossil fuels, have more free time, have a lower risk of being murdered, a radically narrower class divide, and live longer. And ironically, for a country that began as an English penal colony, Australians have six times fewer people behind bars than the United States. Finally, Transparency International ranks the Australian government as one of the most transparent on earth.

Australia is not a perfect country by any stretch of the imagination, and it has its fair share of problems. But on the whole, and by the measures we have available, Australia offers a better standard of living than America due to the fact that almost all its citizens participate in their own governance.

## ESTABLISH A NATIONAL (AND INTERNATIONAL) $15 MINIMUM WAGE

For a developed nation, the United States has one of the lowest minimum wages in the world. As we discussed in chapter 3, the majority of Millennials are stuck in minimum wage jobs. A low minimum wage adversely affects women and people of color. It has an especially negative effect on single women and most notably single mothers, of which the Millennial generation has the largest share in recent history.

According to Christine Owens, writing for *The Hill*, if a $15 minimum wage were instituted, "the typical worker who would see a raise is a thirty-six-year-old woman with some college level coursework who works full-time but still struggles to pay the bills."

> If a $15 minimum wage were instituted, "the typical worker who would see a raise is a thirty-six-year-old woman with some college level coursework who works full-time but still struggles to pay the bills."

The real trickle-down effect of low and stagnant wages in our inflationary economy, where prices continue to climb, is that children are hurt by an increasing amount of time their parent or parents must spend working. This increases the likelihood that kids will spend some amount of time each year in poverty.

In 2012, two hundred brave fast food workers walked off the job in New York, demanding a $15 minimum wage and a union. Since then, the Fight for $15 has become a rallying cry across the United States and around the world. The resulting nonprofit organization and website (FightFor15.org) has amassed the support of thousands of workers in over three hundred cities on six continents.

Two states, California and New York, and the District of Columbia have since amended their labor codes to raise their minimum wage to $15 an hour. Additional states have approved minimum wage increases from $12 to $14.75 an hour.[8]

When New York State finally raised its minimum wage to $15 an hour, industry whined, and financially strapped workers rejoiced. According to a Center on Wage and Employment Dynamics policy brief, the wage increase gave 36.6 percent of the statewide workforce an average pay increase of over 23 percent![9] The report finds that, despite the expected backlash from business, the total payroll increase cost to business in New York State will be a paltry 3.2 percent.

The Raise the Wage Act of 2017 was introduced by Representatives Bobby Scott (D-VA) and Keith Ellison (D-MN) and Senators Bernie Sanders (I-VT) and Patty Murray (D-WA). If passed, the act would not just phase in a $15 minimum wage but it would index the minimum wage to the median wage beginning in 2025, so that each year thereafter the minimum wage would automatically rise based on the growth of the median wage. The act has, of course, garnered considerable criticism from big business, business publications, and conservative Republicans.

According to the National Employment Law Project, the positive effect of a $15 minimum wage on workers would be dramatic while the impact to business would be minimal.[10]

A $15 minimum wage is just that—the bare minimum that should be paid for a human being's time, energy, and work.

## INSTALL A NEW
## ECONOMIC OPERATING SYSTEM

The type of economics we practice in the United States and much of the Western world is based on the work of a Scottish economist named Adam Smith, who lived during the 1700s. His book *The Wealth of Nations* laid the framework for the modern discipline of capitalist economics.

### SMITH BASED HIS WORK ON THREE CORE
### ECONOMIC PRINCIPLES, EACH OF WHICH
### IS A COMPLETE FALLACY:

1. Resources are limitless and conversely the ecosystem's ability to absorb pollution is limitless. Because there are no limits to oil, fresh water, timber, steel, aluminum, etc., an economy based on the growing consumption of these goods can continue indefinitely.
2. Slavery has, is, and will always be available in some substantial form in order to provide the basis of labor for the rest of the economy. Smith believed that slaves were property, and thus built his economic model around this idea while never acknowledging that without this cost-free labor force his model would fail.
3. The accumulation of capital in the form of land, goods, and wealth, also known as property, is the basis for any stable, sustainable, growing economy. But as is patently obvious, this model of an accumulation culture cracks and shatters under the weight of ever more people and ever fewer material resources.

For the most part, modern capitalism is still running on this operating system and the three core mistruths that Smith developed. Rather than running on an economic operating system that was developed 250 years ago it's time we install a new economic OS.

What would a new operating system look like? Most important, it would not likely be capitalism or socialism. It would contain elements of both and elements of neither. Like space travel, the Internet, and the smartphone, this operating system would represent a revolution—a complete new paradigm to that which previously existed.

## BROADLY SPEAKING, OS WORLD ECONOMY V2.0 WOULD:

1. Promote less work
2. Abandon gross domestic product and gross national product
3. End corporations having personhood
4. Emphasize shared resources over resource accumulation
5. Assign value to natural capital
6. Provide parity pricing to all labor globally
7. Make free higher education available to all citizens
8. Be driven by ecological design
9. Measure its own success by provision—i.e., the number of humans and their level of basic needs met

The Millennial tsunami has already created and catalyzed a great many new innovations: Craigslist, car sharing, couch surfing, Airbnb, freecycling, tool libraries, Groupon, Uber, Lyft, Facebook, and so on. To get to the level of structural change in our economy will require both revolutionary and evolutionary work.

Is it possible? We will only know if we try.

One thing is for sure, though: new tools are emerging that could pave the way.

## BRING ON THE BLOCKCHAIN

At the time of this writing, cryptocurrencies are all the rage. Be it Bitcoin, Litecoin, Ethereum, Dash, or one of hundreds of other blockchain-based currencies, these new forms of money are creating a financial frenzy that looks like a dot-com bubble v2.0.

Peer-to-peer digital cryptocurrencies, in some ways, could offer an extension of the new economic principles discussed in this chapter. They are encrypted, have an open ledger system that allows transparency of transactions, and maintain the privacy of the owner of the currency. These are all potentially game changers. But these new currencies also have limitations.

The most obvious limitation is that, in their current incarnation, these currencies require a tremendous amount of computing power. In the case of Bitcoin, the needed computing power was originally distributed among many individual "miners" who each had relatively small amounts of processing power. Those individual processors worked to verify the transactions on the ledger, also known as the "chain," thus creating new "blocks."

As blocks were built, the chain, or ledger, got longer and required more processing speed and power. Today, much of the processing for the Bitcoin blockchain is done in either Iceland, where there is cheap geothermal electricity, or China, where coal-fired power plants are powering the servers that are creating new blocks. Meanwhile, because they have their own immense server farms and because they want to manage the flow of monetary data, both Amazon and Google have begun their foray into creating their own currencies.

While it is impossible to predict which, if any, of the current crypto-currencies will be winners or losers, it is likely that the encryption and blockchain techniques used therein will soon be used for many other purposes. Ethereum, for example, is the basis for a suite of software that is called decentralized apps, also known as dapps. A dapp connects the user and the provider directly, cutting out the middleman. For example, if Twitter were a dapp, the application would run across thousands or even millions of computers worldwide and would therefore be more resistant to censorship. In theory, dapps could require far less processing power than the actual currency blockchains, which require dealing with billions, trillions, quadrillions, or even nonillions of financial transactions.

Blockchain could also offer a way to create smart contracts wherein each party has certain rights, the privacy of which is secure, and the validity of which exists irrespective of national borders, laws, or treaties. Smart contracts could offer a way to prove land ownership, to keep intellectual property, and to cocreate and build things that are beneficial to multiple parties.

Cryptography, encryption, and peer-to-peer ledger chains are new tools that can help keep personal data private and ensure that organizational operations of companies and governments remain transparent. Beyond freeing currency, using these tools to enable fundamental political change could be a powerful step toward a better, more equitable future. That's a good thing.

But we must also hedge against the overhyped bright, shiny, fix-all kind of thinking. One of the biggest advocates of making information free is Peter Sunde, the founder of the Pirate Bay, the infamous torrent site that hosts lots of copyrighted material and allows it to be shared for free.

When I ask Sunde what he thinks about blockchain currencies, his answer is surprising. "I think that there's this myth that technology itself will solve things," he says. "You're building another system; sure, it's transparent if you have the resources, but the technology is not really solving a big problem. But the narrative is that you're solving a big problem." He says digital tools like the blockchain are just that— tools. He believes that real change comes from strong leadership and many committed individuals doing the hard work.

"From the revolution, you need some sort of an evolution," he concludes.

## IT'S ABOUT TIME

If we consider for a moment the lessons from historians like *Generations* author Neil Howe, Millennials are headed face-first into a storm of splintered crises that will likely culminate in a single large global emergency. As Howe warns, all the largest wars in history have occurred during a crisis turning.

We face a danger similar to that which threatened Germany in 1933, and that most republics have faced in eras of upheaval and crisis. At the time, Germany was a functioning quasi-democratic state called the Weimar Republic. Then, in the span of three days and nights in 1934, the government was purged and the nation transformed into a fascist state helmed by a despotic madman named Adolf Hitler.[11] As the people of Germany learned, when citizens stop participating in their own governance, the end of a nation is not an enigma but rather an inevitability.[12]

The desperation and hate that has fomented in our country today makes this nation extremely vulnerable. Unless we all act together and soon, the fate of America is, at best, tenuous.

When the collective vision, the shared mission, and the dream of a huge portion of the population is shattered, the tendency is to move toward division. When fear is the prevailing emotion, the people who are afraid are more easily manipulated. During such eras, the populace gravitates to strong paternal leaders who align them against the "enemy." Herein lies a grave danger to our nation and our world.

As the crisis we experience plays out, we must keep in mind at each twist and turn that the future is yet unwritten. During times of great social upheaval, there are always people preparing the next phase of society. They are sometimes called social designers. We think of Leonardo da Vinci and Ada Lovelace as artist and scientist, respectively, but they were laying the framework for the next turning of the clock—the next era of society. These people had such profound influence over society as to literally sketch and code its future into being.

Today the word *revolution* connotes a short-term reaction to a despot. But revolution used in the context of this book goes back to the Latin root of the word *revolutio*—a "turn." If you're a Millennial, or, rather, a member of this Hero Generation, your legacy will be to lay the foundation for the next turning.

Designing the future is the work of a lifetime. Unlike the pathological, plastic, disposable, accumulation culture that preceded you, Millennials, the next era of social structures and infrastructure must be built to withstand the test of time. Your inventions must have permanence, stability, and be built on a foundation of bedrock such that time cannot easily break, wither, or erode it.

The past ten millennia have been built on conquering the earth, dominating nature, and subjugating other humans. When one area was desolated, humans moved on. "Go West, young man" was the call of Manifest Destiny, so people did. And now the West and the East and the North and the South are all used up and our population is still wanting for more. Humans will soon number ten billion. To live as we do in America today, those ten billion people will need six more planets' worth of resources.

A new modus operandi for our species is needed. And it must be the antithesis of a throwaway society built by white, gray-haired, privileged men drunk on avarice and stoned on self-lust.

The Millennial vision for a new future exists, and your generation's social designers are already hard at work building that future. Here, articulated by four powerful Millennial leaders, is a sense of that future.

**Renaldo Pearson, a social engineer in residence at Harvard and a black history scholar:**

> They say, "I wonder what I would have done during the civil rights movement if I would have been there." Well, here's your time.
>
> We're literally seeing the landmark achievements of the civil rights movement rolled back. We're seeing the very survival of the human species under siege. I believe that this is a decisive moment in the American story. A new chapter is being written right now. Which side are you on?

**Steven Olikara, founder and president of the Millennial Action Project:**

> The future we need to build is much different than what exists today. Let's build a political culture that doesn't see someone of a different political stripe as evil. But where we have a politics that

calls us to serve our better angels and one that makes cooperation more of the norm and not the exception. I think democracy
reform and civic engagement is really the calling of our time.

**Christin "Cici" Battle, director of Young People For:**

I would love to see a world (and I do see it, it's really close)
in which the folks who've been marginalized for so long are
represented. Those should be the leaders, they should be
women, they should be trans women, they should be black folks,
and they should be indigenous folks leading the country so that
we can fulfill a promise that has been empty for so long. So, the
vision I see is not just young people, but for all people.

**Tulsi Gabbard, US congresswoman (D-HI):**

My vision for the future and for our country is a place where
people are able to treat each other with Aloha, which means
respect, care, and compassion. A place where we can come
together and disagree without being disagreeable. And where we
can overcome these divides that are tearing our country apart
because at our core we care for each other, for our future, for this
place that we call home.

  If we can do that, then we can find solutions to so many of
these devastating challenges that we face in our country and in
the world but it's not going to happen unless *you* step up and do
something about it.

## WE ALL HAVE A DREAM

There is one woman who represents the Millennial generation more than any other, and she's been around for a while. In fact, the very image of her speaks to the values of tolerance, inclusion, fairness, freedom of expression, acceptance of those who are different, hope, and belief in a brighter future.

I'm talking about the Statue of Liberty. We all know her iconic edifice, but there a few things you may not know about her.

First, you may not know she was a gift from France, where she was fully assembled and stood over Paris for a year before being shipped to the United States. You may also not know that at her bare feet lie broken chains, which symbolize that in this new land of America no person will be shackled and ruled over by the enslavers, despots, kings, czars, fascists, and mad tyrants of the Old World.

The Statue of Liberty was placed at the gateway to America to welcome immigrants. And in many ways, Millennials, you are like immigrants: you long to break free of the chains that bind you and the old power structures that seek to disenfranchise you. Your new ideas, your bold vision, and your youth are the very lifeblood that this country and this world desperately need.

The Statue of Liberty was a gift to celebrate the one-hundredth anniversary of this social experiment, this thing we call America. "Why," you might ask, "was this centennial worthy of a 305-foot-tall copper-plated work of art?"

America was the first country made up of people from all other nations wherein a form of inclusive governance was created in which liberty, aka freedom, was held as an "inalienable right." When this nation began, it was considered a radical, disruptive, and imperfect experiment. There were many who believed it would never succeed. And there were perhaps just as many, if not more, who believed that it *had* to succeed.

You see, the Dream of America is not the same as the "American Dream." It's not about a gender-normative, Madison Avenue–created, consumption-based, suburban existence with a white picket fence, two kids, and two cars. On the contrary, it's something much more vital.

One expression of the Dream of America was written by a thirty-four-year-old political activist named Emma Lazarus in a poem called "The New Colossus," which is emblazoned on the pedestal upon which the Statue of Liberty stands. In her poem, Lazarus wrote:

> *Give me your tired, your poor,*
> *Your huddled masses yearning to breathe free,*
> *The wretched refuse of your teeming shore.*
> *Send these, the homeless, tempest-tost to me,*
> *I lift my lamp beside the golden door!*

In other words, Lady Liberty stands to welcome all manner of people who have been disenfranchised and disempowered by old structures of power to a place where they can come together to build a better world. For almost two and a half centuries, we, the people of America, have struggled to make that dream come true. And in many respects, it has not yet been realized.

But we're on the precipice of a new era. This new era is neither a black nor a white America; it's not a red or blue America; instead, it's an America that represents the world. And, conversely, we live in a world that every day becomes more similar to America. Perhaps that's because freedom, liberty, tolerance, justice, and the pursuit of happiness know no borders. Perhaps it's because, in spite of our differences and the lines our forebears drew in the sand, we're really just one people living on one planet, hurtling through space and time together.

France gave America a statue to encourage us to keep going. Over 150 years later, that statue remains to remind us that our grand social experiment isn't over. It must continue. Because if it can succeed here, then it can succeed anywhere. The true dream is one that is universal, global, and simple. In essence, it's that we can live harmoniously together.

The real revolution is to make this dream come true.

There is one generation of people that, due to their unique position in history, is poised to finally realize that dream. That generation is you, Millennials. Your mission is to complete the cycle of history, to pull your sword from the stone, to conquer the darkness in our world, to bring in the light, and to become heroes. You hold in your hands the fate of the next millennia.

Go forth, Millennials! And take this world by storm.

# WEBSITES
# FOR THE REVOLUTION

www.RevolutionGeneration.us

www.Represent.us

www.TurboVote.org

www.FairVote.org

www.Equal.Vote

www.NationalPopularVote.com

www.SheShouldRun.org

www.EmilysList.org

www.RunFor.us

www.YoungPeopleFor.org

www.MillennialAction.org

www.RaceForward.org

www.Demos.org

www.RockTheVote.org

www.MoveOn.org

www.FightFor15.org

redistricting.lls.edu

www.MoveToAmend.org

www.KisstheGround.com

www.VoteTulsi.com

www.OurRevolution.com

www.JoshTickell.com

# DOCUMENTARIES
# FOR THE REVOLUTION

*The Revolution Generation* (www.RevolutionGeneration.us)

*The Corporation* (thecorporation.com)

*Capitalism: A Love Story* (michaelmoore.com/movies/)

*Casino Jack and the United States of Money* (www.takepart .com/casinojack/)

*An Unreasonable Man* (www.anunreasonableman.com)

*Heist: Who Stole the American Dream?* (www.heist-themovie.com)

*The Big Fix* (www.thebigfixmovie.com)

*Human Flow* (www.humanflow.com)

*13th* (Netflix.com)

*Inside Job* (Available on Amazon)

*Kiss the Ground* (www.KisstheGround.com)

# BOOKS
# FOR THE REVOLUTION

*Out of the Wreckage: A New Politics for an Age of Crisis*, by George
Monbiot, Verso.

*America the Possible: Manifesto for a New Economy*, by James
Gustave Speth, Yale University Press.

*Change the Story, Change the Future: A Living Economy for a
Living Earth*, by David C. Korten, Berrett-Koehler Publishers.

*Rules for Revolutionaries: How Big Organizing Can Change
Everything*, by Becky Bond & Zack Exley, Chelsea Green
Publishing.

*Civilizing the Economy: A New Economics of Provision*, by Marvin
T. Brown, Cambridge University Press.

*Strapped: Why America's 20- and 30-Somethings Can't Get Ahead*,
by Tamara Draut, Anchor; reprint edition.

*Dreamers: An Immigrant Generation's Fight for Their American
Dream*, by Eileen Truax, Beacon Press.

*The New Jim Crow: Mass Incarceration in the Age of
Colorblindness*, by Michelle Alexander, The New Press.

*Ratf\*\*ked: Why Your Vote Doesn't Count*, by David Daley,
Liveright Publishing Corporation.

*A Brief History of Neoliberalism*, by David Harvey, Oxford
University Press.

*The New Confessions of an Economic Hit Man*, by John Perkins,
Berrett-Koehler Publishers.

*This Changes Everything: Capitalism vs. the Climate,* by Naomi
Klein, Simon & Schuster.

*Kiss the Ground: How the Food You Eat Can Reverse Climate
Change, Heal Your Body & Ultimately Save Our World,* by Josh
Tickell, Enliven Books/Atria.

# ACKNOWLEDGMENTS

My deepest gratitude to my Millennial muse, also known as my wife, Rebecca. That you remain a positive, undaunted believer in the possibility for transformation of both the human soul and the soul of our country is a never-ending source of inspiration to me and so many others.

Thank you to my daughter, Athena, and my son, Jedi. Both of you are too young to understand why your father was gone for weeks on end, only to come home and get up nightly at 2:00 a.m. to sneak into the office and write. I hope that you will forgive my absence, my exhaustion, and, eventually, that you will understand the urgency of this cause. I pray that this work and the works of many others in the "revolution" are in time to save your future.

Thank you to my publisher, Zhena Muzyka, for instantaneously believing in this project. *But, Z, seriously, thank you even more for staying with me as this work morphed during the tumultuous times we have seen.* It has been an incredible journey that has revealed your strengths as a publisher. Thank you to Judith Curr at Atria Books (we'll miss you!) and the entire staff at Simon & Schuster, especially Haley Weaver and Albert Tang.

A very special thanks to our in-house Millennial, "chill expert" Alexa Coughlin, coproducer of *The Revolution Generation* movie and creator of the graphics in this book. A special thanks to the entire staff at Big Picture Ranch, as well as to the crew of *The Revolution Generation* movie, including cinematographer Simon Balderas and Sam Gall, who traveled with me for much of this project. Thank you to Jason Martinez for your constant care of the bits and bytes of the footage and for producing the audio version of this book. Thank you, Lauren Selman, for believing in this.

A special thanks to the early Millennial readers of the manuscript, including Genevieve Wollenbecker, Kylene Ramos, Mari Miyoshi, and Brooke Kettering.

THANK YOU to our entire Elevate coproduction team for living through the largest wildfire in California's history, for losing everything you had (except the hard drive for *The Revolution Generation* movie), for coming back, picking up the pieces, and making one hell of a film. Mikki Willis and Nadia Salamanca, you are my heroes! Gabriel Valda and Anthony Ellison, thank you for your countless hours and your editorial gifts. Michael Goorjian, thank you for your words. Thank you, Zack Kilberg, for single-handedly making the difference.

Thank you also to our executive producers for supporting this project, including Andrea Van Beuren and Shailene Woodley.

Finally, thank you to the numerous excellent NGOs working tirelessly on this issue. May it be through your often uncredited and silent efforts that this revolution saves us all.

# NOTES

## Introduction

1. Professor James Thurber, interview with the author, 2010.
2. Congressman Jim McDermott (D-WA), interview with the author and on-camera appearance in Josh and Rebecca Tickell, *The Big Fix*, 2011.
3. Kenneth P. Vogel, Dave Levinthal, and Tarini Parti, "Obama, Romney Both Topped $1B," *Politico*, December 7, 2012, https://www.politico.com/story/2012/12/barack-obama-mitt-romney-both-topped-1-billion-in-2012-084737.
4. "Structural Change," Investopedia, February 12, 2018, www.investopedia.com/terms/s/structural_change.asp.
5. Asma Khalid, "NPR Poll: After Parkland, Number of Americans Who Want Gun Restrictions Grows," NPR, March 2, 2018, www.npr.org/2018/03/02/589849342/npr-poll-after-parkland-number-of-americans-who-want-gun-restrictions-grows.
6. Tristan Baurick, "'Cancer Alley' Community Fights Back against Air Pollution: Report," *New Orleans Times-Picayune*, March 8, 2018, http://www.nola.com/environment/index.ssf/2018/03/cancer_alley_community_fights.html.
7. Marvin T. Brown, *Civilizing the Economy: A New Economics of Provision* (New York: Cambridge University Press, 2010).

## Chapter One: Meet the Real Millennials

1. Diana Hembree, "Personal Finance Expert: Far from Entitled, Millennials Resemble 'The Greatest Generation,'" *Forbes*, April 30,

2017,   forbes.com/sites/dianahembree/2017/04/30/personal-finance
-expert-far-from-entitled-millennials-are-similar-to-the-greatest
-generation/#535a4fa4d0c7.

2. Michelle Conlin, "Rising Student Debt Locking out U.S. Millennials from Home," Reuters, July 13, 2017, reuters.com/article/us-usa
-studentloans/rising-student-debt-locking-out-u-s-millennials-from
-home-ownership-fed-idUSKBN19Y2K2.

3. Leah McGrath Goodman, "Millennial College Graduates: Young,
Educated, Jobless," *Newsweek*, May 27, 2015, www.newsweek.com
/2015/06/05/millennial-college-graduates-young-educated-jobless
-335821.html.

4. There's nothing wrong with being unmarried, but economically
speaking, married people are better off. Taxes, loans, and the economy in general are structured for the benefit of the married. Thus, a
largely unmarried generation misses out on many of those economic
benefits.

5. Richard Fry, "5 Facts about Millennial Households," Pew Research
Center, September 6, 2017, www.pewresearch.org/fact-tank/2017/09
/06/5-facts-about-millennial-households/.

6. US Census Bureau, "Age and Sex of All People, Family Members
and Unrelated Individuals Iterated by Income-to-Poverty Ratio and
Race: 2016," August 9, 2017, census.gov/data/tables/time-series/demo
/income-poverty/cps-pov/pov-01.html.

7. Josh Sanburn, "Census: Millennials Struggling with Poverty, Unemployment," *Time*, December 4, 2014, www.time.com/3618322
/census-millennials-poverty-unemployment/.

8. "The Price Tag of Being Young: Climate Change and Millennials'
Economic Future," Demos.org, August 22, 2016, www.demos.org
/publication/price-tag-being-young-climate-change-and-millennials
-economic-future.

9. Sanburn, "Census."

10. Richard Fry, "Millennials Surpass Gen Xers as the Largest Generation in U.S. Labor Force," Pew Research Center, May 11, 2015, www.pewresearch.org/fact-tank/2015/05/11/millennials-surpass-gen-xers-as-the-largest-generation-in-u-s-labor-force/.

11. Sanburn, "Census."

12. US Census Bureau, "America's Families and Living Arrangements: 2016," January 1, 1970, census.gov/data/tables/2016/demo/families/cps-2016.html.

13. Camille L. Ryan and Kurt Bauman, *Educational Attainment in the United States: 2015*, US Census Bureau, March 2016, census.gov/content/dam/Census/library/publications/2016/demo/p20-578.pdf.

14. Sanburn, "Census."

15. Tamara Draut, interview with the author, July 26, 2016.

16. Fry, "5 Facts about Millennial Households."

17. Richard Fry, D'vera Cohn, Gretchen Livingston, and Paul Taylor, "The Rising Age Gap in Economic Well-Being: The Older Prosper Relative to the Young," Pew Research Center, Social & Demographic Trends Project, November 7, 2011, www.pewsocialtrends.org/2011/11/07/the-rising-age-gap-in-economic-well-being/.

18. "Millennials Comprise Highest Share of Single Mothers," NAWRB, September 6, 2017, www.nawrb.com/2017/09/06/snapshot-millennial-households/.

19. Amy Traub, Robert Hiltonsmith, and Tamara Draut, "The Parent Trap: The Economic Insecurity of Families with Young Children," Demos.org, December 13, 2016, www.demos.org/publication/parent-trap-economic-insecurity-families-young-children.

20. The Earned Income Tax Credit (EITC), the primary tax code for giving low-earning parents a break, tops out at $6,318 per child. Additionally, the Child Tax Credit (CTC) tops out at $2,000 per child. But both are

available *only if you qualify*. Meanwhile, the income penalty for having just one child is over $14,000 in lost wages due to childcare needs and out-of-pocket childcare expenses. In other words, in a best-case scenario, tax offsets *might* cover half the increased financial burden of having a kid. Added to this is the fact that the cost of living is substantially higher than it was in the 1970s, when much of that tax code was first written. See "40 Years Ago: The Earned Income Tax Credit," National Low Income Housing Coalition, November 10, 2014, nlihc.org/article/40-years -ago-earned-income-tax-credit; and "2017 EITC Income Limits, Maximum Credit Amounts and Tax Law Updates," IRS, March 5, 2018, https://www.irs.gov/credits-deductions/individuals/earned-income -tax-credit/eitc-income-limits-maximum-credit-amounts.

21. *Xinhua Zidian* (Beijing: Shang Wu Yin Shu Guan, 2004), 205.

22. Allan Savory, "How to Fight Desertification and Reverse Climate Change," TED Talk, February 2013, www.ted.com/talks/allan_savory _how_to_green_the_world_s_deserts_and_reverse_climate_change.

23. Allan Savory, interview in Josh and Rebecca Tickell, *Kiss the Ground*, 2018.

24. Hans Rosling, "Global Population Growth," TED Talk, June 2010, www.ted.com/talks/hans_rosling_on_global_population_growth.

25. Alexandra S. Richey et al., "Quantifying Renewable Groundwater Stress with GRACE," *Water Resources Research* 51, no. 7 (July 2015): 5217–38.

26. Nicola Jones, "How the World Passed a Carbon Threshold and Why It Matters," *Yale Environment 360*, January 26, 2017, e360.yale.edu /features/how-the-world-passed-a-carbon-threshold-400ppm-and-why -it-matters.

27. Peter Brewer and James Barry, "Rising Acidity in the Ocean: The Other $CO_2$ Problem," *Scientific American*, September 1, 2008, www .scientificamerican.com/article/rising-acidity-in-the-ocean/.

28. Victoria J. Fabry, Brad A. Seibel, Richard A. Feely, and James C. Orr, "Impacts of Ocean Acidification on Marine Fauna and Ecosystem Processes," *ICES Journal of Marine Science* 65, no. 3 (April 1, 2008): 414–32, https://doi.org/10.1093/icesjms/fsn048.

29. Josh Tickell, *Kiss the Ground: How the Food You Eat Can Reverse Climate Change, Heal Your Body & Ultimately Save Our World* (New York: Enliven Books/Atria, 2017).

30. Chris Arsenault, "Only 60 Years of Farming Left If Soil Degradation Continues," *Scientific American*, www.scientificamerican.com/article /only-60-years-of-farming-left-if-soil-degradation-continues/.

31. Mark Schwartz, "Biological Warfare Emerges as 21st Century Threat," *Stanford Report*, January 11, 2001.

32. Alexei Yablokov, "Comments on Russia's Atomic Suitcase Bombs," *Frontline*, www.pbs.org/wgbh/pages/frontline/shows/russia/suitcase /comments.html.

33. Kim Zetter, "An Unprecedented Look at Stuxnet, the World's First Digital Weapon," *Wired*, November 3, 2014, www.wired.com/2014 /11/countdown-to-zero-day-stuxnet/.

34. Baher Kamal, "Climate Migrants Might Reach One Billion by 2050," Inter Press Service, August 21, 2017, reliefweb.int/report/world /climate-migrants-might-reach-one-billion-2050.

35. Ye Xie and Gavin Serkin, "China May Tip World into Recession: Morgan Stanley," Bloomberg, July 13, 2015, www.bloomberg .com/news/articles/2015-07-13/china-may-tip-world-into-recession -morgan-stanley-s-sharma-says.

36. Elizabeth Kolbert, *The Sixth Extinction: An Unnatural History* (New York: Henry Holt and Company/Picador, 2015).

37. Nicole Friedman, "'Snake People' Invade the Internet," *Wall Street Journal*, August 15, 2015, www.wsj.com/articles/snake-people-invade -the-internet-1439575068?mod=e2fb.

38. Landon Dowdy, "Why Do Millennials Get Such a Bad Rap at Work?" CNBC, August 22, 2017, www.cnbc.com/2015/04/20/are-millennials -lazy-entitled-narcissists.html.

39. Eloise Keating, "Millennials in a Hurry Causing Workplace Conflict: Survey," Smart Company, September 28, 2015, www.smartcompany .com.au/people-human-resources/millennials-in-a-hurry-causing -workplace-conflict-survey/.

40. Neil Howe, interview with the author, July 21, 2016.

41. Krystin Arneson, "'Selfie' Is Oxford Dictionary's Word of the Year. Where Did It Come From?" *Bustle*, November 19, 2013, www .bustle.com/articles/9170-selfie-is-oxford-dictionarys-word-of-the -year-where-did-it-come-from.

42. David Houghton, Adam Joinson, Nigel Caldwell, and Ben Marder, "Tagger's Delight? Disclosure and Liking Behaviour in Facebook: The Effects of Sharing Photographs amongst Multiple Known Social Circles," Birmingham Business School Discussion Paper Series, March 2013, epapers.bham.ac.uk/1723/1/2013-03_D_Houghton.pdf.

43. Miller McPherson, Lynn Smith-Lovin, and Matthew E. Brashears, "Social Isolation in America: Changes in Core Discussion Networks over Two Decades," *American Sociological Review* 71, no. 3 (2006): 353–75, doi:10.1177/000312240607100301.

44. Clare Murphy, "Young More Lonely than the Old, UK Survey Suggests," BBC News, May 25, 2010, news.bbc.co.uk/2/hi/health /8701763.stm.

45. "Suicide," National Institute of Mental Health, www.nimh.nih.gov /health/statistics/suicide.shtml.

## Chapter Two: How Y(ou) Came to Be

1. For an in-depth explanation of STAR Voting and information on its first US-based political election field tests, see chapter 7.

2. Jon Savage, *Teenage: The Creation of Youth Culture* (Dorset, UK: Pimlico, 2008).

3. Boy Scouts of America, *The Boy Scout Handbook* (Irving, TX: Boy Scouts of America, 2011).

4. See Carmelo Lisciotto, "The Hitler Youth," Holocaust Education & Archive Research Team, 2008, http://www.holocaustresearchproject .org/holoprelude/hitleryouth.html.

5. "Chart of US Gross Domestic Product, 1929–2004," economics -charts.com/gdp/gdp-1929-2004.html.

6. "Live Births and Crude Birth Rates Michigan and United States Residents Selected Years, 1900–2016," Michigan Department of Health and Human Services, www.mdch.state.mi.us/osr/natality/tab1.1.asp.

7. Gail Dines, *Pornland: How Porn Has Hijacked Our Sexuality* (Boston: Beacon Press, 2014).

8. Ibid.

9. James Maycock, "War within War," *Guardian*, September 14, 2001, theguardian.com/theguardian/2001/sep/15/weekend7.weekend3.

10. "American History: The 1960s, a Decade That Changed a Nation," Learning English, November 17, 2011, https://learningenglish .voanews.com/a/american-history-the-1960s-10-years-that-changed-a -nation-134041543/114624.html.

11. Lester C. Thurow, "Beware of Reagan's Military Spending," *New York Times*, May 31, 1981, https://www.nytimes.com/1981/05/31/business /beware-of-reagan-s-military-spending.html.

12. Richard Halloran, "Battle Lines Drawn over 1985 Military Spending," *New York Times*, November 30, 1983, https://www.nytimes.com /1983/11/30/us/battle-lines-drawn-over-1985-military-spending.html.

13. Mike Moffatt, "The 1980s American Economy," ThoughtCo., April 23, 2018, www.thoughtco.com/us-economy-in-the-1980s-1148148.

14. Jimmy Carter, "National Energy Program Fact Sheet on the Presi-

dent's Program," April 20, 1977, The American Presidency Project, www.presidency.ucsb.edu/ws/?pid=7373.

15. Tom Murse, "A Brief History of White House Solar Panels," ThoughtCo., January 8, 2018, www.thoughtco.com/history-of-white -house-solar-panels-3322255.

16. "US Field Production of Crude Oil," US Energy Information Admin- istration, April 30, 2018, www.eia.gov/dnav/pet/hist/LeafHandler.ashx ?n=pet&s=mcrfpus2&f=a.

17. Steve LeVine, "The US Bet Big on American Oil and Now the Whole Global Economy Is Paying the Price," *Quartz*, February 1, 2016, qz.com/604756/the-us-bet-big-on-american-oil-and-now-the-whole -global-economy-is-paying-the-price/.

18. William Strauss and Neil Howe, *The Fourth Turning: An American Prophecy* (New York: Three Rivers Press, 1998).

19. danah boyd, *It's Complicated: The Social Lives of Networked Teens* (New Haven, CT: Yale University Press, 2014).

20. Anjali Enjeti, "Generation X's Parenting Problem," *Huffington Post*, May 13, 2015, www.huffingtonpost.com/the-mid/generation-x-parenting -problem_b_7258314.html.

21. California State Department of Education, "Toward a State of Esteem: The Final Report of the California Task Force to Promote Self-Esteem and Personal and Social Responsibility," Education Resources Infor- mation Center, January 1990, eric.ed.gov/?id=ED321170.

22. Joseph Campbell, *The Hero with a Thousand Faces* (Mumbai: Yogi Impressions, 2017).

### Chapter Three: Smart, Educated, and Jobless

1. Bootie Cosgrove-Mather, "TV Guide Names Top 50 Shows," CBS News, April 26, 2002, www.cbsnews.com/news/tv-guide-names-top-50-shows/.

2. Tamara Draut, *Strapped: Why America's 20- and 30-Somethings Can't Get Ahead* (New York: Anchor Books, 2007).

3. G. William Domhoff, "Power in America," Who Rules America?, whorulesamerica.ucsc.edu/power/.

4. Allison Schrager, "The Good News about the Hollowing Out of America's Middle Class," *Quartz*, August 2, 2017, qz.com/1005068/the-upper-middle-class-is-the-new-middle-class/.

5. "The American Middle Class Is Losing Ground," Pew Research Center, Social & Demographic Trends Project, December 9, 2015, www.pewsocialtrends.org/2015/12/09/the-american-middle-class-is-losing-ground/.

6. Domhoff, "Power in America."

7. Robert Michael Smith, *From Blackjacks to Briefcases: A History of Commercialized Strikebreaking and Unionbusting in the United States* (Athens: Ohio University Press, 2003).

8. Domhoff, "Power in America."

9. Stephen H. Norwood, *Strikebreaking & Intimidation: Mercenaries and Masculinity in Twentieth-Century America* (Chapel Hill: University of North Carolina Press, 2002).

10. John Logan, "The Union Avoidance Industry in the United States," *British Journal of Industrial Relations* 44, no. 4 (December 2006): 651–75.

11. Martin Jay Levitt with Terry Conrow, *Confessions of a Union Buster* (New York: Crown, 1993).

12. "Deindustrialization and the Rise of the Sunbelt," Lumen Learning, courses.lumenlearning.com/ushistory2ay/chapter/deindustrialization-and-the-rise-of-the-sunbelt-2/.

13. Louis D. Johnston, "History Lessons: Understanding the Decline in Manufacturing," *MinnPost*, February 22, 2012, www.minnpost

.com/macro-micro-minnesota/2012/02/history-lessons-understanding
-decline-manufacturing.

14. Robert Mackay, "More Auto Layoffs, More Wives at Work," *Elyria Chronicle Telegram*, May 30, 1980, newspaperarchive.com/elyria
-chronicle-telegram-may-30-1980-p-18/.

15. Jon Hilsenrath and Bob Davis, "America's Dazzling Tech Boom Has a Downside: Not Enough Jobs," *Wall Street Journal*, October 12, 2016, www.wsj.com/articles/americas-dazzling-tech-boom-has-a
-downside-not-enough-jobs-1476282355.

16. John Perry Barlow, "The Economy of Ideas," *Wired*, March 1, 1994, www.wired.com/1994/03/economy-ideas/.

17. Draut, interview with the author.

18. Derek Thompson, "A World Without Work," *Atlantic*, July/August 2015, www.theatlantic.com/magazine/archive/2015/07/world-without
-work/395294/.

19. US Census Bureau, "POV-01: Age and Sex of All People, Family Members and Unrelated Individuals Iterated by Income-to-Poverty Ratio and Race,"August 9, 2017, census.gov/data/tables/time-series
/demo/income-poverty/cps-pov/pov-01.html.

20. Number of children derived from "POP1 Child Population: Number of Children (in Millions) Ages 0–17 in the United States by Age, 1950–2016 and Projected 2017–2050," Forum on Child and Family Statistics, www.childstats.gov/americaschildren/tables/pop1.asp.

21. According to Pew, there were sixteen million Millennial moms in 2015, but that number was and likely still is increasing by one million per year. It's logical that for each mother there is also a father, and in most but not all cases the father is a Millennial. Therefore, I estimate approximately forty million Millennial parents. See "More Than a Million Millennials Are Becoming Moms Each Year," Pew Research

Center,   pewresearch.org/fact-tank/2017/01/03/more-than-a-million
-millennials-are-becoming-moms-each-year/.

22. Traub, Hiltonsmith, and Draut, "The Parent Trap."

23. Alexandra Cawthorne, "The Straight Facts on Women in Poverty," Center for American Progress, October 8, 2008, www.americanprogress
.org/issues/women/reports/2008/10/08/5103/the-straight-facts-on
-women-in-poverty/.

24. Hanna Brooks Olsen, "How Young People Became the New Face of Poverty in America," *Daily Dot*, December 11, 2015, www.dailydot
.com/via/american-poverty-millennials-student-debt/.

25. US Census Bureau, "POV-01: Age and Sex of All People, Family Members and Unrelated Individuals Iterated by Income-to-Poverty Ratio and Race"; Josh Sanburn, "4 Ways Millennials Have It Worse Than Their Parents," *Time*, December 4, 2014, time.com/3618322
/census-millennials-poverty-unemployment/.

26. Draut, *Strapped*.

27. Ibid.

28. Drew DeSilver, "5 Facts about the Minimum Wage," Pew Research Center, January 4, 2017, www.pewresearch.org/fact-tank/2017/01/04
/5-facts-about-the-minimum-wage/.

29. James B. Barnes, "61% of Those Making Minimum Wage Are Millennials Living in Poverty: Here's the One Thing That Would Get Them Out," *Thought Catalog*, March 8, 2014, thoughtcatalog.com/james
-b-barnes/2014/03/61-of-those-making-minimum-wage-are-millennials
-living-in-poverty-heres-the-one-thing-that-would-get-them-out/.

30. "Comparing the Inflated Cost of Living Today from 1950 to 2014: How Declining Purchasing Power Has Hurt the Middle Class Since 1950," My Budget 360, www.mybudget360.com/cost-of-living-2014
-inflation-1950-vs-2014-data-housing-cars-college/.

31. Ray Boshara, William R. Emmons, and Bryan J. Noeth, "The Demographics of Wealth: How Age, Education and Race Separate Thrivers from Strugglers in Today's Economy," Federal Reserve Bank of St. Louis, July 2015, www.stlouisfed.org/~/media/Files/PDFs/HFS/essays/HFS-Essay-3-2015-Age-Birth-year-Wealth.pdf?la=en.

32. Lori Wallach, "NAFTA at 20: One Million U.S. Jobs Lost, Higher Income Inequality," *Huffington Post*, January 6, 2014, www.huffingtonpost.com/lori-wallach/nafta-at-20-one-million-u_b_4550207.html.

33. Drew DeSilver, "5 Facts about the National Debt," Pew Research Center, August 17, 2017, www.pewresearch.org/fact-tank/2017/08/17/5-facts-about-the-national-debt-what-you-should-know/.

34. "Corporate Profits After Tax with Inventory Valuation Adjustment (IVA) and Capital Consumption Adjustment (CCAdj)," Federal Reserve Bank of St. Louis, FRED Economic Data, fred.stlouisfed.org/graph/?g=dGc; "Corporate Profits After Tax (without IVA and CCAdj)/Gross Domestic Product," Federal Reserve Bank of St. Louis, FRED Economic Data, https://fred.stlouisfed.org/graph/?g=1Pik.

35. David Harvey, *A Brief History of Neoliberalism* (Oxford, UK: Oxford University Press, 2005).

36. Eric Fry, "Here's Why the Price of a College Education Makes No Sense Anymore," *Business Insider*, September 13, 2010, www.businessinsider.com/a-college-education-of-diminishing-returns-2010-9.

37. Sabrina Eaton, "Betty Sutton Says That on Average, 15 U.S. Factories Close Each Day," Politifact, November 7, 2011, www.politifact.com/ohio/statements/2011/nov/07/betty-sutton/betty-sutton-says-average-15-us-factories-close-ea/.

38. "How to Schedule Staff for Different Industries," Time Clock Wizard, January 17, 2017, www.timeclockwizard.com/how-to-schedule-staff-effectively.

39. Alexia Elejalde-Ruiz, "How Erratic Schedules Hurt Low-Wage Work-

ers," *Chicago Tribune*, January 11, 2016, www.chicagotribune.com /business/ct-volatile-schedules-0907-biz-20150904-story.html.

40. This is a reference to the famous 1963 Milgram Experiment, in which Yale psychologist Stanley Milgram carried out "obedience" studies to determine whether everyday people were capable of inflicting genocide. The basic result was: yes, they are. See simplypsychology .org/milgram.html.

41. John R. Thelin, A *History of American Higher Education* (Baltimore: Johns Hopkins University Press, 2011).

42. Lily Rothman, "Putting the Rising Cost of College in Perspective," *Time*, August 31, 2016, time.com/4472261/college-cost-history/.

43. Lauren Carroll, "Jeb Bush: Student Loan Debt Has Doubled under Obama," Politifact, August 14, 2015, www.politifact.com/truth-o-meter /statements/2015/aug/14/jeb-bush/jeb-bush-student-loan-debt-has -doubled-under-obama/.

44. Zack Friedman, "Student Loan Debt in 2017: A $1.3 Trillion Crisis," *Forbes*, February 21, 2017, www.forbes.com/sites/zackfriedman/2017 /02/21/student-loan-debt-statistics-2017/.

45. Ryan McMaken, "Here's the Reason Why Student Loans Aren't Being Paid Off," *Business Insider*, February 9, 2017, www.businessinsider .com/why-student-loans-arent-being-paid-off.

46. Nick Perry, "With No Way out of Trouble, More Students Likely to Default," *Seattle Times*, October 6, 2008, www.seattletimes.com/seattle -news/with-no-way-out-of-trouble-more-students-likely-to-default/.

## Chapter Four: The Politics of Y(outh)

1. Nick Penzenstadler and Susan Page, "Exclusive: Trump's 3,500 Lawsuits Unprecedented for a Presidential Nominee," *USA Today*, June 1, 2016, www.usatoday.com/story/news/politics/elections/2016/06/01 /donald-trump-lawsuits-legal-battles/84995854/.

2. Patrice Taddonio, "Watch: Inside the Bailout That Saved a Collaps-
   ing Trump Organization," *Frontline*, October 3, 2016, https://www
   .pbs.org/wgbh/frontline/article/watch-inside-the-bailout-that-saved
   -a-collapsing-trump-organization/; Max J. Rosenthal, "How Trump
   Went Bust and Got Rich Using Other People's Money: A Time-
   line," *Mother Jones*, October 14, 2016, https://www.motherjones
   .com/politics/2016/10/how-donald-trump-destroyed-his-empire-and
   -dumped-ruins-others-timeline/; David S. Hilzenrath and Michelle
   Singletary, "Trump Went Broke, but Stayed on Top," *Washington
   Post*, November 29, 1992, https://www.washingtonpost.com/archive
   /politics/1992/11/29/trump-went-broke-but-stayed-on-top/e1685555
   -1de7-400c-99a8-9cd9c0bca9fe/?utm_term=.948cc599aff1.

3. Hilary Hanson, "Hillary Clinton Accused of Using Static Noise
   to Conceal Fundraising Speech," *Huffington Post*, April 9, 2016,
   www.huffingtonpost.com/entry/hillary-clinton-static-noise-speech_us
   _570930dae4b0836057a16748.

4. You may download Senator Sanders's speech here: www.sanders
   .senate.gov/newsroom/press-releases/full-congressional-record
   -transcript-of-sanders-filibuster.

5. Harvey, *A Brief History of Neoliberalism*.

6. Ibid.

7. Ibid.

8. George Monbiot, "Neoliberalism—the Ideology at the Root of All
   Our Problems," *Guardian*, April 15, 2016, www.theguardian.com
   /books/2016/apr/15/neoliberalism-ideology-problem-george-monbiot.

9. Senator Bernie Sanders (I-VT), interview with the author, September
   2010, Washington, DC.

10. "2016 Presidential Primaries, Caucuses, and Conventions: Democratic
    Convention," Green Papers, October 25, 2017, www.thegreenpapers
    .com/P16/D.

11. William A. Galston and Clara Hendrickson, "How Millennials Voted This Election," Brookings, November 21, 2016, www.brookings.edu /blog/fixgov/2016/11/21/how-millennials-voted/.

12. Jesse Moore, "The Millennial Vote: A Turning Point," *Huffington Post*, October 24, 2016, www.huffingtonpost.com/jesse-moore-/the -millennial-vote-a-tur_b_12623404.html.

13. Graham K. Brown, "Did the Bernie Bros Cost Clinton the Election?" GrahamKBrown.net, November 14, 2016, grahamkbrown.net/2016 /11/14/did-the-bernie-bros-cost-clinton-the-election/.

14. Emma Lord, "The Millennial Electoral Maps Might Give You Hope, but Our Generation Has a Lot of Work to Do," *Bustle*, November 9, 2016, bustle.com/articles/194296-the-millennial-electoral-maps -might-give-you-hope-but-our-generation-has-a-lot-of-work.

15. Alan Flippen, "Black Turnout in 1964, and Beyond," *New York Times*, October 16, 2014, www.nytimes.com/2014/10/17/upshot/black-turnout -in-1964-and-beyond.html.

16. Pema Levy, "The Voting Rights Act May Be Coming Back from the Dead," *Mother Jones*, May 8, 2017, www.motherjones.com/politics /2017/05/supreme-court-voting-rights-texas/.

17. Ari Berman, "Welcome to the First Presidential Election Since Voting Rights Act Gutted," *Rolling Stone*, June 23, 2016, www.rollingstone .com/politics/news/welcome-to-the-first-presidential-election-since -voting-rights-act-gutted-20160623.

18. Tomas Lopez, "'Shelby County': One Year Later," Brennan Center for Justice, June 24, 2014, www.brennancenter.org/analysis/shelby -county-one-year-later.

19. Levy, "The Voting Rights Act May Be Coming Back from the Dead."

20. Justin Levitt, "Who Draws the Lines?" All About Redistricting, redistricting.lls.edu/who.php.

21. "A Primer: How Electoral Districts Are Drawn," *Newsday*, January

9, 2012, www.newsday.com/opinion/oped/a-primer-how-electoral-districts-are-drawn-1.3439300.

22. David Daley, *Ratf\*\*ked: Why Your Vote Doesn't Count* (New York: Liveright, 2017), xiii.

23. Ibid.

24. Ryan Lovelace, "Trump: GOP 'Rigged,' but I Don't Care Because I Won," *Washington Examiner*, May 5, 2016, www.washingtonexaminer.com/trump-gop-rigged-but-i-dont-care-because-i-won/article/2590545.

25. Center for American Progress, "100 Ways, in 100 Days, That Trump Has Hurt Americans," April 26, 2017, www.americanprogress.org/issues/general/news/2017/04/26/431299/100-ways-100-days-trump-hurt-americans/.

26. "1980–82 Early 1980s Recession," Slaying the Dragon of Debt, bancroft.berkeley.edu/ROHO/projects/debt/1980srecession.html.

### Chapter Five: How They Hacked Your Brain

1. Shannon Greenwood, Andrew Perrin, and Maeve Duggan, "Social Media Update 2016," Pew Research Center, November 11, 2016, www.pewinternet.org/2016/11/11/social-media-update-2016/.

2. James B. Stewart, "Facebook Has 50 Minutes of Your Time Each Day. It Wants More." *New York Times*, May 5, 2016, www.nytimes.com/2016/05/06/business/facebook-bends-the-rules-of-audience-engagement-to-its-advantage.html.

3. Kelly Wallace, "Teens Spend a 'Mind-Boggling' 9 Hours a Day Using Media, Report Says," CNN, November 3, 2015, www.cnn.com/2015/11/03/health/teens-tweens-media-screen-use-report/index.html.

4. Matt Egan, "Facebook and Amazon Hit $500 Billion Milestone," CNN, July 27, 2017, money.cnn.com/2017/07/27/investing/facebook-amazon-500-billion-bezos-zuckerberg/index.html.

5. Thomas H. Kee, "Shares of Facebook and Microsoft Meet Resistance,

but One Is Still a Bargain," *Marketwatch*, May 4, 2017, marketwatch
.com/story/shares-of-facebook-and-microsoft-meet-resistance-but-one
-is-still-a-bargain-2017-05-04.

6. Paul La Monica, "Why Facebook Could One Day Be Worth $1 Trillion," CNN, April 28, 2016, money.cnn.com/2016/04/28/investing
/facebook-trillion-dollar-market-value/index.html.

7. Mathew Ingram, "Mark Zuckerberg Is Giving Away His Money, but with a Twist," *Fortune*, December 2, 2015, fortune.com/2015/12/02
/zuckerberg-charity/.

8. J. Walker Smith and Ann Clurman, *Generation Ageless: How Baby Boomers Are Changing the Way We Live Today . . . and They're Just Getting Started* (New York: HarperCollins, 2007).

9. Caitlin Johnson, "Cutting Through Advertising Clutter," CBS News, September 17, 2006, www.cbsnews.com/news/cutting-through
-advertising-clutter/.

10. Barlow, "The Economy of Ideas."

11. boyd, *It's Complicated*.

12. Kate Taylor, "Millennials Spend 18 Hours a Day Consuming Media—And It's Mostly Content Created by Peers," *Entrepreneur*, March 10, 2014, www.entrepreneur.com/article/232062.

13. J. Howard Beales, "The FTC's Use of Unfairness Authority: Its Rise, Fall, and Resurrection," Federal Trade Commission, May 30, 2003, www.ftc.gov/public-statements/2003/05/ftcs-use-unfairness
-authority-its-rise-fall-and-resurrection.

14. "Advertising to Kids and the FTC: A Regulatory Retrospective That Advises the Present," Federal Trade Commission, www.ftc.gov/sites
/default/files/documents/public_statements/advertising-kids-and-ftc
-regulatory-retrospective-advises-present/040802adstokids.pdf.

15. Beales, "The FTC's Use of Unfairness Authority."

16. Ibid.

17. *Consuming Kids: The Commercialization of Childhood*, Media Education Foundation, October 29, 2008, mediaed.org/transcripts /Consuming-Kids-Transcript.pdf.

18. Ibid.

19. Paul M. Connell, Merrie Brucks, and Jesper H. Nielsen, "How Childhood Advertising Exposure Can Create Biased Product Evaluations That Persist into Adulthood," *Journal of Consumer Research* 41, no. 1 (June 1, 2014): 119–34, academic.oup.com/jcr/article-abstract /41/1/119/1810274?redirectedFrom=fulltext.

20. Sarah Spinks, "Inside the Teenage Brain," *Frontline*, January 31, 2002, pbs.org/wgbh/pages/frontline/shows/teenbrain/etc/script.html.

21. Renata Tomaz, "The Invention of the Tweens: Youth, Culture, and Media," *Intercom: Revista Brasileira de Ciências da Comunicação* 37, no. 2 (July /December 2014), scielo.br/scielo.php?pid=S1809-58442014000200177 &script=sci_arttext&tlng=en.

22. Audrey Watters, "How Steve Jobs Brought the Apple II to the Classroom," *Hack Education*, February 25, 2015, hackeducation.com /2015/02/25/kids-cant-wait-apple.

23. Ibid.

24. Ibid.

25. Ibid.

26. Jeremy Reimer, "Total Share: Personal Computer Market Share 1975–2010," *Jeremy's Blog*, December 7, 2012, jeremyreimer.com /m-item.lsp?i=137.

27. Allen D. Kanner, "Today's Class Brought to You By . . ." *Tikkun*, January 2008, commercialfreechildhood.org/sites/default/files/kanner _todaysclass.pdf.

28. Ibid.

29. "The United States of Energy," student worksheet, American Coal

Foundation, teachcoal.org/wp-content/uploads/2011/10/USofEnergy
-teachingguide2.pdf.

30. Rachel Dretzin, "The Merchants of Cool," *Frontline*, February 27, 2001.

31. Ibid.

32. Ibid.

33. Andrew Janowitz et al., "Statista—The Statistics Portal for Market Data, Market Research and Market Studies," *Statista*, www.statista.com.

34. Josh Golin, interview with the author, July 25, 2016.

35. Faye Harris, "The Rise of the Micro-Influencer," *Huffington Post*, December 6, 2017, www.huffingtonpost.com/faye-harris/the-rise-of-the-microinfl_b_10625136.html.

36. Joanna Geary, "Tracking the Trackers: What Are Cookies? An Introduction to Web Tracking," *Guardian*, April 23, 2012, www.theguardian.com/technology/2012/apr/23/cookies-and-web-tracking-intro.

37. Olivia Solon, "Facebook Can Track Your Browsing Even after You've Logged Out, Judge Says," *Guardian*, July 3, 2017, www.theguardian.com/technology/2017/jul/03/facebook-track-browsing-history-california-lawsuit.

38. Haley Tsukayama, "What Those Creepy-Sounding App Permissions Mean—and When to Be Wary," *Washington Post*, August 20, 2014, www.washingtonpost.com/news/the-switch/wp/2014/08/20/what-those-creepy-sounding-app-permissions-mean-and-when-to-be-wary/?utm_term=.f8adb3c35cba.

39. Alex Hern, "Facebook's 'Ethnic Affinity' Advertising Sparks Concerns of Racial Profiling," *Guardian*, March 22, 2016, www.theguardian.com/technology/2016/mar/22/facebooks-ethnic-affinity-advertising-concerns-racial-profiling.

40. Tony Bradley, "Facebook AI Creates Its Own Language in Creepy Preview of Our Potential Future," *Forbes*, July 31, 2017, www

.forbes.com/sites/tonybradley/2017/07/31/facebook-ai-creates-its-own
-language-in-creepy-preview-of-our-potential-future/#7d282f91292c.

41. Amit Chowdhry, "Facebook's DeepFace Software Can Match
Faces with 97.25% Accuracy," *Forbes*, March 18, 2014, www.forbes
.com/sites/amitchowdhry/2014/03/18/facebooks-deepface-software
-can-match-faces-with-97-25-accuracy/.

42. "DeepFace," Wikipedia, August 30, 2017, en.wikipedia.org/wiki
/DeepFace.

43. Chowdhry, "Facebook's DeepFace Software Can Match Faces with
97.25% Accuracy."

44. Ibid.

45. "Who's Hotter?" Facemash, atenwood.com/facemash/.

46. Nir Eyal with Ryan Hoover, *Hooked: How to Build Habit-Forming
Products* (New York: Portfolio, 2014).

47. O. Turel, Q. He, G. Xue, L. Xiao, and A. Bechara, "Examination of
Neural Systems Sub-Serving Facebook 'Addiction,'" *Psychological
Reports* 115, no. 3 (December 2014): 675–95, www.ncbi.nlm.nih.gov
/pubmed/25489985.

48. Bruce E. Levine, "How Our Society Breeds Anxiety, Depression,
and Dysfunction," *Salon*, August 26, 2013, www.salon.com/2013/08
/26/how_our_society_breeds_anxiety_depression_and_dysfunction
_partner/.

49. Adam D. I. Kramer, Jamie E. Guillory, and Jeffrey T. Hancock,
"Experimental Evidence of Massive-Scale Emotional Contagion
through Social Networks," *Proceedings of the National Academy of
Sciences* 111, no. 24 (June 17, 2014): 8788–90, www.pnas.org/content
/111/24/8788.

50. Ibid.

51. Julio Gil-Pulgar, "In the Battle Between Google, Facebook, and
Amazon against Banks: Bitcoin Will Be the Winner," Bitcoin.com,

January 24, 2017, news.bitcoin.com/in-the-battle-between-google-facebook-and-amazon-against-banks-bitcoin-will-be-the-winner/.

52. "Turns Out Many Consumers Are Interested in Banking with Google, Amazon, and Facebook," *Fortune*, January 11, 2017, fortune.com/2017/01/11/google-facebook-amazon-banking/.

53. Elizabeth Dilts, "Third of Global Consumers Open to Google, Amazon Banking: Survey," Reuters, January 11, 2017, www.reuters.com/article/us-wealth-financialservices-survey/third-of-global-consumers-open-to-google-amazon-banking-survey-idUSKBN14V2I2.

54. Matthew Hussey, "The Banks of Google, Facebook, and Amazon," TNW, May 5, 2016, thenextweb.com/facebook/2016/05/05/banks-google-facebook-amazon/.

55. Chris Matthews, "Here's Why Big Banks Are Lending to Fewer Blacks and Hispanics," *Fortune*, June 2, 2016, fortune.com/2016/06/02/banks-lending-minorities/.

56. Sy Mukherjee, "Blacks Are Still Significantly Less Likely to Get Approved for a Mortgage Than Whites," *Fortune*, July 19, 2016, fortune.com/2016/07/19/mortgage-lending-racial-disparities/.

57. Steven Finlay, "We Should Be as Scared of Artificial Intelligence as Elon Musk Is," *Fortune*, August 18, 2017, fortune.com/2017/08/18/elon-musk-artificial-intelligence-risk/.

58. Katie Rogers, "Mark Zuckerberg Covers His Laptop Camera. You Should Consider It, Too." *New York Times*, June 22, 2016, www.nytimes.com/2016/06/23/technology/personaltech/mark-zuckerberg-covers-his-laptop-camera-you-should-consider-it-too.html.

59. Scott Shane and Mark Mazzetti, "Inside a 3-Year Russian Campaign to Influence U.S. Voters," *New York Times*, February 16, 2018, www.nytimes.com/2018/02/16/us/politics/russia-mueller-election.html.

60. Cynthia McFadden, William M. Arkin, Kevin Monahan, and Ken Dilanian, "U.S. Intel: Russia Compromised Seven States Prior to

2016 Election," NBC News, February 28, 2018, www.nbcnews.com /politics/elections/u-s-intel-russia-compromised-seven-states-prior -2016-election-n850296.

61. Shane and Mazzetti, "Inside a 3-Year Russian Campaign to Influence U.S. Voters."

62. Ibid.

63. Jeremy B. White, "Vladimir Putin Says Russians Accused of Hacking US Election 'Do Not Represent' the Country," *Independent*, March 4, 2018, www.independent.co.uk/news/world/americas/us-politics /vladimir-putin-internet-research-agency-troll-farm-robert-mueller -indictment-13-russians-a8239386.html.

64. Sara Murray and Jeremy Herb, "Trump Still Unconvinced Russia Meddled in 2016 Election," CNN, February 14, 2018, cnn.com/2018 /02/13/politics/trump-unconvinced-russia-meddled-election/index .html.

65. White, "Vladimir Putin Says Russians Accused of Hacking US Election 'Do Not Represent' the Country."

66. Jeffrey Gottfried and Elisa Shearer, "News Use across Social Media Platforms 2016," Pew Research Center, Journalism Project, May 26, 2016, www.journalism.org/2016/05/26/news-use-across-social-media -platforms-2016/.

67. Jane Wakefield, "Social Media 'Outstrips TV' as News Source for Young People," BBC News, June 15, 2016, www.bbc.com/news /uk-36528256.

68. Michael Nunez, "Former Facebook Workers: We Routinely Suppressed Conservative News," *Gizmodo*, May 9, 2016, gizmodo .com/former-facebook-workers-we-routinely-suppressed-conser -1775461006.

69. Sam Thielman, "Facebook News Selection Is in Hands of Editors Not Algorithms, Documents Show," *Guardian*, May 12, 2016,

www.theguardian.com/technology/2016/may/12/facebook-trending
-news-leaked-documents-editor-guidelines?CMP=Share_iOSApp
_Other.

70. Rand Waltzman, "The U.S. Is Losing the Social Media War," *Time*, October 12, 2015, time.com/4064698/social-media-propaganda/.

71. Golin, interview with the author.

72. Ibid.

73. Anne Ryman, "Digital Billboards Put Ads in Front of Students. Are They Harvesting Personal Info, Too?" KGW8 News, February 25, 2018, www.kgw.com/article/news/nation-now/digital-billboards -put-ads-in-front-of-students-are-they-harvesting-personal-info-too /465-b4e94bcc-523e-4e29-b7d0-76f1ce99e6c2.

74. See, for example, www.schoolpartnerships.com.

75. Azam Khan, "3 Reasons Email Marketing Is the Most Effective at Reaching College Kids," *Adweek*, October 21, 2011, www.adweek.com /digital/3-reasons-email-marketing-is-the-most-effective-at-reaching -college-kids/.

76. They are: desertification, overpopulation, water scarcity, climate, ocean acidification, chemical agriculture, terrorism, refugees, global recession, and mass extinction. For a more detailed list, see chapter 1.

## Chapter Six: From the Ashes Rise

1. Eighty-three percent of Millennials registered to vote (Natasha Guzmán, "How Many Millennials Are Registered to Vote? The 2016 Election Has Stolen Their Attention," *Bustle*, November 3, 2016, www.bustle.com /articles/191458-how-many-millennials-are-registered-to-vote-the -2016-election-has-stolen-their-attention); 23.7 million young voters participated in the 2016 election, which is 50 percent of citizens aged eighteen to twenty-nine in the US ("An Estimated 24 Million Young People Voted in 2016 Election," Center for Information & Research

on Civic Learning and Engagement, November 9, 2016, civicyouth
.org/an-estimated-24-million-young-people-vote-in-2016-election/);
50 percent of Millennials voted (David Sable, "Elections Are Won by
Votes, Not Likes and Shares," *Huffington Post*, November 28, 2016,
www.huffingtonpost.com/david-sable/elections-are-won-by-vote
_b_13286198.html).

## Chapter Seven: How to Fix America (and the World)

1. Mark Joseph Stern, "Yes, We Could Effectively Abolish the Electoral
College Soon. But We Probably Won't." *Slate*, November 10, 2016,
www.slate.com/blogs/the_slatest/2016/11/10/the_electoral_college
_could_be_abolished_without_an_amendment.html.

2. T. S. Last, Edmundo Carrillo, and Megan Bennett, "Webber Elected
Santa Fe Mayor in First Ranked-Choice Voting," *Albuquerque Journal*, March 7, 2018, www.abqjournal.com/1142413/webber-leads-in
-first-round-of-ranked-choice-voting.html.

3. Sari Horwitz, "More Than 30 States Offer Online Voting, but Experts Warn It Isn't Secure," *Washington Post*, May 17, 2016, www
.washingtonpost.com/news/post-nation/wp/2016/05/17/more-than
-30-states-offer-online-voting-but-experts-warn-it-isnt-secure/?utm
_term=.c7ead784cd3b.

4. Brian Barrett, "America's Electronic Voting Machines Are Scarily Easy
Targets," *Wired*, August 2, 2016, www.wired.com/2016/08/americas
-voting-machines-arent-ready-election/.

5. Ibid.

6. David Pogue, "When Will We Be Able to Vote Online?" *Scientific
American*, February 1, 2016, www.scientificamerican.com/article
/when-will-we-be-able-to-vote-online/.

7. Lily Kuo, "Electronic Voting Is Failing the Developing World
While the US and Europe Abandon It," *Quartz*, March 10, 2013,

qz.com/61209/e-voting-is-failing-the-developing-world-while-the-us-and-europe-abandon-it/.

8. "Why America Needs a $15 Minimum Wage," National Employment Law Project, April 26, 2017, www.nelp.org/publication/why-america-needs-a-15-minimum-wage/.

9. Michael Reich, Sylvia Allegretto, Ken Jacobs, and Claire Montialoux, "The Effects of a $15 Minimum Wage in New York State," Center on Wage and Employment Dynamics, March 2016, irle.berkeley.edu/files/2016/The-Effects-of-a-15-Minimum-Wage-in-New-York-State.pdf.

10. Ibid.

11. Florian Wilde, "Divided They Fell: The German Left and the Rise of Hitler," *International Socialism* 137 (January 9, 2013), isj.org.uk/divided-they-fell-the-german-left-and-the-rise-of-hitler/.

12. BEZS XPNB VYFT QCPN AIJC KZQJ ZBZK SECO NXFA BCNW KULL DUOR OVXL LOTQ XTHY JMND TQBT CISY EZTG UXAA KYZC PSVF XXMF INWX HADI IX